INFORMATION AND COMMUNICATION TECHNOLOGY IN ORGANIZATIONS

INFORMATION AND COMMUNICATION TECHNOLOGY IN ORGANIZATIONS

Adoption, Implementation, Use and Effects

Harry Bouwman
Bart van den Hooff
Lidwien van de Wijngaert
Jan van Dijk

SAGE Publications
London ● Thousand Oaks ● New Delhi

First published in Holland with the title *ICT in Organisaties. Adoptie, Implementatie, Gebruik en Effect.*
Amsterdam, Boom Uitgeverij, 2002

First published in Great Britain 2005

SAGE Publications
1 Oliver's Yard
55 City Road
London EC1Y 1SP

SAGE Publications Inc
2455 Teller Road
Thousand Oaks, California 91320

SAGE Publications India Pvt Ltd
B-42 Panchsheel Enclave
New Delhi 110 017

Library of Congress Control Number 2004116092

A catalogue record for this book is available from the British Library

ISBN 1-4129-0089-1
ISBN 1-4129-0090-5 (pbk)

Typeset by Pantek Arts Ltd, Maidstone, Kent
Printed in Great Britain by Athenaeum Press, Gateshead

Contents

Authors

Harry Bouwman is an associate professor at the information and communication technology (ICT) section of the Faculty of Technology and Management at Delft Technical University. He studied political science at the Free University of Amsterdam. In 1986 he took his doctoral degree at the Catholic University of Nijmegen. He worked at, among other places the University of Amsterdam, the University of Utrecht, Michigan State University and at TNO Strategy, Technology and Management. His publications cover videotext (*Relaunching Videotex*, 1992), multimedia, (*Multimedia tussen hoop en hype/Mutlimedia between Hope and Hype*), 1993; *Multimedia en Route*, 1996), ICT clusters (*Silicon Valley in de Polder*, 2000) and ICT and communication science (*Communicatie in de Informatiesamenleving/Communication in the Information Society*), and he wrote scientific articles on these subjects, as well as on (mobile) telecommunication and on e- and m-commerce. He is currently involved in research into the development of business models for services provided by organizations cooperating within complex value systems.

Bart van den Hooff is an assistant professor at the Communication Science Department of the University of Amsterdam, and a researcher at the Amsterdam School of Communications Research ASCoR. In 1997, he took his doctoral degree with distinction, with the thesis 'Incorporating electronic mail: adoption, use and effects of electronic mail in organizations'. After taking his degree he worked for some time as a consultant (at M&I/PARTNERS in Amersfoort), and returned to the world of academia in 1999. Both in his teaching and in his research he focuses on issues surrounding the adoption, use and effects of ICT in organizations, in particular the role ICT plays in processes of organizational learning and knowledge sharing.

Lidwien van de Wijngaert studied Communication Science at the University of Amsterdam, and conducted research at the Telematica Institute in Enschede. Since August 1999 she is working as an assistant professor at the Institute for Information Science at the Faculty of Mathematics and Information Science of the University of Utrecht. Her research focuses on the significance of ICT to users and their context. She publishes on a regular basis in books and scientific journals such as *New Media & Society* and *Information Services and Use* and she is a regular speaker at scientific conventions, both at home and abroad. Since March 2001 she has been an associate consultant at Dialogic in Utrecht.

Jan van Dijk is professor of Applied Communication Science at Twente University, specializing in the Sociology of the Information Society. Between 1980 and 2000 he was associate professor at the Social Science Faculty at the University of Utrecht. Van Dijk has been conducting research into the social aspects of new media since 1984. He focuses primarily on the social, cultural and political aspects. His best known books are *De Netwerkmaatschappij* (1991–2001)/*The Network Society* (1999), *Nieuwe media en politiek* (1997)/*Digital Democracy* (2000). He is currently conducting research into the influence of networks and network organizations, into interactive television and into digital inequality. He advises the European Commission in his capacity of member of the European Union's (EU's) Information Society Forum.

Preface

The decision to write a book about a common field of interest is easily taken. The process involved in transforming that idea into an end-product (the book itself) is another matter. Some steps in that process are taken quickly, others require a certain amount of time and discussion. And although not all these discussions are relevant to the reader, in this preface we want to address a number of subjects on which our discussions have focused – as well as the decisions in which they have resulted. The title of the book is, of course, the very first subject of discussion: *Information and Communication Technology in Organizations: Adoption, Implementation, Use and Effects*.

Is this a book about what in Europe we call ICT (information and communication technology)? Well, yes and no. Technology – whether it is Internet-technology or information and communication technology makes little difference to us – appears to be at the centre. After all, it is one of the central words in the title. We view technology as no more than a tool to organize things differently, streamline processes and carry out tasks more easily. Technology is an *enabler*. The use of technology is given shape in all kinds of social processes, whereby economic and political (both within businesses and *real* politics) considerations play a role.

Is it about organizations? Again, yes and no. Organizations are the context in which adoption, implementation and use of ICT are given shape. The effects of the adoption, implementation and use of ICT can be felt directly within the organization, but there is also an impact on the relationships between the organization and its environment: its suppliers, competitors and customers.

Information and Communication Technology in Organizations. Why *in*, should this not be *between*, or *within*? The use of the word in seems to imply that we limit ourselves to what happens within the boundaries of an organization. Nothing could be further from the truth. Increasingly, organizations are part of a complex network of organizations that sometimes work together and sometimes compete with each other, blurring the boundaries of organizations. Not only is there co-operation across organizational boundaries, an increasing number of people are working in organizations on a temporary basis, or people work together in virtual teams or communities of practice. Although we start with what happens inside organizations, we do not end there.

Adoption, implementation, use and effect. As such this is a nice linear way of describing all that goes on when new technologies are implemented in an organization. But although this analytical division helps us organize the chapters of this book, in practice the processes involved are anything but linear. They are complex processes that contain a great number of feedback loops, that often grind to a halt and that are sometimes even abandoned altogether.

And that is just the title. You can imagine that, in the light of the differences in our backgrounds, we have discussed a number of issues at great length. We have no desire to bore our readers with that, but there are a few things that we do wish to emphasize.

To begin with, we have a shared perspective. The book that you see before you was written from a shared socio- and communication-scientific point of view with regard to the domain of ICT and organizations.

This is not a book, then, that spends a great deal of time discussing various ICT-related development methods, nor does it address new standards and protocols or talk about the latest in co-operation tools. Although we pay attention to technology, this is not a book *about* technology. It is a book that we feel may help developers, systems architects, programmers, ICT managers, and so on, gain insight into the human and organizational dimension of ICT. Technical experts may be disappointed by the way we discuss their area of expertise: we do not go beneath the surface and will not discuss *the New New Thing*, to paraphrase Michael Lewis. That is not our ambition. Technology is but one of the factors we address.

Nor is this a book about management. There are no *how to do* lists, simple decision models, suggestions on investment decisions, plans of action or guidelines. We do believe, however, that managers will find this book very useful, as it helps them understand the complexity with which they are faced at an everyday level. We claim to provide an overview of all sorts of individual, social, organizational and economic factors that play a role in the adoption, implementation, use and effects of ICT in organizations. In Chapter 1 we present our basic ideas on the subject. In Part II we will get back to it in greater detail.

We have decided to divide the book into three parts. In the first and general part we introduce our basic model of processes and factors. In Part II we discuss the four process steps. In Part III we address the two crystallization points of developments in ICT and organizations, to wit e-commerce/e-business and e-government.

With regard to the first part, we have struggled with which question to address first: organizations or technologies. We have decided to discuss the technological component of ICT first. The reason we have made this choice is that a description of trends and developments and of individual technologies and applications makes it easier to establish a connection when discussing organizations. Again, technology is not the most important subject, but it is where things get started, in real life as in this book. The second part sticks to the four process steps: adoption, implementation, use and effect.

The two chapters in the final part are very different in nature. The chapter on e-commerce/e-business sheds more light on current discussions and topics with regard to the use of ICT in organizations. As we have addressed various examples with regard to the adoption, implementation, use and effects in Part II we have decided not to do so here, but instead discuss the current state of affairs surrounding e-commerce/e-business. In the chapter on e-government we have adhered more closely to the process/factor model presented in Chapter 1, for several reasons. First, we did not discuss government and ICT at great length elsewhere in the book. Secondly, for reasons that will become clear when reading Chapter 9, government organization is a special kind of organization. Thirdly, government tends to follow the business community's lead in terms of benefiting from the possibilities of ICT.

Chapter 10 includes some of our final thoughts on the book, the concept of multiplicity and a research agenda. Central to the whole book and to this chapter is that we advocate a multi-theory, multi-level, multi-method, multi-moment approach of research into the adoption, implementation, use and effect of information and communication technology in organizations.

We have written the book with our students in mind. They are students in Communication Studies (Amsterdam), Communication Science (Twente), Information Studies (Utrecht) and Technical Management (Delft). We wish to thank students who were given the opportunity to respond earlier to concept chapters and lectures based on our ideas for their comments and reactions. However, the book is also relevant to students with other backgrounds, such as management, business administration, economics or organizational psychology and psychology.

We would not have been able to write this book without the support and efforts of a number of people we would like to thank: Eric Andriessen, Ronald Batenburg, Frank Bongers, Edward Faber, Marieke Fijnvandraat, Timber Haaker, Carola Hageman, Christiaan Holland, Els van de Kar, Marijn Janssen, Carleen Maitland,

Marian van der Poel, Tom Postmes, Marc Steen, Chip Steinfield, Gert Stronkhorst, Martin Tanis, Karianne Vermaas, Rene Wagenaar, Uta de When Montalvo, Helen Van der Horst, Dirk de Wit, Rieneke van der Woerd, Janneke Wolters and colleagues from Amsterdam, Delft, Enschede and Utrecht. Furthermore we would like to thank the anonymous reviewers and Delia Alfonso, and Anne Summers from Sage.

Needless to say, we are always open to suggestions as to how to improve this book. We are fully responsible for any errors, so feel free to let us know of any.

Harry Bouwman
Bart van den Hooff
Lidwien van de Wijngaert
Jan van Dijk
[September 2004]

Acknowledgements

The authors and publishers are grateful for permission to reprint the following material in this book:

Figure 1.1: Adapted from B.J. van den Hoof (1997) *Incorporating Electronic Mail: Adoption, Use and Effects of Electronic Mail in Organizations.* Amsterdam: Otto Cramwinckel.

Figure 1.3: Adapted from J.H.T.H. Andriessen (1989) 'Nieuwe Media in Organisaties: Gebruikt of Niet? (New Media in Organizations: Used or Non-used?)', in H. Bouwman and N. Jankowski (eds), *Interactive Media op Komst (The Rise of New Media).* Amsterdam: Otto Cramwinckel.

Figure 1.4: Adapted from B.J. van den Hoof (1997) *Incorporating Electronic Mail: Adoption, Use and Effects of Electronic Mail in Organizations.* Amsterdam: Otto Cramwinckel.

Figures 3.3, 3.4, 3.5, 3.6, 3.7, 3.8: From Mintzberg, *Structure in Fives: Designing Effective Organizations*, 1st Edition, © 1983. Adapted by permission of Pearson Education, Inc., Upper Saddle River, NJ, USA.

Figure 4.1: From R.T. Frambach (1993) 'An integrated model of organizational adoption and diffusion of innovations', *European Journal of Marketing*, 27 (50): 22–41, the Emerald Group.

Figure 6.4: Reprinted from Information and Management Vol 40, '*Why do People...*', pp. 191–204, Legris et al., ©2003, with pemission from Elsevier.

Figure 6.5: From V. Venkatesh, M.G. Morris and F.D. Davis (2003) 'User acceptance of information technology: Toward a unified view', *MIS Quarterly*, 27 (3): 477. © Regents of the University of Minnesota. Reprinted by permission.

Figure 6.6: Reprinted by permission from W.J. Orlikowski 'The duality of technology: Rethinking the Concept of Technology in Organizations', *Organizational Science*, 3 (3): 398–427, (1992), The Institute for Operations Research and the Management Sciences (INFORMS), 901 Elkridge Landing Road, Suite 400, Linthicum, Maryland 21090–2909, USA.

Figure 6.7: Reprinted by pemission from G. DeSantis and M. Poole, 'Capturing the complexity in advanced technology use: adaptive structuration theory', *Organizational Science*, (5): 121–147, (1994) the Institute for Operations Research and the Management Sciences (INFORMS), 901 Elkridge Landing Road, Suite 400, Linthicum, Maryland 21090–2909, USA.

Table 1.1: Adapted with the permission of The Free Press, a division of Simon & Schuster Adult Publishing Group, from Everett M. Rogers (1983) *Diffusions of Innovations*, 3rd edn. © 1961, 1972, 1983 by The Free Press. All rights reserved.

Abbreviations

2.5 G	See GPRS
3 G	See UMTS
AGPS	assisted GPS (combination of GPS and MPS)
AST	Adaptive structuration theory
B2B	Business to business
B2C	Business to consumer
Bluetooth	Standard for unlicensed wireless communication
bps	Bits per second (transmission speed)
CAD-CAM	Computer-Added Design–Computer-Aided Manufacturing
CCO	Cisco Connection Online
CD-rom	Compact Disc – read only memory
CMC	Computer-mediated communication
CPE	Customer premises equipment, like telephone, PC, DVD player and so on
CRM	Customer Relation Management
CSCW	Computer-Supported Collaborative Work
DSL	Digital Subscriber Line
DVD	Digital Versatile Disc
EAI	Enterprise Application Integration
ebXML	Electronic Business using Extensible Markup Language
EDGE	Enhanced Data rates for GSM Evolution
EDI	Electronic Data Interchange
ERP	Enterprise Resource Planning
EU	European Union
FAQ	Frequently Asked Questions
FTP	File Transfer Protocol
Gbps	Gigabit per second (transmission speed)
GDSS	Group Decision Support System
GP	General Practitioner
GPRS	General Packet Radio Service
GPS	Global Positioning System
GSM	Global System for Mobile Communications (or Groupe Spéciale Mobile)
HTML	Hypertext Markup Language
HTTP	Hypertext Transport Protocol
IAD	Iterative Application Design
ICT	Information and Communication Technology
IEEE	Institure of Electronics Engineers
IM	Instant Messaging

IRC	Internet Relay Chat
ISDN	Integrated Services Digital Network
ISO	International Standards Organization
IT	Information Technology
ITU	International Telecommunication Union
JAIN	JAVA (for) Advanced Intelligent Network
JAVA	Object oriented platform independent language related to C. JAVA refers to coffee. Product of Sun Microsystems
JINI	JINI is an interface between JAVA and applications and services.
JXTA	JAVA P2P protocol
Kbps	10^3 Bits per second (transmission speed)
LAD	Linear Application Developement
LAN	Local Area Network
LBS	Location-Based Services
Mbps	Megabit per second (transmission speed)
MEMS	Micro-Electro-Mechanical Systems
MIS	Management Information System
MP 3 files	Files that contain digital music and coded on basis of the MPEG standard
MPEG	Motion Picture Expert Group
MPS	Mobile Positioning System
NBS	New Benefit System
OECD	Organization for Economic Co-operation and Development
PAN	Personal Area Network
PC	Personal Computer
PDA	Personal Digital Assistants
PKI	Public Key Infrastructure
R&D	Research and Development
REH	Rational Expectations Hypothesis
ROM	Return on Management
SDM	System Development Method
SET	Secure Electronic Transactions
SGML	Standard Generalized Markup Language
SIDE	Social Identification model of De-individuation Effects
SIESTA	Strategic Investment Evaluation and Selection Tool Amsterdam
SIP	Social Information Processing theory
SME	Small and Medium-sized Enterprises
SMPT/MIME	Simple Mail Transfer Protocol/Multipurpose Internet Mail Extensions (Internet e-mail protocol)
SMS	Short Message System
SOAP	Simple Object Access Protocol
TCP/IP	Transmission Control Protocol/ Internet Protocol

Terabit	10^{12} bits
TMC	Traffic Management Channel
TRA	Theory of Reasoned Action
TTP	Trusted Third Party
UDDI	Universal Description, Discovery and Integration
UDP	User Datagram Protocol (connectionless version of TCP, suitable for broadcasting, video etc.)
UML diagram	Universal Modelling Language diagram
UMTS	Universal Mobile Telecommunication Services
UNIX	operating system
URL	Uniform or Universal Resource Locator
UTAUT	Unified Theory of Acceptance and Use of Technology
WAN	Wide Area Network
WAP	Wireless Application Protocol
Web XML	XML standard for the Internet
WiFi	Wireless Fidelity – or IEEE 802.11 standard family
WLAN	Wireless LAN
WSDL	Web Service Definition Language
WWW	World Wide Web
X.400	e-mail standard
XML	Extensible Markup Language
XSL	Extensible Style Language, a specification for separating style from content when creating HTML or XML pages (webopedia.com)
XSLT	Extensible Style Language Transformation, the language used in XSL style sheets to transform XML documents into other XML documents

PART I

1 ICT and organization: processes and factors

1.1 INTRODUCTION

The convergence of telecommunication and computer technology has given rise to what, at least within Europe, is generally called information and communication technology or ICT. The emergence of ICT has radically altered a number of aspects of both the way we live and the way we work. In today's working environment, an office without a personal computer (PC) is unthinkable, and those of us who cannot be reached at work by e-mail have some explaining to do – as does a company that does not have its own website. In the domestic environment, ICT is beginning to play an important role as well, most obviously in the form of the Internet. Going to the CD store is no longer necessary for the ICT-literate, who buy their music cheaper at an online store such as CD Now (Amazon), or who do not have to pay at all by using software like KazaA, or simply e-mail for the large-scale exchange of MP3 files. In certain postcode areas customers of the British supermarket chain Tesco no longer have to get up out of their chairs in order to do their shopping (www.tesco.com), it is possible to obtain cinema tickets through www.bios.nl, we can watch the news whenever we want to on www.cnn.com, we come into contact with like-minded people through one of the countless virtual communities, and so on.

The goal of this book is not to provide a state-of-the-art (and therefore soon-to-be-obsolete) picture of all the blessings ICT has in store for us. First of all, we focus exclusively on the organizational domain, leaving the 'domestic' role of ICT to others. Secondly, our aim is to show what role ICT can play within the organizational domain, which we will do by not only focusing on the (positive as well as negative) effects of ICT on organizations, but by discussing all the phases that precede these effects as well – the decision to use ICT, the implementation of applications in the organization and the everyday use of these applications. The goal of this book is to provide a scientifically sound picture of the significance of ICT to today's organizations: the entire process of adoption, implementation, use and effects is analysed. On the one hand, that means that this book focuses on the scientific analysis of the role of ICT in organizations while, on the other, it offers useful tools for everyday practice.

In this chapter we define the domain of this book. We describe the process of adoption, implementation, use and effects of ICT in organizations using the work of a number of important authors and researchers in this area. Next, we will address the factors that have an influence on the course of this process. This chapter provides a guideline for the chapters in Part II, where we will discuss each of the phases in this process in greater detail. In addition, this chapter offers the framework for the analysis of specific ICT applications in Part III, where we discuss e-business and e-government.

1.2 ORGANIZATION, COMMUNICATION AND TECHNOLOGY

Literature on ICT is often characterized by a certain degree of technological determinism, and often seems to be based on the assumption that the blessings of technology are virtually self-evident, that they can be determined rationally and objectively, and that all one has to do in order to realize these blessings is implement the specific technology in one's organization. On the other hand, at times there appears to be a certain level of 'organizational and social determinism' in the literature as well. In the latter case, the applicability of ICT in an organization is almost exclusively evaluated on the basis of the organization's current processes and structures and what people do with these technologies. Only those technologies are implemented that match the existing processes and structures as well as people's behaviour.

Needless to say, both points of view have their shortcomings. First, the effects of a technology on people and organizations can never fully be established in advance. So anyone who decides only to use technologies that match the known needs of an organization will discover that there will still be all sorts of changes in the organization: it turns out that the technology offers unexpected possibilities for innovation, is adapted in its daily usage to needs that were unknown beforehand and, as a result, may offer even more new possibilities, and so on. Secondly, it has become sufficiently clear that the introduction of a new technology does not automatically lead to the realization of all kinds of positive effects of that technology. What emerges is an interesting interaction between technology and organization, and it is this interaction that is the central theme of this book.

The entire process of the adoption, implementation, use and effects of such a technology is a process of mutual interaction: what do users want to do with the new technology and what are they able to do with it, and what changes in the organization's processes and structures are brought about by the new technology? This means that the use of ICT in organizations is a dynamic interaction between the process of technological innovation that leads to new ICT applications and reinvention of existing applications, and the process of organizational innovation that consists of the actual adoption and implementation of an ICT application in an organization, the use of these applications and the effect this has on the work and communication in the organization.

Van den Hooff (1995; 1997) uses the model presented in Figure 1.1. This model can serve as a tool to determine the suitability of a specific form of ICT within an organization, and also provides insight into the interaction between the characteristics of the technology and (processes within) an organization.

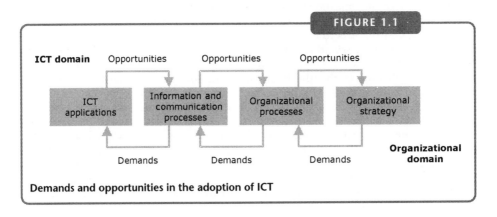

FIGURE 1.1

Demands and opportunities in the adoption of ICT

This model combines two lines of reasoning. The first line of reasoning springs from the *organizational* domain and focuses on the *demands* that an organization's processes put on information and communication media. These processes can be divided into primary and supporting processes (see Chapter 3). These processes make up the key activities of an organization, and are typically guided by strategy processes. They put certain demands on communication processes – a highly time-critical process, for instance, requires speedy communication, and a process in which many parties at geographically dispersed locations are involved requires communication across great distances. To meet these demands, certain information and communication technologies have to be selected with characteristics that match these demands.

The other line of reasoning springs from the *ICT* domain, and focuses on the *opportunities* certain technologies (or media) offer to change or improve communication processes. What contribution can these technologies make to improving the communication and supply of information within an organization or between an organization and its environment, what general effects can be distinguished, and how can the positive effects for a certain organization be realized and the negative ones controlled? Changes in information and communication processes in turn offer possibilities for changes in organizational processes, which can ultimately affect the organization's strategic position.

The central argument made here, is that a proper evaluation of the value of an ICT application should combine both lines of reasoning: both points of view presented in Figure 1.1 have their value, and in everyday practice the implementation of ICT in organizations will be a combination of the two. Successful application of ICT in an organization concerns an awareness of the organization's needs, the possibilities of the technology and the extent to which the two match. Later we will see that this balancing act can be somewhat more complex in practice, when we discuss the role of strategic management and ICT support (see Chapter 5). During the process of adoption, implementation, use and effects it is important to keep matching these possibilities and demands, and thus to ensure that:

- on the one hand, ICT applications are adopted that match existing structures and processes within the organization, making sure that technological choices fit the existing situation; and
- on the other hand, those possibilities of the applications that do not directly match the current situation are also kept in mind. The technical possibilities may lead to innovation of processes and structures, and provide insight into those effects of the application that may not have been expected or intended (both positive and negative).

In short, the use of ICT in organizations requires knowledge regarding both organizations and technology. That is why, in this introductory part of our book, we discuss both of these core elements of the process: ICT technology is the main subject of Chapter 2, while Chapter 3 focuses on a number of relevant basic concepts of organizational science. In the following paragraphs we will discuss the central starting points we will use in our analysis of the organizational innovation process of adoption, implementation, use and effects of ICT.

1.3 INNOVATION, ORGANIZATION AND DIFFUSION

The adoption, implementation, use and effects of ICT in organizations, constitutes the diffusion of an innovation in a social system – in other words, a diffusion process (Rogers, 1983). Our book, however, concerns a specific kind of diffusion process: an organizational diffusion process, and one that involves ICT. In this section, we will demarcate step by step the domain of this book: from a description of diffusion in a general sense, to a description of the adoption, implementation, use and effects of ICT in organizations.

Diffusion of innovations

Everett M. Rogers is the 'godfather' of scientific research into the diffusion of innovations. In his book *Diffusion of Innovations* (1983) he brings together a large number of varying studies in this area to create a general framework. The basis of this framework is Rogers's definition of diffusion (1983: 5): '*Diffusion* is the process by which an innovation is communicated through certain channels over time among the members of a social system.' From this definition, Rogers derives the four central elements of a diffusion process: an innovation, communication channels, time and a social system. Each study on diffusion, Rogers argues, contains these four elements.

An *innovation* is an idea, practice or object that is perceived as new by an individual or by another 'unit of adoption' (Rogers, 1983: 11). This is, then, a subjective matter: the extent to which a unit of adoption perceives the innovation as new is central here, regardless of whether that is true from any 'objective' point of view. The rate at which different innovations get adopted by members of a social system can vary strongly, and depends, among other things, on a number of characteristics of the innovation itself (Rogers, 1983: 214–32):

- *relative advantage*, the extent to which an innovation is considered 'better' than the idea, practice or object it is supposed to replace;
- *compatibility*, the extent to which an innovation is consistent with existing values, previous experiences and the needs of potential users;
- *complexity*, the extent to which the innovation is perceived as difficult to understand and complex to use;
- *trialability*, the extent to which an innovation can be tested and experimented with on a limited scale; and
- *observability*, the extent to which the use and effects of an innovation are visible to other members of the social system.

In general, innovations that the members of a social system perceive to score higher in terms of relative advantage, compatibility, trialability and observability, and lower in complexity, will be adopted more rapidly within that social system than other innovations.

Communication channels are essential, since Rogers defines diffusion as a 'particular type of communication process' (ibid.: 17). Communication channels are the actual carriers of the diffusion process, the roads along which the innovation travels through the social system. These channels can be *mass media* (particularly effective when it comes to distributing information regarding the innovation) or *interpersonal channels* (relationships within social networks, especially effective in persuading others to adopt

– or reject – an innovation). The roles of individuals, and relationships between those individuals, in a social communication network constitute an important influence on the course of a diffusion process.

The role of *time* in the diffusion process manifests itself as the point in time at which an individual (or another adoption unit) decides to adopt the innovation: their innovativeness. In addition, time plays a role in the speed with which an innovation is being diffused within a social system: the rate of adoption. Rogers identifies five 'adopter categories' based on their relative innovativeness:

- *innovators*, who are actively looking for information regarding new ideas and who adopt these innovations at a very early stage;
- *early adopters*, who often play the role of opinion leaders within the community of which they are a member, and who adopt innovation at a relatively early stage, but are less venturesome than innovators;
- *early majority*, those units of adoption that adopt an innovation before the 'average' person or organization does so;
- *late majority*, the group that is somewhat sceptical and waits until the 'average' person or organization has adopted the innovation before deciding to do so themselves; and
- *laggards*, conservative individuals or organizations with few external contacts and a primarily suspicious attitude towards new ideas, who will not adopt an innovation until a very late stage (or not at all).

In general, Rogers states, these categories each constitute a certain proportion of the members of a social system. Figure 1.2 presents this distribution, together with three typical 'diffusion curves'. In the first phase of the process only a small portion of the members of a social system (the innovators) will adopt the innovation (so the rate of adoption is still low) but, once the early adopters have joined in, the curve rises steeply (the diffusion process is gaining momentum) – and by the time the late majority has also adopted the innovation only the laggards are left, who will take considerable time

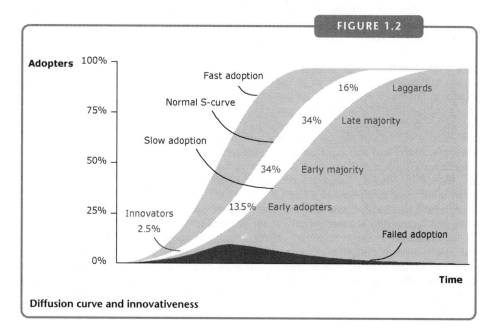

FIGURE 1.2

Diffusion curve and innovativeness

before embracing the innovation (as a result the adoption process slows down again). The three complete curves presented in this figure vary in terms of the rate of adoption, the speed with which an innovation is being diffused within a social system: the steeper the curve, the higher the adoption speed. The incomplete curve represents a failed diffusion process, where diffusion has never really lifted off and the rate of adoption remains marginal.

The *social system* is the environment within which the diffusion process takes place. Rogers (1983: 24) defines this as follows: 'A social system is defined as a set of interrelated units that are engaged in joint problem solving to accomplish a common goal'. The structure of communication networks within a social system exerts an important influence on the course of the diffusion process, as do the values and culture within the system and the various roles that the members of the social system play within the system: opinion leaders, for example, are people who are able to influence the attitude and behaviour of others with regard to an innovation. These opinion leaders (who are often among the early adopters) are key figures in the diffusion process. Opinion leaders are found both at management level and on the work floor.

Each of Rogers's four elements is thus made up of a number of variables that influence the course of the diffusion process. In the light of the subject of this book, this is an important thing to realize. After all, this book is about the factors that influence the adoption, implementation, use and effects of ICT in organizations. This means that the diffusion process which is the subject of this book is not a generic diffusion process, but a specific kind: an organizational diffusion process – the social system in which we study the diffusion process is an organization.

Innovation in organizations

With regard to the diffusion in an organizational context, Rogers (1983: 138) argues that this process has a number of differences compared to diffusion processes that take place in other social systems. Diffusion of innovation in organizations is an innovation process: 'certainly, innovation is a process, a sequence of decisions, events and behaviour changes over time' (Rogers, 1983: 138). In this innovation process Rogers distinguishes five phases, which are listed in Table 1.1.

According to Rogers, an organizational innovation process possesses some special characteristics that warrant special attention for this process over other diffusion processes. The *innovation decision* in an organizational innovation process is *contingent*, which means that the choice of an individual member of an organization depends very much on the decision made by the organization. So, two 'units of adoption' are involved in an organizational innovation process: both the organization as a whole, and its individual members. In addition, the roles in communication networks in an organization are often a mixture of formal roles (the position within the organization: managers or project leaders) and social roles (opinion leaders, 'key communicators'): managers and executives are often opinion leaders who have an influence on people, both on and off the work floor, and on people's attitudes and behaviour concerning innovations. Such individuals often determine to a large degree what is considered 'appropriate' behaviour with regard to adoption and use, and they also determine what resources (both politically and financially) are made available for implementation (Johnson and Rice, 1987).

It is essential to distinguish the different units of adoption, and we will elaborate this distinction in Chapter 4 (when the adoption phase is discussed in more detail). The distinction that Rogers makes in different phases in the innovation process is useful, but other authors distinguish different phases in this process – as we will see in the next section, where we address the adoption, implementation, use and effects of ICT in organizations.

TABLE 1.1

Phases in the innovation process in organizations (Rogers, 1983: 363)

Phase in the innovation process	Main activities
I. Initiation	Gathering information, conceptualizing and planning for the adoption of an innovation
1. Agenda setting	Defining the general organizational problems that lead to a need for innovation; looking for suitable innovations in one's environment
2. Matching	A problem is considered with an innovation, and the fit between them is planned and designed.
Decision to adopt	
II. Implementation	All events, actions and decisions involved in putting the innovation to use.
3. Re-definition/restructuring	(1) The innovation is adapted to the organization's situation and the problem at hand, and (2) organizational structures relevant to the innovation are adapted to the innovation.
4. Clarification	The relationship between the innovation and the organization is clear as the innovation is put into full and regular use.
5. Routinization	The innovation eventually loses its separate identity and becomes an element in the organization's ongoing activities.

Diffusion of ICT in organizations: from adoption up to and including effects

Andriessen (1989) specifically addresses the organizational innovation process in relation to ICT – or, as he calls it, 'new media'. Andriessen's vision is based on Cozijnsen and Vrakking (1986), who distinguish six phases in the development and introduction of 'new media' (see Figure 1.3).

FIGURE 1.3

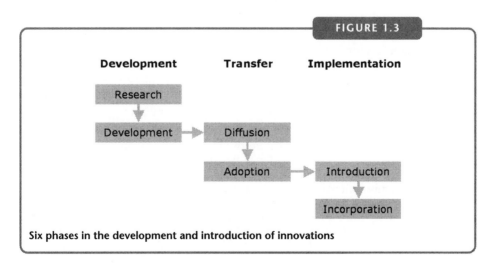

Six phases in the development and introduction of innovations

In this process, a design for an innovation emerges at a certain point in time as the result of research activities, certain daily activities or a creative idea. This design is subsequently developed into a product, service or new process. That concludes the development stage, and then the innovation is marketed and diffusion takes place among possible users of the innovation. In this book, the potential users are organizations who decide whether or not to introduce the product, service or new method of working in their organization. This decision is made on the basis of the information they have at their disposal concerning the innovation, on the one hand, and on their perceived need for such an innovation, on the other. This brings us to the implementation stage: first the innovation has to be introduced to potential users within the organization, after which they can begin to use it, turning it into a regular part of the organization's daily processes. Andriessen focuses on the last three phases in this model: adoption, introduction and incorporation. He argues that the development of each phase is determined by a number of different factors. His approach is represented in Figure 1.4.

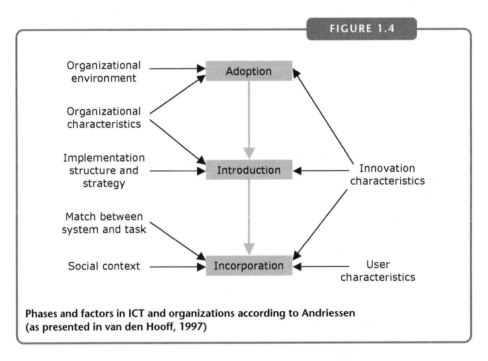

FIGURE 1.4

Phases and factors in ICT and organizations according to Andriessen
(as presented in van den Hooff, 1997)

In the first phase in Andriessen's model, the organization is the unit of adoption: in the *adoption* phase the focus is on 'exploration, research, consideration and decision making in order to introduce a new system (we prefer the term innovation) within the organization' (Andriessen, 1989: 19). Once this decision has been made, the innovation has to be introduced to the prospective users. This takes place in the *introduction* phase, when the innovation is implemented in the organization. Here, the second unit of adoption has to make a decision: on the basis of the information presented in the introduction phase, the individual user has to decide whether or not to adopt the innovation. Once the innovation has been adopted on a large scale, and actual use of the innovation is established, the process moves into its third stage: the *incorporation* phase. In this third phase, the innovation becomes part of the organization's daily ongoing activities.

Andriessen's model provides a way to chart the factors influencing the introduction of new information and communication technologies. In this model, however, no attention is paid to the consequences of the adoption, introduction and incorporation of an innovation in an organization. In this book these effects are a central subject – what is the use of ICT for an organization and what are the consequences with regard to tasks and communication within (and between) organizations? Van den Hooff (1997) uses a model that explicitly incorporates these effects. In his research into the use of e-mail in organizations he distinguishes the following phases: adoption (the organizational decision whether or not to use e-mail), use (the actual use of e-mail in the organization) and effects (the consequences of the use of e-mail for both the execution of tasks and communication). Van den Hooff also distinguishes a number of factors influencing each of these phases:

- characteristics of the *task* for which potential users could use the application (complexity, number of people involved, importance of time and distance, and so on);
- characteristics of *e-mail* itself ('richness', speed, user-friendliness, and so on);
- characteristics of the (potential) *user* (innovativeness, position within the organization, role in communication networks, and so on);
- characteristics of the *organization* (size of the organization, structure and culture, environment, and so on); and
- characteristics of the *implementation* strategy (degree to which it matches other characteristics).

Although van den Hooff does include the implementation strategy in his model as one of the factors influencing the process, unlike Andriessen he pays little attention to the specific role of the implementation phase in the organizational innovation process.

A four-phase model of the diffusion of ICT in organizations

In short, we need a model that explicitly pays attention both to the implementation of ICT in the organization and to the effects of its use. In this book we will use a model with four phases:

- adoption;
- implementation;
- use; and
- effects.

Adoption
Following Andriessen (1989: 19), we define the adoption phase as follows: 'the phase of investigation, research, consideration and decision making in order to introduce a new innovation in the organization'.

The adoption phase is the start of the process, the phase in which the organization explores what the market has to offer in terms of solutions, what its needs are with regard to such applications and what strategic benefits and efficiency gains it hopes to achieve, and finally decides whether or not to adopt a specific application. In our view, the adoption phase is primarily a decision-making process, resulting in a decision whether or not to introduce an innovation to the members of the organization – in other words, the decision whether or not to implement the innovation.

In our view, adoption is primarily an *organizational* decision-making process: on the basis of an organizational choice the decision is made whether or not to introduce an ICT application to the members of an organization. Obviously, the individual members of the organization then have their own decision to make: every one of them has to decide whether or not they are going to use the application. In our model, however, this decision takes place after the implementation phase: it is only after the application has been introduced to the users that they are in a position to make this decision. In addition, the outcome of this 'decision' becomes clear when individuals start *using* the application – or not, as the case may be. In other words, adoption is a phase that primarily takes place at the organizational level. In Chapter 4, where we will discuss this phase in greater detail, we will take a closer look at the problems associated with the various levels of analysis.

Implementation

Implementation follows the decision to adopt an innovation, and can be conceptualized as the phase where a positive decision is made operational: the decision on the part of an organization to use an ICT application is translated into a number of activities aimed at establishing the actual use of the application in the organization. The implementation phase can be defined as follows: the phase of internal strategy formation, project definition and activities in which an adopted application is introduced within the organization, with the aim of removing reservations and stimulating the optimum use of the application. Although the implementation phase may appear to be a primarily technical matter (realizing the physical infrastructure, installing the software, and so on), it is, in fact, a phase that primarily has to do with organizational issues. The implementation strategy is aimed at countering any resistance there may be against the ICT application, familiarizing the users with the application and training them in such a way that they will use it in a meaningful way. On the basis of this implementation strategy one or more implementation projects will be defined (depending on the scale of the organization and the application) in which the actual implementation takes shape.

The implementation phase plays a crucial role in the way the entire diffusion process takes place, as it determines the extent to and way in which the ICT application will be used within the organization. In relation to the phases that precede and follow the implementation phase (the adoption and use phases respectively), the importance of the implementation phase can be described in terms of the ability to translate the organizational adoption decision into many individual decisions to adopt the innovation – in other words to persuade the individual members of the organization to use the innovation. In chapter 5, we will discuss the crucial role of the implementation phase in the diffusion process in further detail.

Use

An organization can arrive at a well-considered decision to adopt an innovation, and pursue a thorough implementation strategy to introduce an ICT application, but in the end the crucial variable is the extent to which members of the organization actually use the application. This brings us to the 'use' phase, which we define as follows: the phase in which the members of an organization start applying the ICT application in their daily operational activities.

First, the *extent* to which the application is being used is of evident importance here. Is it an application that will become a significant part of the organization's daily routine, such as e-mail? Or is it a very specific application, such as, for instance, a simulation tool for designing airplanes, which will only be used by a limited number of departments? Such questions emphasize the importance of linking the use of an application to the goals that have been formulated during the adoption and implementation phases – a small-scale use does not have to mean that the application is not a success if the application was never intended to be used on a massive scale in the first place.

Secondly, the *way* in which the application is being used is important as well – what are the communication tasks for which it is being used, and within what communication processes is it being used? Is it a tool that was primarily designed for short messages (an 'information bulletin' on the intranet) or an application that plays a role in the strategic decision-making process (a video-conferencing application, for example)? Here, too, the actual use has to be linked to the relevant objectives – often the day-to-day experiences with the application will cause employees to use it in ways that were not expected or intended during the adoption and implementation phases. In these processes of 'adaptation' or 'reinvention' the application is modified to meet the needs of the people who use it. We will discuss these processes in greater detail in Chapter 6.

Effects

The actual value of an ICT application for an organization is largely determined by the effects this application has on the organization. We can define the 'effects' phase as follows: the phase in which the consequences of the use of an ICT application for the organization become manifest – consequences for the individual execution of tasks within the organization, for communication processes and structures within and between organizations, and for the position of the organization within its environment. To map these consequences we can use the distinction drawn by Sproull and Kiesler (1991) between first- and second-level effects. *First-level effects* relate to the consequences of ICT use for individual tasks: gains in productiveness and efficiency are typically first-level effects. Such effects refer to the fact that internal and external communication processes become more efficient, the fact that important information becomes more easily available in the organization, the fact that time and distance become less of a barrier in communication, and so on. As Sproull and Kiesler themselves put it: 'First level effects of communication technology are the anticipated technical ones – the planned efficiency gains or productivity gains that justify an investment in new technology' (Sproull and Kiesler, 1991: p. 4). *Second-level effects*, on the other hand, relate to the social structure of the organization: for example, changes in the communication structures in and between organizations as a result of the use of ICT. Changes in the social structure of the organization, for example, new or changing communication patterns, new roles within social networks or new patterns of dependency between actors, are examples of second-level effects. The adoption and use of ICT applications (communication media, finally) will have both first- and second-level effects.

Hammer and Mangurian (1987) distinguish three kinds of consequences of ICT for organizations: effects on the *efficiency* of processes, effects on the *effectiveness* these processes and effects in terms of *innovation*, that is, the generation and implementation of new ideas. These three kinds of effects can be related to the acceleration of certain processes (*time*), the expansion of the geographical reach of the organization (*distance*), and the *relationships* the organization maintains with its environment. We will discuss the model by Hammer and Mangurian in Chapter 3, and in Chapter 7 we will take a closer look at each of the effects mentioned above. Although both distinctions presented here can be used to clarify the effects of ICT, they have their shortcomings as well. In Chapter 7, we will critically review these distinctions of ICT effects.

1.4 ORGANIZATION, ENVIRONMENT AND INDIVIDUALS

Earlier we described adoption as a primarily organizational process, while the use of an application is primarily an individual affair: the individual employees either use or do not use an application and, as a consequence, so does 'the organization' as a whole. In short, the entire process of adoption, implementation, use and effects of ICT in organization involves various levels of analysis, and before we discuss the course of the process in greater detail we need to provide some clarification with regard to these different levels. We will do so using Figure 1.5.

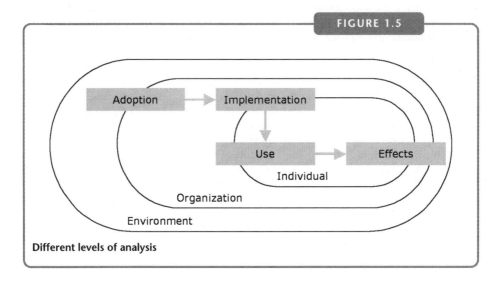

FIGURE 1.5

Different levels of analysis

Figure 1.5 shows that three levels of analysis are involved in this process: the organization, the individual employees within the organization and the organization's environment (suppliers, customers, competitors, government institutions, and so on). The four phases we distinguish here are related to these levels of analysis as follows:

1 *Adoption* to a large degree consists of the interaction of an organization with its environment: exploring the market for available ICT applications, collecting information and comparing applications. This phase also very much takes place at the organizational level: the needs and strategy of the organization have to be determined and matched with the results of the exploration. After all, this is an *organizational* decision-making process.

2 *Implementation* is primarily an organizational process of internal strategy formation, project definition and execution. However, the involvement of the individual users with this process is an important variable in the way it takes shape, and is an important determinant of its results.

3 The *use* of an innovation, as mentioned above, is primarily a matter of the individual users. The extent to which and the way in which an ICT application is used is determined by the sum of its use by the various individual users. It is also possible, however, to consider ICT use at an organizational level – for example in the case of electronic data interchange (EDI) systems, where the actual 'users' are the organi-

zation's logistical processes (or the system being used for them). As explained earlier, however, this phase is mainly about the individual user.

4   The *effects*, finally, are found at all three levels: at an individual level, the use of ICT has an impact on the users' work, information supply and communication; at an organizational level it affects the structures and processes; and, finally, there are consequences with regard to the interaction between the organization and its environment – and its position within that environment.

In the further analysis of the course of the process, and the factors that influence that process, it is important to keep in mind this conceptual distinction between the various levels of analysis. We will get back to this in the chapters on the various phases in the process, in Part II of this book.

The course of the process

By dividing the process of diffusion of ICT in organizations into four phases we have created a framework for all the important elements of this process: the decision to use an application, its implementation in the organization, the actual use of the application by members of the organization, and the effects it has on the tasks, communication and strategic positioning of the organization.

It may be clear by now that the course of this process is influenced by a large number of factors. Based on the concepts discussed thus far, the following section will discuss which factors play a role in the course of the diffusion process and indicate in what ways the influence of these factors manifests itself.

 **FACTORS INFLUENCING THE ADOPTION, IMPLEMENTATION, USE AND EFFECTS**

In the previous section we have discussed a number of models describing the 'innovation process' of ICT in organizations and identifying the various factors influencing the development of that process. When we consider these various visions together, a large number of factors emerge, which we will integrate into four perspectives from which to describe the process of adoption, implementation, use and effects:

*   The *organizational* perspective: all factors related to the nature of the organization and the environment in which it operates.
*   The *technological* perspective: all factors related to the information and communication technology itself: hardware and software, networks, standards, and so on.
*   The *economic* perspective: all factors related to financial considerations (costs and benefits) that play a role in the decision-making process surrounding ICT – and the effects of ICT.
*   The *user* perspective: all factors concerning the individual user – his or her characteristics, tasks, organizational position – as well as factors having to do with the psychological processes surrounding ICT – from the decision-making process through to the use and effects.

Although each of these perspectives is important in explaining the course of the process, they operate at different levels and their importance varies at different points in the process. In the adoption phase, for instance, costs and benefits play an important role in deciding whether or not to introduce a certain application. In other words, the economic perspective is very important here – and in the effect phase it is also important, when it becomes clear whether or not the costs and benefits that were calculated beforehand turn out to be realistic. The user perspective, on the other hand, plays an important part in the implementation phase (involving users in the process), as well as in the use and effects phases.

In addition to this difference in phases there is a difference in the level of analysis: economic and technical developments occur primarily in the organization's environment (and are most important at the environmental and organizational levels), while the user perspective obviously plays a role at the individual level.

In the following sections we will discuss the perspectives at greater length, and we will address the question why they are more important in some phases than in others. In addition, we will look at the nature of the perspectives and the themes that play a role.

The organizational perspective

The organizational perspective concerns the factors related to the nature of organizations and the environment in which they operate. This perspective is important during all phases of the application of ICT within an organization – from adoption through to the effects, the organizational environment is an important factor.

Our focus is not on organizations whose primary products or services are ICT related, but on the organizations that use ICT. In these organizations, ICT supports the processes which ultimately lead to the organization's primary products or services. The reason why ICT is so important to many organizations is that it allows them to work more effectively, more efficiently and, for example, across greater distances than competing organizations. An ICT application can have even greater effects on the nature of the organization. In time, for instance, both the structure and culture of an organization can change due to the effects of ICT (see, for example, Fulk and DeSanctis, 1999). Vertical control becomes less important in organizations, while horizontal co-ordination becomes more important, and people increasingly co-operate across formal organizational boundaries.

In part II of this book we will, among other things, look at the process of adoption, implementation, use and effects of ICT from the organizational perspective. We will pay attention, for example, to the following questions:

*   *Adoption*: at what levels are decisions made with regard to the introduction of an ICT application? What is the relationship between organizational context and individual decisions? What is the influence of organizational culture and structure on the decision-making process – and on its outcomes? What role is played by the innovativeness of an organization, and by what factors is that innovativeness determined? Based on what criteria can an organization estimate the extent to which a specific ICT application matches the organization's characteristics?
*   *Implementation*: what is the relationship between the organization's strategy and the implementation of ICT? What are the differences and similarities between organizational and technical implementation? What phases can we distinguish in organizational implementation? What strategies can be used to counter organizational resistance to a process of change – such as the implementation of ICT?

- *Use*: to what degree are ICT applications being used within organizations, and for what purpose? What strategies can an organization use to ensure that ICT is being used in such a way that the organization benefits the most? What is the influence of an organization's characteristics on the use of ICT by members of the organization? What do we mean by strategic use of ICT?

- *Effects*: what effects does ICT have on the nature and organization of business processes? What is the significance of ICT to vertical control and horizontal co-ordination in organizations? What influence does ICT have on the relationship between an organization and its environment – as well as on the relationships within the organization and the broader economic and social context within which organizations operate? What interactions between organization and technology are the result of the use of ICT?

Technological perspective

Obviously, the technological perspective on ICT is an important one as well. Although the interaction between technology and organization is central here, and our focus is primarily on the organizational aspects of this interaction, it is important to keep in mind the relevant technological developments in ICT. Technology especially plays an important role in the first two phases (adoption and implementation). However, in the effect phase technology is also relevant, when we look at how the use of an ICT application affects the application itself – the above-mentioned adaptation or reinvention process.

Although technology is in itself important, in this book we primarily consider it to be an enabler of various organizational processes. As far as the successful application of ICT is concerned, the technology itself is an important precondition. Technology offers the possibility to redesign processes or to offer entirely new products or services. When we look at technologically advanced markets such as the ICT market, we generally see a certain technology push: technology is often developed not to meet market demands, but from a technological innovation point of view. It only becomes clear later what the significance can be to people and organizations. A certain degree of technology push can be considered inevitable and is even desirable: needs can only be known to a limited extent in advance, and if one only responds to existing needs there will be little genuine innovation.

An important concept with regard to the implementation of ICT within organizations is *accessibility*. This accessibility can be described at three levels: physical accessibility, suitability and affective accessibility. Physical accessibility has to do, for example, with the availability and reliability of a technology. In addition, attention has to be paid to issues such as standards. In many cases standards do not properly match, as a result of which different systems cannot be combined. Also, new technologies often turn out to be incompatible with the technology that is already being used within an organization. With regard to suitability the question is whether there is a good fit between the task that has to be performed (for example, ordering new materials) and the possibilities the technology has to offer. Finally, accessibility has to do with the user-friendliness of an innovation – the extent to which it is relatively easy to use.

In Chapter 2 we will further discuss the technological perspective. We will discuss, among other things, the following issues:

- *Adoption*: what technological characteristics have an influence on the decision whether or not to adopt? On what factors does the relative advantage of an ICT application depend? What role is played by technological standards in the adoption phase? What is the role of the interaction between 'technology push' and 'market pull' in the decision whether or not to adopt?

- *Implementation*: what are the differences and similarities between technical and organizational implementation? What role is played by system development methods with regard to the implementation? What methods can we distinguish? What characteristics of the technology influence the formation of the implementation strategy? In what way must business processes be redesigned to arrive at a meaningful implementation of ICT?

- *Use*: how do users handle new technology in practice? To what extent do (objective or subjective) technological characteristics of ICT influence the choice and use of ICT? What exactly is the role of the application's accessibility? To what extent does user experience lead to new ways to use a certain application? What interaction processes can occur between technology, organization and user when ICT becomes operational?

- *Effects*: to what extent does the use of ICT lead to effects with regard to both technology and organization? To what degree do such effects in turn lead to further technological development or adaptation? To what extent do the technological characteristics of ICT help explain the occurrence or absence of certain effects related to the use of ICT?

Economic perspective

The economic perspective on ICT is primarily concerned with the costs and benefits (in a broad sense) that are associated with the adoption, implementation, use and effects of ICT. Investments in ICT are generally considerable, and it is often hard to quantify the benefits. Considerations of this nature are particularly relevant in the adoption and effects phases.

In addition, it is important to note that the use of ICT is strongly connected to a macro-economic development towards a network or information economy. A number of fundamental concepts within economic theory is given a new or different meaning in this process (Shapiro and Varian, 1999). An important concept within this network economy, for example, is connectivity. People and computers are becoming more and more interconnected through the use of ICT. Another effect of the use of ICT is that the concept of scarcity is given an entirely different meaning. When more people participate in a network, that network gains in value (network externalities). Whereas in the old economy, exclusiveness raises the price of a product, in the network economy to share is to generate greater value. At any rate, the product that is ICT is an entirely new phenomenon on the market, and market developments lead to major shifts between the various market parties. Tendencies towards differentiation as well as towards concentration can be distinguished.

Another theme that can be described from the economic perspective is the productivity paradox. Does it make sense to keep investing large amounts of money in ICT when it hardly appears to benefit productivity? Or is there an increase in productivity after all, but is that increase difficult to detect due to various other developments – and, if that is the case, how should we measure productivity? These kinds of paradoxes make it clear that it is harder than it would seem to determine the effects of ICT from an economic perspective.

In Part II of this book we will describe the economic perspective in the various phases of the implementation of ICT within organizations:

- *Adoption*: how can an organization arrive at a reliable estimate of the costs and benefits on which to base its decision whether or not to adopt? To what extent is it possible to estimate both the costs and the benefits beforehand? How important are economic criteria anyway in such a decision-making process? What role is played in the decision-making process by the use other organizations and individuals make of a certain application? How can the adoption of ICT be conceptualized as 'collective action'?

- *Implementation*: how can an organization keep the costs of the implementation of a new application under control? In what way can project structure and strategy help doing so?

- *Use*: to what extent are rational costs/benefits considerations relevant to the decision whether or not to use ICT? What costs are associated in practice with the use of ICT – how much do organizations really spend on ICT?

- *Effects*: does the use of ICT lead to tangible strategic benefits? How can the various kinds of benefits be quantified? Is there an increase in productivity as a result of the use of ICT, or no effect at all – or even a decrease? Or is it possible to establish such effects at all? To what extent can qualitative benefits be expressed in economic terms?

User perspective

The user perspective concerns the factors associated with the daily use of ICT. The question is, for instance, whether or not there is a fit between the task the user wishes to perform and the possibilities offered by the technology (see, for example, Daft and Lengel, 1986a). This has especially to do with the way ICT is being used and the kinds of tasks for which it is used. The degree to which it is being used is, of course, also important: the extent to which the positive effects of ICT can be realized depends to a large degree on the extent to which the information and communication processes are actually used in the performance of organizational tasks.

One of the most important themes within the user perspective is media choice. As we mentioned earlier, this has to do with finding the right fit between the nature of the task and the possibilities of the technology. A central question is how to arrive at that right fit. What tasks can be performed best using which technology? A related question is how important that fit is – in addition to such rational considerations, issues like context (especially social influences from colleagues and others), experience and background are also found to play an increasingly important role when it comes to explaining the use of ICT applications. Another issue is, for instance, if and in what way processes regarding information and communication are altered due to the use of ICT. The use of ICT, for instance, can change the way access to information, power and status are distributed among the communication partners.

The willingness to change and the way people deal with change are individually determined. People vary enormously in their attitudes towards innovation (from innovator to laggard), an element of the individual psychological disposition that is of great importance with regard to adoption, implementation and use. Also, strategies can be developed to deal with user resistance, to ensure the successful implementation of new technology.

The user perspective will also be discussed thoroughly in Part II of this book, with questions such as:

- *Adoption*: what is the relationship between the individual and the organizational decision to adopt? In what way is the decision influenced by the characteristics of the individual? How do individual users influence one another?

- *Implementation*: to what extent should users be involved in the implementation process, and in what way? What role is played by the characteristics of individual employees in determining the implementation strategy? In what way must a system be introduced in order to deal with user resistance as well as possible?

- *Use*: what is the influence of individual characteristics such as innovativeness, knowledge and experience on the use of ICT? To what extent are the (individual perceptions of the) characteristics of tasks important with regard to the choice and use of ICT? To what extent are individual characteristics a part of an interaction process between organization, technology and user? What role is played by influences from other users – either through their behaviour, or through their opinions and values? To what extent and in what way is ICT actually used by users in organizations?

- *Effects*: what are the effects of the use of ICT on individual efficiency and effectiveness? What influence does the use of ICT have on qualitative criteria such as job satisfaction? What are the effects of social networks and the position of the individual in those networks? Does ICT lead to social impoverishment? Does the use of ICT lead to information overload and how do users deal with this?

1.6 CONCLUSION

A large number of factors exert an influence on the process of adoption, implementation, use and effects of ICT in organizations. Consequently, we consider this process from the various points of view described above. There is considerable overlap between the various perspectives, and to some extent they are also mutually dependent. By looking at the various phases in the introduction process of a new system within an organization from a number of different perspectives, we arrive at an integrated vision with regard to that process.

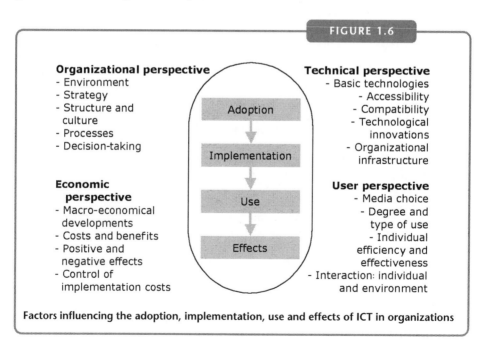

FIGURE 1.6

Organizational perspective
- Environment
- Strategy
- Structure and culture
- Processes
- Decision-taking

Technical perspective
- Basic technologies
- Accessibility
- Compatibility
- Technological innovations
- Organizational infrastructure

Adoption

Implementation

Economic perspective
- Macro-economical developments
- Costs and benefits
- Positive and negative effects
- Control of implementation costs

Use

Effects

User perspective
- Media choice
- Degree and type of use
- Individual efficiency and effectiveness
- Interaction: individual and environment

Factors influencing the adoption, implementation, use and effects of ICT in organizations

This position has led to the model that is presented in Figure 1.6. In a nutshell, this model provides the contents of Part II of this book. In the centre of this model we find the phases of the process. The various perspectives each contain a number of factors that play a role in that process – both in terms of influence on the adoption, implementation and use, and in terms of the potential effects. In Figure 1.6 these factors are presented merely in terms of examples – in the course of Part II of this book each of the perspectives will become more concrete.

In this chapter the central processes and factors concerning the adoption, implementation, use and effects of ICT in organizations have been identified. They have been approached primarily from the point of view of an interaction between organization and technology – a continuous search for a balance between organizational demands and technological possibilities. The focus has been on the organizational side of the story, on the organizational innovation process.

We have divided the innovation process into four phases: adoption, implementation, use and effects. Each of these phases plays a specific role in the way ICT is diffused in organizations, in the way it is being used and in the value it brings (or does not bring) to organizations. It is important to note that this a process that takes place at various levels of analysis: the organization's environment, the organization itself and the individual members of the organization.

The way this innovation process develops is influenced by a large number of factors, which means that the process must be considered from a number of different, but complementary, perspectives: the development of the innovation process is influenced by organizational, technological, economic, user-related and psychological factors.

Before moving on to Part II, where we will take a closer look at the process from each of the aforementioned perspectives, we need to have a better understanding of the main organizational and technological developments. Thus far, we have treated both areas as a kind of black box. In the following two chapters we will examine them more closely. The central assumption of this book is that an ongoing interaction is taking place between organizational and technological innovation. Therefore, both aspects deserve separate attention, and need first to be discussed in more detail before further analysing the process of adoption, implementation, use and effects of ICT in organizations.

2 Technology

Information and communication technology plays an important role when people try to overcome the limitations of time and distance to communicate, exchange information or work together. There are various technologies that play a role in that process, technologies that are used to establish communication over a distance (telecommunication) and technologies that are used to store, process and provide data (information technology). The convergence of telecommunication and computer technology has resulted in what is called information and communication technology (ICT). Information and communication technology is a general term used to describe a large number of different technologies and applications. In this chapter we will discuss the most important technological trends, look back at how companies have adopted information and communication technologies and how they have gradually converged. Next, we will discuss an analytical model that can be used to examine these technologies more closely. Finally, we will look at the various applications that are being (or can be) used within organizations. We will begin by presenting a brief outline of our vision on technology and its significance. We will address the following issues:

- technological determinism versus technology as the outcome of various individual and social decisions;
- negative and positive social effects of technology; and
- technology push and pull.

2.1 TECHNOLOGY IN CONTEXT

The way people perceive the role and significance of technology very much depends on how they perceive reality. The dominant perception in popular culture is that by its very nature the influence of technology is deterministic. The search for the best solutions to (technological) problems is best left to inventors and engineers. They will provide the desired solution, which is usually a technical one. According to this vision the introduction of new technologies leads to higher levels of production, improved communication and more effective and more efficient process management.

An alternative vision is the one that argues that technology is the outcome of a process involving many factors and actors. This vision can be positioned somewhere between technological and organizational or social determinism. The way technology takes shape and is being developed, implemented and used depends on various economic, social and political considerations. Although technology as such is produced by knowledge institutes and research laboratories, the decisions surrounding research and development (R&D) programmes are made on the basis of economic and social arguments: what are the benefits to the user and how does the technology fit in with the organizational strategy. Within an R and D context, increasing attention is paid to the potential social or individual and organizational use of technologies, the question of how user demands can best be met, the correct usage and to what knowledge is needed to utilize the technological achievements. Ultimately, the use of technology is being shaped, among other things, by the way it adapts to personal, organizational and social demands. This is often referred to as the social shaping of technology.

In addition to the distinction between technological determinism and approaches based on the social decision-making process surrounding technology, there are some approaches that emphasize the positive effects of technology, the contributions of technology to a more pleasant life, whereas others focus on the negative aspects, not only in terms of information overload, stress and the need to keep up (see Chapter 7 for a more elaborate discussion), but also in terms of, for instance, negative ecological effects. Some regard the negative consequences of ICT-related innovation as a threat to progress, pointing out the damaging effects, for instance, in terms of the environment, the excessive use of energy, health risks, privacy issues, increased work pressure, alienation, and so on. Others argue that technology is the driving force behind developments within society. Technology is making our lives more pleasant, processes are becoming more efficient and effective, and people have more leisure time and greater flexibility. Doubtless, there is something to be said for both points of view.

A third distinction is the one between technology push and technology pull (see also our discussion in Chapter 1 on opportunities versus demand, and our elaboration on this topic in Chapter 4). Technology push presumes that the development of knowledge and technology is a more or less autonomous process. This autonomous process results in all sorts of innovations that are of such quality that the user will be easily convinced of their usefulness and will therefore decide to accept and use the innovations or, even, in extreme cases, will be forced to use the technology because alternatives are eliminated. This last was for instance the case in France when the Minitel was introduced and it was no longer possible to look up telephone numbers in a White or Yellow Pages. According to the technology push concept, all the provider has to do is draw the user's attention to the innovations in the appropriate manner. This approach, which has been used for years by a large number of big technology companies, is hardly effective in reality. The opposite approach is called technology pull, and it is based on the assumption that the acceptance and use of technology can only be explained from the user's point of view. Here too, the truth lies somewhere in the middle. Without fundamental research new technological developments will not take place, but a successful translation of technology into applications is only possible when individual, organizational and social decision-making processes are taken into account. Increasingly, there is awareness that ICT developments are only possible through a dialogue with the user. Often failure successfully to implement a technology and persuade people to adopt it is caused by disregard for what the user wants or by the erroneous assumption that the artificial user as defined by the designer resembles the actual user. Users are being involved more and more in definition studies, in the pre-testing of designs, both on paper and in simulations, and of prototypes, as well as in market studies. Hardware and software developers realize that technology has to facilitate user behaviour.

We believe that technology and its use to a large extent depend on how and where the technology is being applied. Its development and use depends on social processes and influences, on organizational and personal preferences, and on factors involving push and pull. Without going into great detail, we believe that the way technology is being developed and shaped, as well as the way technologies are being introduced and used, to a large extent depends on individual, organizational and social influences and decisions, in other words, on economic, social and political factors. It may be clear that these decisions are subject to opposing and even conflicting interests. What is important is that a process of mutual influence ultimately shapes technology and organization. We will address this perspective, also known as adaptive structuration, in Chapter 6.

The many actors, factors, and so on make it difficult to predict which technologies will be used when and by whom. Especially with regard to fundamental technologies, for instance, in the areas of physics, biotechnology or software, it is not always easy to tell what the long-term significance to information and communication technology will be. In the future, data transport will no longer have to be electronic, it can also be mechanical, chemical or biological, for instance using micro-electronic-mechanical systems (MEMS) or cell material in bio-informatics. Nevertheless, it is easier to pinpoint trends at a fundamental level than to predict what ICT services and/or software people will use. These fundamental technologies are important to observe and to analyse in terms of future developments, however we do not hold the position that developments in technology, important as they are, are the only and principal driver, as assumed in technology deterministic visions.

2.2 TECHNOLOGICAL TRENDS

Trends at a fundamental technological level determine what computer manufacturers, network providers, software developers and application designers can offer. We have listed what we think are the most important trends:

- Digitization is the process whereby information is translated into ones and zeros, making the transferring, switching, manipulating and checking data more effective and efficient. Digital information is easier to process and store. It is possible to send digital information across great distances without any loss of quality. The greater the number of bits (the measure of digital information) can be processed per second, the more powerful and efficient a service that is delivered through a computer or a network, or a combination of the two.

- Increased processing capacity of computer chips. It is here that Moore's Law applies. In 1965, Moore, one of the founders of Intel, the large computer chip manufacturer, wrote in *Electronics Magazine* that in the past six years the number of circuits on transistors had doubled. This means that the processing capacity is increasing. Moore predicted that this would be a continuing trend, while at the same time the price of computer chips would drop. Since 1965 the average length of this period has fallen to two years. This is an indication of the scope of technological improvement. An example of this is the density of computer memory-chips. In 1980, a computer memory-chip could contain 64 kilobits, in 1990 this had grown to 4 megabit and around the turn of the century it had passed the 1 gigabit mark. Moore's Law will remain valid in the foreseeable future, at least until 2015, when the physical limits of the electronic behaviour of solid material are expected to have been reached (Bouwman *et al.*, 2000).

- Miniaturization and reduced use of energy. One of the main reasons that equipment can become ever smaller is the increased processing capacity. Another essential factor is a more efficient use of energy. Batteries have posed a serious limitation on the size and presentation of equipment for some time now. Recent developments in the field of new materials allow for even smaller batteries. Furthermore, researchers are developing systems that can use people's body heat to generate sufficient energy for some applications.

• Digitization, miniaturization and a more efficient use of energy have, for example, made the use of mobile communication equipment possible. The mobile phone, until recently above all a terminal for telephony, is increasingly becoming a vessel for all kinds of digital services. The current simple data services (sending messages) will certainly be replaced by more advanced applications based on Internet technology. This is the third-generation mobile communication, often referred to as Universal Mobile Telecommunications System (UMTS). Mobile data communication is not only possible using UMTS, but also with Bluetooth or wireless LAN (WLAN). Software platforms enable interchange of data between WLAN (WiFi or IEEE802.11 standard family), UMTS and Bluetooth. Bluetooth offers new opportunities for a reliable wireless signal transfer between various small and cheap applications over a small distance (from 10 cm up to 10 metres).

Applications that use Bluetooth do not have to be in each other's field of vision. The connections can be made on an ad hoc basis, without the user being aware of it. Printers, PCs, mobile phones, personal digital assistants (PDAs) and other peripheral equipment can be connected wirelessly. Future outlooks are directed towards the personal area and wearable networks, with the so-called personal area networks (PANs), Piconet or I-centric services, which automatically adapt to individual requirements (Popescu-Zeletin *et al.*, 2003).

• Increased technical integration. Computer technology is increasingly being built not only into the mobile phone, but into a variety of other appliances, such as cars and household utensils (washing machines, central heating systems, temperature control systems and so on). These systems are often referred to as embedded systems. These embedded systems make it possible to use several functions at the same time. The display of a telephone provides information with regard to the caller, a photocopier can be used as a fax or printer.

• Increased use of sensors and location technologies. In many embedded systems sensors are being used. Sensors regulate the temperature in office buildings, or indicate when the toner of a photocopier has to be replaced. In addition, sensors can be used to determine the whereabouts of certain employees. Location technologies become more important, especially in relation to mobile and wireless networks. There are different kinds of location techniques: cellular location techniques and the Global Positioning System (GPS), and the European alternative, Galileo. There are different kinds of cellular location techniques that all make use of the communication and position between the mobile phone and the base station.

• Positioning using GPS (Global Positioning System and Galileo) is enabled by the signal satellites are constantly beaming down. The signal has a fixed pattern and contains the exact position of the satellite and a time reference. A terminal calculates its position in relation to the position of the satellite with a certain degree of accuracy (3-30m). The GPS or Galileo receiver module can be integrated into a mobile phone. A new development is a mix of cellular location techniques and GPS, that is assisted GPS. Assisted GPS (AGPS) integrates the functionality of GPS and a cellular telecommunications network and adds functionality to this by adding a Mobile Positioning System (MPS). The MPS collects the differential GPS data from the receiver and other assistance data and uses the Global System for Mobile Communication (GSM) network (or any other network like UMTS) to communicate with the mobile handset. The mobile handset can send the measured GPS signal back to the MPS using the same network (Hambeukers, 2001). The performance of location methods depends on the context of the user's indoor, outside, urban or rural surroundings.

• Increasing 'intelligence'. Networks and systems are becoming ever smarter. Information and communication systems are highly complex and they have to be able to adapt quickly to new developments and user demands. Increasingly, relevant functionalities are built into the software rather than the hardware. Software plays an important role in the management of information and communication systems. Management software can either be integrated into the network or built into peripheral equipment. The location is important for the monitoring of services and applications. When the software is stored at a central location inside the network it is managed by the network or service provider. When it is located inside peripheral equipment, for instance, a mobile phone or PC, that responsibility lies with the end-user. One example of this is the answering machine: the user can see how many messages there are, he or she can turn the device on or off at will, and so on. Only the user controls the device. Voice mail, on the other hand, is implemented in the network and is managed by the service provider or the central telephone exchange within the organization.

Another example of increasing intelligence is the development of software agents, a specific form of distributed software applications. Agents are given an important role in the search for and selection of information. Searching the Internet is sometimes compared to sifting through someone's garbage. Currently, most people use a system whereby information is requested and they have to wait for the information to be sent to them. This means network facilities are being used. Sending agents onto the network to gather information at the right place and time can help reduce the time network facilities are being occupied. Based on the user's demands and profile, agents choose their own time to search the Internet and retrieve relevant information. Applications of this principle can be found in e-commerce, online services, selective information retrieval, network management, and so on.

- Increased interoperability between services instead of applications. Instead of applications that have to be bought, installed or downloaded from a central location and so on, services will be delivered via the Internet. Web services, based on standards such as WSDL (Web Service Definition Language) and UDDI (Universal Description, Discovery and Integration) from Microsoft, JINI (a JAVA-based technology), and JXTA (JAVA P2P protocol) from SUN and open standards as SOAP (Simple Object Access Protocol) and XML (Extensible Markup Language) will enable services such as single sign-on, authentication, notification and messaging, personalization, integrated search, management and data exchange and delivery by integration of web services with legacy systems. These services however require clear architectures, both in the business, information and application domains. Multi-tier architectures provide a message-based and modular architecture aimed at increasing flexibility, usability and scalability in comparison to centralized, mainframe and file-sharing systems. A typical multi-tier architecture makes a distinction between a client tier (presentation of limited functionality to the end-user), a middle tier, which include the application logic and the business rules and might contain messaging and transaction processing technology (so called middleware), and the data tier, which includes the databases.

Currently, databases are often object oriented and distributed. An object-oriented database consists of objects, or data elements together with strict definitions of their attributes and the methods (or operations) to be performed on them (Kim, 1990). A distributed database consists of data files located at different sites on a computer network, which need to be synchronized periodically to ensure that every user has consistent data. The use of such databases makes it possible to provide access to the same information using different channels, not only via the Internet, but also, for example, via online databases and call centres or in print. Processing within a multi-tier architecture can be done on a server in the middle tier or on a client. When most of the processing is done on the client this is referred to as a thick client; when most of the processing is done on the service one speaks of a thin client. Thick clients have high control and maintenance costs, security problems, leads to autonomous processing of information, minimal communication with servers and, when communication takes place, high bandwidth use. Thin clients have low control and maintenance costs, low security risks, continuous communication and low bandwidth use.

Development of web services helps to separate business logic from implementation by making use of standardized service interfaces. Web services in fact perform encapsulated business functions. Web services make use of XML messages to communicate between client and server, making use of networks and protocols for transport. Simple Object Access Protocol provides an envelope around XML messages in order to exchange structured information. Web Service Definition Language is a protocol that shows the possibilities of a web service. Universal Description Discovery and Integration provides a kind of White, Yellow and Green Pages for localizing and registering web services and companies that offer these services (Janssen, 2003).

Developments in the domain of web services will lead to horizontal disintegration of value chains within organizations and outsourcing and commodification of IT.

- Increased security. Security begins with improved and safer identification and verification mechanisms. In a variety of organizational processes identification (who am I speaking to) and authorization (what is and is not this person allowed to do) is extremely important. Other security issues are the integrity of, for instance, data traffic, privacy and protection against third party intrusion. Increasingly, biometric methods, such as the electronic fingerprint, retina scan and voice recognition, will be used for verification. The development of various standards (Private Key Infrastructure [PKI], Secure Electronic Transactions [SET]) plays an important role in payments and electronic transactions.

- Natural interfaces. The man–machine interface, in other words, the way the end-user uses peripheral equipment – PC or telephone – will change drastically as well. User input through keyboard or mouse, followed by output on screen, can be replaced by voice-controlled interaction: voice recognition and synthesis. Software built into the equipment will enable simple communication between user and machine, especially in situations where the communication follows a more or less set pattern. At the same time machines will receive more information regarding the users and behave accordingly, for example by sending back information that fits the user profile.

The general trend in ICT is that technology is becoming 'smaller, faster, smarter, more natural, safer, and cheaper'. Fundamental technological developments that depend on the physical characteristics (think, for instance, of Moore's Law) are easier to predict than those that depend on software development, for instance future developments in the web service domain. After all, software development is above all a human activity. In organizations, many applications are based especially on software developments.

2.3 CONVERGENCE

The various technological trends have caused a number of different developments to take place, both in the computer (information technology – IT) and the telecommunications sector. In particular digitization has led to a convergence of technologies and industries. We shall briefly discuss the main technological developments in the IT and telecommunications sectors.

From calculator to Internet

Information and communication technology is not something that happened in the last 20 or 30 years. Information technology is a development that was started over 100 years ago. When we look at office automation, for example, we see that 'information technology' has been used for a number of purposes since the end of the nineteenth century (after van den Ende, 1998a):

- The (re)production and storage of documents. For a long time pen and paper were used to provide access to documents for others or for later use. At the end of the eighteenth century the typewriter and the Dictaphone joined them. Carbon paper and mimeograph, in addition to printing books, made it possible to distribute documents among several users. Also, card systems were introduced that allowed documents to be easily located.

- Accounting, calculations and data processing. Accounting machines, calculators and punch card machines have a very long history. In 1833, the English mathematician Babbage was working on a mechanical calculator. In 1876, Hollerith developed an electro-mechanical device that operated with punch cards. Babbage had envisaged similar cards as input for his calculator. Hollerith's invention stood at the cradle of what was later to become IBM. The first fully electronic calculators such as ENIAC and Colossus (the first American and English computers) caused the developments in the area of electronic calculating to accelerate further. After the development of transistors and integrated circuits (computer chips), the first prototypes of the computer were followed by mainframes, minicomputers and PCs (Winston, 1998). More and more software was developed for these electronic calculators, such as word processors, spreadsheets, databases and integrated systems like MS Office and Enterprise Resource Planning (ERP) systems.

- Communication. With regard to both internal and external communication across distances a number of new possibilities emerged at the beginning of the twentieth century: the telephone (and before that the telegraph), pneumatic dispatch and later electronic communication systems. Especially telephony played an important role in the expansion and acceleration of communication systems within and between organizations. Computer technology also had a growing impact on the way communication networks operated. The emphasis has shifted away from communication based on analogue technologies towards digital forms of communication. In 1964, Paul Baran presented the first concept of what later was to become the Internet. Computer technology also influences the way telecommunication networks are being managed. The central concept in this respect is the intelligent network: a network that makes it possible to separate the actual traffic from its control processes. This makes things like voice response systems, voice mail, call forward and audio-conferencing possible.

The introduction of all these technologies has had an influence on the way companies operate nowadays. The twentieth century can be divided into a number of periods (van den Ende, 1998a):

- 1880–1914, the rise of the modern administration: the introduction of typewriters, for example, created new types of jobs, but it also helped create a division in the kind of jobs typically held by either men or women. Women were employed as typists or switchboard operators. Men focused increasingly on managerial tasks, resulting in a separation between management and company ownership (de Wit and Huiter, 1998).

- 1914–57, the mechanized office: as a result of the introduction of more new technologies and of the economic crisis, the emphasis increasingly shifted towards work distribution and improved efficiency. Scientific management (or Taylorism) emerged. An example of Taylorism was the centralization of administrative activities in large offices, where punch cards, accounting machines and addressographs were used (de Wit and van den Ende, 1998).

- 1957–80, the rise of the computer: in the period after the Second World War the central administrative departments developed into computing centres with the arrival of (mainframe) computers. These computing centres (the forerunners of the automation departments) operated a few big, unwieldy computers. During this period the first software was developed (van Oost and van Hoorn, 1998). Many processes were automated for the first time. This development was characterized by the so-called island automation. There was little or no co-ordination between various projects, causing all sorts of problems.

- 1980–2000, computer revolution: as a result of, among other things, the above-mentioned technical trends and the improved price/quality ratio, the 1980s were characterized by the emergence of the personal computer. The last decade of the twentieth century was characterized by an increasingly large-scale access to networks and the Internet. Technology push is increasingly being replaced by a focus on people and organizations, and the integration of various systems has become an important objective (van den Ende, 1998b).

Table 2.1 provides an overview of the developments that have taken place in the office environment since the late nineteenth century. The table is certainly not exhaustive but it highlights a number of important moments and developments. Technology, in interaction with organizational processes, has played a role in the way organizations have developed.

TABLE 2.1

Developments of ICT in the twentieth century

Period	1880–1914	1914–1957	1957–1980	1980–2000
Characterization	Modern administration	Mechanized office	Rise of the computer	Computer revolution
Technical developments	Office technology	Central administration	Mainframe computers	Personal computers and networks
Organizational developments	Job distribution between men and women. Rise of middle management	Scientific management, centralization of administrative activities	Increase of scale	Analysis of business processes schematization
Communication	Telex, telephone	Radio		Internet, e-mail, video-conferencing
Storage/filing			Tape, magnetic tape	Optical storage media
Processing	Punch cards	Accounting machines	Spreadsheets	ERP systems
Reproduction	Mimeograph	Addressing machines	Matrix printers	Laser printers
Production	Typewriter, Dictaphone		Word processors	

From back office to front office

The final phase of this development is illustrated by the fact that the internal automation (back office) is increasingly connected to communication (front office) between organizations and their environment: partners, suppliers, customers, and so on. Applications aimed at communicating with suppliers or customers have increasingly become integrated with administrative business systems. Nowadays, this integration is referred to as e-business. We will take a closer look at this in Chapter 8. Information technology and communication opportunities are becoming interconnected in other functional domains as well.

Before discussing the various applications and services we will address the question as to how applications operate through communication networks, resulting in the so-called information, communication and transaction services. We will first discuss the layer model.

2.4 LAYER MODEL

Communication networks make up the bottom layer in the layer model (see Figure 2.1). In the simplest version the layer model illustrates the relationship between (1) the physical infrastructure: the cables in the ground or the ones connecting PCs, (2) the transport services: the services that make sure that the signals are being transferred from sender to recipient via the physical infrastructure (the cables in the ground or the office network), (3) the services being used and (4) the end-user. The end-user has access to the services and applications through a telephone, a computer, possibly with a modem, or mobile peripheral equipment such as a telephone. Due to wide proliferation of the Internet layer models have also consequences for the way IT within and between organizations is defined and implemented. A more layered approach can be found around web-services.

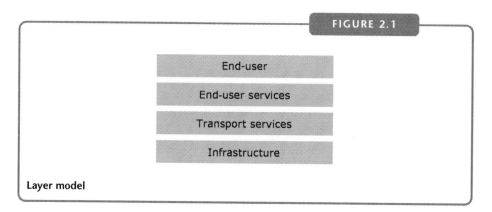

FIGURE 2.1

End-user

End-user services

Transport services

Infrastructure

Layer model

Until the 1980s, every service had its own transport service and infrastructure (Figure 2.2). Telephony was conducted over the telecommunications network, mobile telephony over the mobile network, and data communication over the so-called Datanet-1, an X-25 network or the giga-ethernet that is used in an office environment. All these services were vertically integrated.

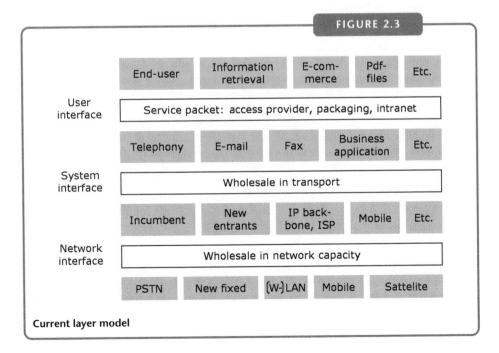

FIGURE 2.2

End-user	End-user	End-user	End-user	End-user	End-user
End-user services	Tele-phone	E-mail	Mobile phone	EDI	Printing
Transport services	Telecom network	ISP network	Mobile network	Data commu-nication	Data commu-nication
Infra-structure	Telecom infrastructure	Telecom infrastructure	Mobile infrastructure	Datanet	LAN

Traditional division between networks

Thus far, the network used to access the service has also been the delivery network: telephony used the fixed telecommunications network, printers could only be operated via the office network, and so on.

This relatively simple world of vertically integrated and separate communication domains, each with its own layer model, no longer exists (Figure 2.3). The rise of information and communication technology has made it possible to connect various networks. It also allows vertical connections to be disentangled. The connection

FIGURE 2.3

	End-user	Information retrieval	E-com-merce	Pdf-files	Etc.
User interface	Service packet: access provider, packaging, intranet				
	Telephony	E-mail	Fax	Business application	Etc.
System interface	Wholesale in transport				
	Incumbent	New entrants	IP back-bone, ISP	Mobile	Etc.
Network interface	Wholesale in network capacity				
	PSTN	New fixed	(W-)LAN	Mobile	Sattelite

Current layer model

between peripheral equipment and network type becomes less and less natural. The network through which a service is being accessed is no longer automatically the delivery network. It becomes possible to receive images that are provided through the Internet on a mobile telephone. The signals can be transferred through the data communication network and/or the fixed telecommunications network, and reception can ultimately take place through the mobile communications network. Telephone calls can be conducted over the Internet. E-mails can be sent to a personal digital assistant through a wireless local area network (wireless LAN – Local Area Network). Pdf files can be downloaded from a database via the Internet and printed locally.

2.5 ICT IN ORGANIZATIONS

One of the results of the above-mentioned technological trends is that text, images and sound are integrated into multimedia applications. Digital storage and manipulation of images and sound requires a large processing capacity. Multimedia is dependent on powerful computer chips and storage and distribution media. The capacity of the 'common PC' is still growing explosively, turning it into a multimedia workstation. Although a few years ago multimedia still depended on external carriers such as compact disc – read only memory (CD-ROM) (which by now has all but found its place in the history books thanks to the digital versatile disc [DVD]), nowadays there is a complete integration of multimedia in standard PC's: the hard drive of a PC contains more information than a CD-ROM. Digital versatile disc players are built into virtually all PCs. Speech recognition systems can be provided on request.

It is not only the computing and storage capacity of PCs that increases, at network level more capacity is available as well. Traditional networks based on copper wires or coaxial cables, used both in public (for instance, the fixed telecommunications network) and in private (in-house) networks, are being replaced by fibre optics networks. With respect to the increase in the capacity of networks people often refer to Gilder's Law. He points out that the bandwidth of networks triples each year. As a result the speed with which data can be transferred increases as well.

There is a trade-off between the quality and the amount of data that can be transferred through a network. Sending a simple e-mail requires fewer bits per second (bps) than sending images. It is not of crucial importance whether the e-mail is received instantly or whether some delay occurs (seconds or even minutes). Nor is it a problem if data containing a scan or floor plan are transferred with some delay or if the images take a few seconds to appear on screen. As far as real-time moving images, for instance during a videoconference, and telephony are concerned, however, such a delay is unacceptable. This type of data has to be available immediately and continuously. This leads to a temporary high level of network occupation. This high level indicates how much information has to be instantly available at any given moment. Real-time video in combination with speech requires a continuous availability (preferably) of 2 Mbps. Transporting high-quality real-time moving images (television) requires 155 Mbps. Multimedia applications require high capacity and a virtually constant availability of network capacity.

Telecommunications standards are increasingly based on or adapted to the TCP/IP protocol. TCP/IP stands for Transmission Control Protocol/Internet Protocol, and indicates how data are transferred over the Internet. By aligning the various standards it becomes easier to connect interorganizational networks as well as internal and external networks.

End-user services

From the point of view of organizations the available of end-user services and applications are most important. Applications and services can be divided on the basis of functionality: consulting information, communicating with others or exchanging information to support certain processes, often transaction processes and applications that are integrated into elements of information, communication and registration services. Furthermore, these applications and services can be used both within an organization (internally) and between an organization and its environment (externally). Also, to distinguish various applications and services it is important to consider the structuring level of processes. Brown and Duguid (2000) make the following distinction: (1) highly structured processes that are relatively easy to describe and to analyse and (2) processes that are hardly structured at all and are difficult to organize. The first group (highly structured processes) includes logistics, sales, financial administration, personnel management, and so on. These are the domain of most enterprise or transaction processing systems, supply chain systems and customer relationship systems, manufacturing systems but also human resources systems. The second group refers to less structured, creative processes, for instance, in the strategy formation of an organization, or the way organizations manage knowledge, and so on. This is the

---

TABLE 2.2

Matrix with examples of applications/services, according to the structuring of processes and internal/external orientation

	Information	Communication	Transaction and registration	Integrated applications
Structured processes Internal	Databases, document management systems, ERP systems, human resource management systems	Electronic boardroom, group decision support system	Monitoring systems (e.g. production control systems, planning systems, sales and stock systems), electronic agenda	Information (file) sharing, application sharing, computer supported collaborative work, workflow management
External	Online-databases, Internet, call centres (inbound)	Call centres (outbound), e-mail, electronic data interchange	Customer relation management (CRM), EDI, electronic fund transfer, ordering systems, supply chain management systems, reservation systems	Multimedia call centres
Unstructured processes Internal	Management information systems, intranet, knowledge management	Electronic boardroom, (mobile) telephone, e-mail, voice mail, computer-conferencing, videoconference, shared whiteboard		CSCW, communities of practices
External	Internet, online databases	E-mail, voice mail, videoconference		Communities of practices

domain of executive support systems, management support and decision-support systems. More and more, knowledge work systems are also accounted for. Our focus in this book will be more on the second type of systems that support less structured processes than the enterprise information systems, which are more the domain of information systems research.

The three dimensions discussed above produce the matrix (in Table 2.2). Without pretending to be exhaustive or complete, we have listed some examples in the cells.

Information services

Databases are at the heart of information services. The use of databases, often object oriented and distributed, makes it possible to provide access to the same information using different channels, not only via the Internet, but also, for example, via online databases and call centres or in print. The application being used is determined by the peripheral equipment. The most familiar example is doubtless the telephone. A large number of call centres can be reached by telephone. Professional organizations provide their information and services in this way, for example, banks providing account information. Another well-known example is the PC. The PC allows people to use Internet services, online databases, and so on. Most of these services are accessed via the traditional telephone network, Integrated Services Digital Network ISDN or Digital Subscriber Line (DSL) or via a local network connected to the public Internet.

In addition to the distinction based on the presentation of information (text, images, sound), a distinction can be drawn between the nature of the information. Some information is produced and used within organizations (databases that are often being used within business systems: enterprise and management information systems [MIS] applications), whereas other information is provided by third parties. This second category of information includes, among other things:

- financial information – currencies, prices, stock exchange information, and so on.
- economic information, for instance, market information, company addresses, business profiles, and so on;
- legal information – complete legal texts, jurisprudence, legal articles, and so on.
- scientific information – especially in the areas of medicine and chemistry there are information services that provide complete scientific articles. Also, there are bibliographical databases;
- government information;
- general news as generated by news services and various editorial boards; and
- educational information such as encyclopaedias, and so on.

A third possible distinction is based on the structuring level of the information. Information that is used in various structured business processes often has a fixed format. There are often precise guidelines as to how data used in specific processes have to be stored.

Many information services and databases are reasonably well structured and easy to search. In the case of databases that support structured, often operational processes, relevant information is instantly available. This is not the case with less structured processes, for instance strategic policy formation. In those cases where relevant information is being recorded in the form of (digitally stored) documentation, there is hardly ever any real order, never mind having easy access to the data. A great deal of information within organizations is person related and can only be consulted on an ad hoc basis. Personal preferences tend to determine the way documents are stored, often in directories that are not publicly available. Alternatively, the information is only stored in the heads of the employees. Documentary information supply aims at providing access to this kind of information, to all kinds of documents that vary in terms of size, structure and depth. Information is an essential part of knowledge. Knowledge management aims at increasing access to knowledge and people's ability to perform certain tasks (Weggeman, 1997, p. 64).

An important development has been the rise of the Internet, the World Wide Web and browsers. This development has led to a situation whereby the Internet provides public (Internet) or private (intranet) access to a large collection of unstructured information. Technological developments also make it possible to actively deliver information to the end-user (web-casting).

Communication services

There are various forms of communication services and applications that are relevant to organizations. An important distinction that can be drawn in this respect is between synchronous and asynchronous applications. Synchronous communication involves the simultaneous 'presence' of the participants in the communication process (for instance a telephone call), whereas in the case of asynchronous communication there is a certain time interval between the message and a reaction to that message ('delayed communication', such as an exchange of letters). Some systems can only be accessed at the same time and location, for instance electronic conferencing systems located in a meeting room. Other applications, such as bulletin boards, do not depend on either time or place. A frequently used division is based on these two dimensions (see Table 2.3).

The best-known example of a communication application is e-mail, or electronic mail. This is an example of an asynchronous application: a message is sent, arrives at the electronic mailbox of the recipient, who opens the message, reads it at a convenient moment and then sends a reply. In the early 1990s this application was relatively new and used especially for internal communication. Nowadays, there are hardly any

TABLE 2.3

Examples of synchronous and asynchronous, and (non-)distributed communication (Krcmar, 1992, Hawryszkiewycz, 1997; Wigand, Picot and Reichwald, 1997, Bongers and Holland, 2001)

	Same time (synchronous)	Different times (asynchronous)
Same place	Face-to-face communication, electronic conferencing systems with local network in a physical location (GDSS), presentation systems	File sharing, design tools, diary management systems, project management software
Different place (distributed)	Telephone, audio- and video-conferencing, shared whiteboard	E-mail, voice mail, computer conferencing (IRC), electronic conferencing through the Internet, bulletin boards, multiple author software, workflow systems, systems based on client server architecture

organizations that do not have e-mail in their communication repertoire. It is only in rare cases that e-mail applications are not linked to external networks. In the beginning the content of e-mails was limited to plain text. Nowadays complete documents (possibly including audio and video) are being transferred through e-mail.

Voice mail is a similar application. Voice mail addresses the problems involved with both parties having to be present at the same time to ensure successful communication. A spoken message is stored, which the recipient can access at his or her convenience – and they can store the message, forward it to others, respond to it immediately, and so on. Also, several people can be reached with one message.

Examples of synchronous applications are 'chatting' and computer conferences. Chat is an application that enables two persons connected to the same network to exchange information synchronously – a kind of written telephone conversation. By the same token computer conferencing can be compared to a teleconference: several persons can communicate simultaneously with the aid of PCs and a network infrastructure. An example of this is instant messaging, an application best described as an Internet as well as a mobile chat box.

As far as organizational communication is concerned, the use of synchronous communication for business purposes ('real' meetings) is far more interesting. Video-conferencing with a quality that can serve as a realistic alternative to physical meetings requires a studio with a camera, codec equipment, and so on. Often the set-up will be a small meeting room where three people can be captured reasonably well on camera. A less complicated solution is provided by desktop video systems whereby a camera is attached to a PC, or video images can be sent from one workstation to another.

The applications that have been discussed so far are examples of applications used in processes that are not really formalized, whereby unstructured information is being exchanged. The nature of the information being exchanged is relatively undetermined. There are, however, applications that use highly structured data in processes, whereby it has been exactly determined which information has to be available, in which format and for whom, for instance in call centre or workflow management systems. A basic principle of workflow management is that it is not just a single activity that is being automated but, rather, the entire process of which the specific task is merely a part. Workflow management makes sure that a user has access to the data he or she requires to perform a specific task in the business process at the right moment. In general terms, workflow management is the automated support of processes. A specific form of structured information exchange is electronic data interchange (EDI). Electronic data interchange deals directly with transactions – for instance, order and billing processes – whereby standardized messages are exchanged between computers. This involves communications between computers rather than people. Based on stock information, for example, a computer can send out a standard order to a supplier's computer, which can then process the order – and possibly even send out the invoice. Electronic data interchange is used in numerous economic sectors, for instance trade, transport, health care and social insurance, and is increasingly based on Internet technology. As has become clear above, EDI is in effect a combination of registration (in databases) and communication (exchanging messages) services. Web services enable Enterprise Application Integration (EAI): the automatic coupling of applications of multiple organizations. Enterprise Application Integration is the next step from EDI towards business-to-business integration. Automated collaboration between organizations is becoming more important, for instance when connecting flight reservation systems with legacy reservation systems of car rental companies or with traffic or route information services.

Transaction or registration services

Transaction and registration services are becoming more and more important for organizations, businesses and governments in dealing with their stakeholders. These services register information aimed at processing transactions. Here, too, a distinction can be drawn between internal and external applications. In the case of internal transactions this involves both the monitoring of all kinds of processes (for instance in workflow systems, planning modules, financial administration, ERP systems, and so on.) and the collection of all sorts of information by employees, for example in a central electronic diary. In the case of external applications, it has to do above all with collecting information from consumers and other parties within the organization's environment, as well as processing electronic transactions: e-commerce.

Internal registration services can focus on technology as well as on business processes. Technology-oriented registration services include, for example, monitoring the occupation levels of the company network, checking the online presence and performance of individuals and/or various technical systems and so on. Following this, registration services can also be used to supervise the progress of various (often geographically dispersed) business processes. At a central location information can be collected regarding the time certain half-finished products have to be available, regarding the progress of the transportation of certain parts, stock information, and so on. Something of this nature takes place each time people pay for their groceries at the supermarket counter: the data collected via the barcode reader are translated instantly into stock information ('one less bottle of cola'). An order is automatically generated every time the available stock drops below a certain level. Often the order will be sent electronically as well, through EDI. Payment can take place electronically, with the payment system checking whether the person is authorized to transfer money to the supplier's bank account.

External registration services in particular have to do with the interaction between the organization and the market, with various parties in its vicinity. An example of this is the collection of information regarding the organization's customers, for instance by monitoring which pages of the organization's website were visited. It can also be information that is collected for customer relation management (CRM). Also, an organization can conduct online market research, for example by asking visitors of the website to fill in an electronic form containing target group-related data (such as name, address, income, interests). These forms are then instantly translated into a record (or several records) in the organization's customer database. In addition to collecting online information (and providing it, see 'information services') the organization can also allow actual online transactions to take place. Anyone ordering a book from, say, Amazon.com, selects the book he or she wants to buy on the basis of author, title, genre, keyword or any other piece of information. The book can be ordered directly online, and the customer can indicate the delivery address and method of payment (credit card, electronic payment, and so on). These data are stored in the database, and the order is generated and subsequently processed automatically. Payments by credit card and electronic payments are processed immediately. At face value this looks like a registration service, and that is exactly what it is: the provider determines the information that is required and the format in which that information has to be submitted.

Integrated applications

Applications and services are increasingly merging into information, communication and registration services. They offer the possibility to consult information, and in many cases to conduct transactions, for example on websites or information kiosks in banks. In addition, these information services offer the possibility to send an e-mail to the organization. People who want to send an e-mail are no longer limited by the traditional 'communication' pattern: one-on-one can just as easily become one-on-many, and in general messages that are sent to newsgroups or bulletin boards can be consulted at a later date – as an information service.

Some well-known applications that integrate different patterns are intranet, groupware, computer-supported collaborative work (CSCW) and group decision support system (GDSS). Intranet and groupware to a large extent are similar applications: they are office applications that integrate information, communication and registration services. These services provide an integrated package of online databases and shared documents and applications – is also referred to as CSCW. Computer-supported collaborative work can range from 'file and information sharing' (having access to the same file or information and being able to modify it (separately), to 'application sharing': working together on one document, creating a design together, and so on.

Intranet can be defined as a local (closed) version of the Internet for organizations (Bouwman, 1998). Generally speaking an intranet will include applications that are found on the Internet: one or several internal websites, e-mail based on Simple Mail Transfer Protocol/Multipurpose Internet Mail Extensions (SMTP/MIME) (the Internet protocol), newsgroups, 'chat' applications, and so on. Information concerning the internal organization, customers, projects, stock supplies and so on can be accessed through the internal website; memos and newsletters are sent by e-mail; expense claims are submitted online; and a jointly produced document is put on a web page (which does require high-quality version management, but that is another story), and so on.

Group decision support systems are specifically aimed at supporting decision-making processes. This involves both providing information during decision-making processes and systematically processing the results of these processes. Some group decision support systems contain all kinds of calculation rules or procedures to ensure decisions are arrived at in a more systematic way and the contributions of the various participants are treated in a more balanced way. This may reduce weight attached to a formal position (for example that of a chairman) in the decision-making process, although emotional arguments do play a role in 'rational considerations' as well.

In addition to playing a role in work situations, combinations of applications are also used in learning situations. Until recently, 'practice and drill' was a leading principle in many of the computer-supported learning situations, but there is an increasing shift towards systems that are based on a process of joint discovery and communication aspects. Knowledge management is moving in the same direction. In communities of practice people working in certain areas exchange information, consult one another or look for ways to document their shared knowledge.

Developments at the level of services

When we look at future developments we can predict that the next generation of information, communication and registration applications and services will be more intuitive and there will be a trend towards genuine multimedia. The intuitive nature is expressed in all forms of usage. Information services are developing from speech-oriented towards image-oriented systems that facilitate person-to-person communication as well as person-to-multiple-persons communication. Co-operation is essential here. Transaction services will play an increasingly important role, especially in light of the expectations surrounding e-commerce. Many support-ing technologies aimed at improving customer identification and facilitating consumer behaviour will be developed. To an extent these processes will be purely logistical, involving in-house stock management at consumer level. On the other hand, there is a link with consumer communities. In the future the distinction between the various services – information, communication and transaction services – will fade and they will become increasingly integrated.

3 Organizations

In this chapter we will discuss the main ingredients and methods of organizations with regard to ICT. First, we will provide a definition and general model of an organization, followed by a discussion of the most important aspects of organizations: goal, structure and culture. We will demonstrate why these aspects should be treated as processes and how they fit in with a social environment. Finally, we will give a brief introduction of the main theories that will emerge repeatedly in this book regarding ICT in organizations.

This chapter is not an introduction to organization science. We will merely discuss a number of ICT-related elementary features of organizations. We are interested in the flow of information and communication within and between organizations, the way others may be interested in the flow of money and assets (economists), power processes (sociologists), co-ordination and management (management experts) and other features of organizations.

3.1 WHAT IS AN ORGANIZATION?

An organization is a unit of formal positions, usually held by individuals, with explicit objectives, tasks, processes and assets (for example people, buildings and machines). In other words, an organization is an abstract system of formal positions, tasks and processes. In cases where tasks are mutually adapted and overlap, we use the term processes. The term group, on the other hand, is usually used to describe a concrete collection of people that do not hold formal positions or work together in more or less formalized processes. At a certain point, however, a group becomes so large that we lose sight of the relationships and activities of its members. Whenever the members of a group cease to interact or know each other directly and start defining formal positions, tasks and processes, a transition takes place from group towards organization. However, an organization does consist of actual people and various subgroups and units. Individuals as well as organizations have their own goals and methods. One of the main problems facing an organization is how to bring these individual goals and methods in line with the goals and methods of the organization.

Information and communication technology blurs the boundaries between organizations, groups and individuals. We see concrete individuals forming groups on the Internet. They establish contact with other individuals and form pairs, threesomes, and so on. A single individual can even run a large-scale company on the Internet this way. When several people do this we witness the rise of the most abstract form of organization in history: the virtual organization (see Chapter 7). It is an organization that exists independently of time, place and physical circumstances, and is entirely based on ICT. In between individual activities and virtual organizations a variety of networks, communities and project groups is formed, partly operating online and partly offline. The boundaries of these new communities and project groups are extremely diffuse. In Chapter 7 we will see that these relationships can completely break open the traditional structures of organizations.

As we mentioned earlier, an organization has goals, formal positions, tasks, rules and resources. Its individual members have their own wishes and behave in certain ways, towards each other and towards the organization as a whole. They do so in a specific environment: they are, after all, more than just members of an organization and representatives of that organization to the outside world. All these elements can be found in the organizational model presented in this chapter. The model distinguishes three organizational aspects (goals, structure and culture), the organization as such (organizing the positions mentioned in the definition with the use of goals, tasks and resources) and the flow of information and communication that is required (see Figure 3.1).

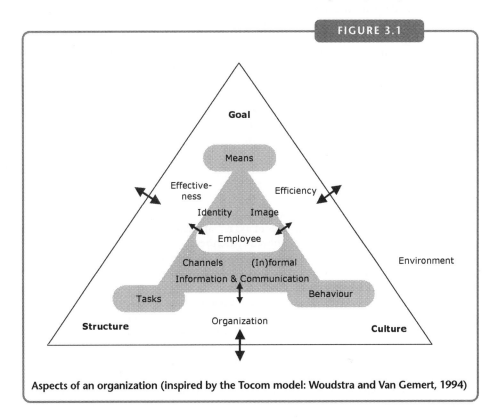

FIGURE 3.1

Aspects of an organization (inspired by the Tocom model: Woudstra and Van Gemert, 1994)

The leading principle of every organization is its goals. The goals can be commercial (profit, customer satisfaction, continuity), social (governing society or providing collective services the way [semi-]governments do) or idealistic (political, cultural and religious organizations). In its strategy the organization decides how to use its various resources in order to achieve its goals. The aim is to work as efficiently and effectively as possible. Information and communication technology plays an increasingly important role in making organizational goals explicit, in propagating them and, above all, in measuring them. Software makes it possible to monitor organizational goals that have been translated into concrete objectives.

Structure is an abstract of the organization's composition. To reach its goals the organization has a number of tasks that have to be performed by its members using the tools that are available. Individual people are assigned specific tasks within a specific hierarchical structure. Most organizations have a top management level, a staff, a middle management level and a work floor. This division of labour determines the organization's formal structure and the roles that people play, as well as the competencies and responsibilities involved. The execution of tasks is being constantly fed by information and communication channels within the organization (see Galbraith, 1973). In recent decades, ICT has played an increasingly important role in this process. Organizations have come to depend on ICT to such an extent that they cease to function entirely when the computer crashes or the network is 'down'.

The third aspect of organizations is culture. The general goals and abstract structure of an organization are, after all, realized by people. These people share a certain set of values and forms of expression that are just as important to the behaviour of the members of an organization as its formal goals, structure and tasks. Values can be closely linked to these formal elements, in which case there is a formal culture with many rules and procedures. Or they can be less closely related, in which case there is a less formal culture: things are taken care of informally or in the corridors. There is a certain relationship between structure and culture. The level of hierarchy determines what the culture of an organization will look like. The culture found in a flat organization is usually different from that found in a hierarchical one. Compare, for instance, the Civil Service, with its highly formalized culture, to the informal structure and culture of a law centre. Within these two types of organizations communication takes place in completely different ways. Some organizations have an oral culture while others prefer to put things in writing, and many nowadays have an e-mail culture. In addition, some organizations have an internally oriented culture whereas others are more open and customer oriented. The arrival of ICT in an organization can have far-reaching consequences for its culture, but it may also be the culture that determines the adoption, implementation and use of ICT. Van den Hooff (1997), for example, discovered that a less formal organizational structure encourages the use of e-mail.

Before discussing the above-mentioned organizational aspects in relation to ICT, we would like to mention two other ways of looking at organizations: the process perspective and the contingency perspective.

The process perspective can be used to describe the concrete elements of an organization. According to a classic book by Michael Porter (1980), an organization is a combination of primary and supporting processes. In these processes values are being transformed, for instance from production via distribution to consumption, or from imported raw materials and production resources to end-products (goods and services). In the overall value system Porter calls these processes value chains. Figure 3.2 presents an adaptation and expansion of Porter's model of the value chain within organizations.

At each point within the value chain ICT can play a supporting role, and it increasingly does so in everyday reality. When a chocolate factory, for instance, purchases cocoa from its suppliers, it can use ordering and registration systems based on EDI (electronic data interchange: see previous chapter). It will do so after its internal monitoring systems indicate that stock is getting low or demand for the company's product (chocolate bars) is on the increase. The information feeding the internal monitoring systems in turn is based on sales figures. After the product is manufactured it has to be delivered to the customer (a supermarket) by a transport company (external logistics): the chocolate bars have to be put on the supermarket shelves as quickly as possible. The required automated supply system is linked directly to the ordering and stock systems, possibly using the same EDI application. When the product has reached the supermarket, marketing and advertising begin, also using external media

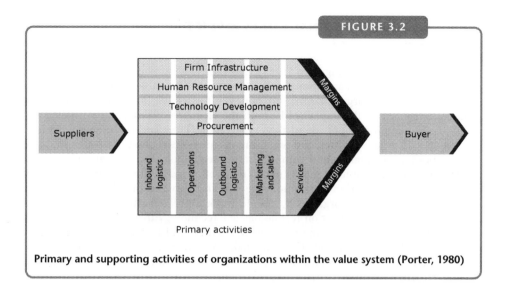

FIGURE 3.2

Primary and supporting activities of organizations within the value system (Porter, 1980)

(newspapers, folders, commercial advertisements). Although at the moment these are still predominantly separate media, in the future they will increasingly be the same websites customers can access using mobile equipment, linked by supermarkets to databases that they use as stock and ordering systems.

More than ever before, organizations are systems that communicate and process information. Information and communication technology is a technology that is perfectly suited to make organizational processes more effective and efficient (see section 2.1). According to this book, incidentally, the way ICT is introduced in organizations is a process as well: adoption, implementation, use and effect. Each chain in the model presented in Figure 3.2 can be supported by an ICT application, for example management information systems, personnel information systems, stock systems, production systems and customer systems.

Another perspective on organizations that we discuss in this book is the contingency perspective. No organization is an island. Every organization has to adapt to its environment (see Figure 3.1). The environment contains a number of factors that, from the point of view of the organization, are contingent: they are circumstantial in nature. This book sees organizations as complex adaptive systems. This means that they are made up of large numbers of people and resources that interact and adapt to each other and to their environment. The implementation of ICT is one of the most difficult challenges facing an organization. It has to take into account its own people and resources as well as people (suppliers, customers) and resources (rules and various resources) in its environment. In the past, organizations were able to operate relatively independently and concentrate on making a good and complete product or service with a limited number of people. Nowadays, organizations can rarely manufacture a complete product on their own. Instead, as a rule organizations have to work together to manufacture a product within a value system. Organizations focus on a part of the value system or value chain and leave the rest to suppliers and other parties involved in realizing a product or service. Thus, organizations are increasingly becoming units within a network that have to adapt to a rapidly changing environment.

3.2 ORGANIZATIONAL GOALS AND ICT

In 1987, Hammer and Mangurian (1987) (see Table 3.1) provided a neat summary of the way ICT can help organizations realize their goals. This table contains three values that are pursued by organizations: efficiency, effectiveness and innovation. These values are realized by the impact of ICT on the elements of time, place/distance and relationships within and outside of the organization. Time and place have a decisive impact on all human activities, and organizations are no exception. It is often said that time is money. Information and communication technology can help an organization realize a greater geographical reach (place) more effectively. After all, organizing is all about establishing relationships among people and between people and resources. When things are better organized, people work more effectively and efficiently. Information and communication technology is a technology that transcends time and place and can help optimize the relationships within and between organizations by connecting the various links in the value chain, by removing redundant links and by replacing old links with new and more efficient ones. In Table 3.1 we have translated these abstraction into nine concrete organizational goals with respect to ICT.

TABLE 3.1

The impact-value grid of the application of ICT in organizations according to Hammer and Mangurian (1987).

		Value		
		Efficiency	Effectiveness	Innovation
Impact	Time	Accelarate business process	Reduce information float	Create service excellence
	Place/distance	Increase market size	Esure global management control	Penetrate new markets
	Relationships	Bypass intermediaries	Replicate scarce knowledge	Build networks

Although, of course, people in organizations try to work as effectively as possible, it is easier to increase efficiency because that involves factors over which, according to the contingency perspective, the organization has more control. Efficiency means achieving the maximum result with minimal resources. This can be done, first, by addressing the factor time and by speeding up organizational processes. In the last 20 years ICT has been very helpful in this regard. Automating production and administration has increasingly allowed organizations to deliver their goods and services more quickly. In addition, organizations have been able to remove links from the production and distribution process and use information systems rather than people to perform certain tasks. In the past, semi-finished products would not be transported to another department until they were finished, which meant that stock would pile up. Nowadays, multifunctional teams often work together on a product, with each member contributing his or her part, and the (information) system serves as a conveyor belt moving the parts along. Thanks to ICT, logistics have improved considerably. With regard to management, control and administration, part of the middle management layer in organizations has disappeared. Supervision has shifted from people towards pre-programmed information and communication systems. At a higher level in the economy and society, entire intermediary organizations can be (partly) replaced by ICT or by other intermediaries that use ICT more effectively. Distribution is a good example. Electronic trade on the Internet is an attempt to sell products directly to the consumer. It is not possible, however, to bypass the intermediary altogether. The products have to be delivered and material distributors can be replaced by other intermediaries or 'information brokers' such as electronic merchants. Generally speaking, however, the number of links is reduced.

A third way to increase efficiency is by expanding the market using the same means of production. Information and communication technology gives organizations a greater geographical reach. Thanks to the Internet, for example, a company that used to cater to a local market can now sell its goods and services on an (inter)national market without having to make large investments. Even a local pop group can now distribute its songs worldwide in MP3 format.

In the last 20 years organizations have predominantly used ICT as a way to increase their efficiency, the main aim being to cut costs, for instance in terms of personnel (van Tulder and Junne, 1988). In the next phase the effectiveness of companies and other organizations could be improved. As we mentioned earlier, this is a goal that is harder to achieve. If ICT were to play a role here it would have to be deeply rooted within the organization. In society as a whole and organizations in particular, this process – the subject of this book – has only just started. The first goal is not to accelerate organizational processes, but to improve their quality. As a result the quality of existing products and services will improve. The introduction of ICT in the car industry, for example, has led to better and more energy-efficient cars. The same is happening now with the production of computers. Existing services can be improved through the use of ICT as well. Tax returns, for instance, are processed faster than they used to be, with fewer mistakes being made. Another example is social security fraud, which has become easier to detect by linking various databases.

Perhaps the most important contribution of ICT to the effectiveness of organizations is the fact that it makes a new kind of organizational approach possible, a combination of a centralized and decentralized approach. Computer networks allow companies to give local units room to manoeuvre and at the same time maintain control by monitoring and registering all the strategic conditions, goals and resources through information systems. Thus, they are able to manage and control at a distance. They can take full advantage of the flexibility and adaptability of local circumstances and at the same time operate and manage the company as a whole, and respond when necessary.

Finally, the effectiveness of organizations can be increased through knowledge management (see Weggeman, 1997; Huysman and De Wit, 2000; Huysman and Van Baalen, 2001). In the information society knowledge is an organization's most important resource. Knowledge management is an attempt to share, manage and develop the expertise of the individual members of an organization for the benefit of the entire organization. This means that the knowledge has to be made explicit, added to existing knowledge and stored in a file or system that is available to the entire organization. Knowledge management also involves a systematic application and evaluation of knowledge. Various ICT applications can help make knowledge explicit and formalize, standardize, apply, store and evaluate it in order to make it available. Examples of this are information systems, online courses and intranets.

Improving the effectiveness of organizations with the use of ICT is a (very) long-term affair. It requires a lengthy process of developing new products, services and methods. These can save time, help overcome distances or improve the organization of the economy and society as such through better relationship management in the broadest sense of the word. In the last ten years, the Internet in particular has given rise to new high-quality services that help save time and are easy to access: for example, medical self-diagnosis, mortgage advice and systems for finding private property, and so on. These are high-quality services because they have translated the extensive expertise of medical doctors, financial experts and stockbrokers into systems that are relatively easy to use. Although these new services save time because users do not have to visit experts, they have not created new markets. To a certain extent they replace existing markets. The quality of these electronic marketplaces is subject to debate. As yet there are few electronic markets that are genuinely new. A beginning is being made with the way these markets themselves are functioning, allowing customers to compare prices online (distance), enabling buyer groups to be formed (relationships for joint purchasing) and facilitating the improvement of the collective logistics.

Finally, ICT creates numerous innovations in relationship management, also known as 'networking'. This refers to the relationships between the organization and its suppliers and customers/clients. These relationships have been included in computer networks that register every contact. Relationships with suppliers are increasingly managed through EDI (electronic data interchange) and customer relationships through CRM (customer relationship management). The application of ICT in particular leads to numerous innovations in the field of marketing. Direct marketing evolves from segmented marketing (for instance on the basis of postal codes) towards individual or one-to-one marketing with the use of interactive techniques.

3.3   ORGANIZATIONAL STRUCTURE AND ICT

The structure of an organization is the abstract configuration of its internal relationships organization as expressed in the division of labour and tasks. These relationships can be visualized in graphic models. The best-known models are the configurations created by Mintzberg (1983; 1989) who first visualized five and later eight organizational structures. We have included the former five configurations in this book because they can be clearly related to typical ICT applications. They are ideal types, in the sense that most organizations are usually made up of combinations of these types, models or configurations. In addition, organizations are constantly developing and may evolve from one model into another.

It is likely that organizations with different structures – for instance small and large organizations – use different ICT applications. In Mintzberg's configurations, organizations are made up of five components (Figure 3.3):

1 strategic top;
2 middle management;
3 technological structure;
4 supporting staff; and
5 operational cores.

FIGURE 3.3

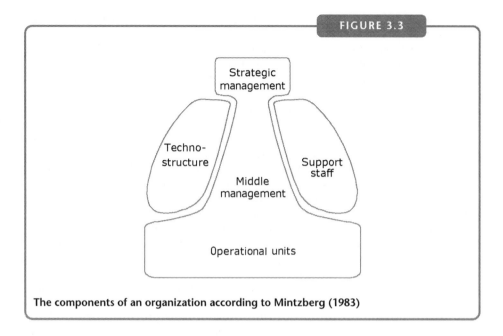

The components of an organization according to Mintzberg (1983)

Mintzberg divides organizations on the basis of:

- size (large, small);
- nature of the work/activity (routine, expert);
- work management (co-ordination method, standardization and supervision);
- distribution of tasks (centralized and decentralized, horizontal and vertical); and
- environment (complex/simple, stabile/volatile).

The first configuration is a simple structure, which Mintzberg calls the entrepreneurial organization. This is a very small company, consisting of an entrepreneur who works alone or employs a small number of people (Figure 3.4). This structure is found, for example, in small Internet companies. Due to the small number of people, the work requires versatility and expertise in a large number of areas. Most of the work has to be

FIGURE 3.4

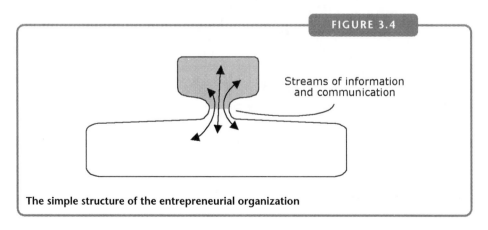

Streams of information and communication

The simple structure of the entrepreneurial organization

carried out by the entrepreneur. There is no staff or technological structure. The leader or entrepreneur is the dominant force. He or she personally co-ordinates the work. There are few formal rules and processes, and communication is informal. There is little or no division of labour because people have to be able to back each other up. Although the organization's environment is volatile, it is simple enough to allow the organization to respond quickly to changes in demand. The organization is customer oriented because it depends on its clients in a very direct way. The ICT applications used in this configuration are not elaborate, they are simple. They are used for relatively straightforward and usually unstructured processes. As a result the ICT applications being used are relatively simple: standard accounting software, a limited use of word processors, especially mobile telephony and voice mail (customers have to be able to reach the organization) and Internet access to find the occasional information. When the organization is a professional ICT or high-tech company the applications may be more advanced, for example a website and software for e-commerce, consultancy and design.

The machine bureaucracy or machine organization (Figure 3.5) is a large organization with an extensive staff and technological structure, and a dominating management. This type of organization is characterized by relatively routine work that is carried out by operational cores. Some examples of this type of organization are the Department of Social Security or an insurance company. The routine work, such as processing a social security claim or insurance form, is extremely formal and standardized. Depending on the bureaucratic nature of the relevant procedures, the work can either be smooth or cumbersome. Authorities and specializations have been clearly defined, however, horizontally (departments, specializations) as well as vertically (the hierarchical line). In this type of (often pyramid-shaped) organization the technological structure and top management 'call the shots'. The technological structure determines the standards and top management indicates how the standards should be imple-

FIGURE 3.5

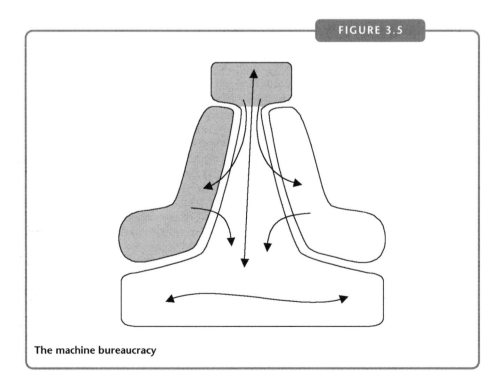

The machine bureaucracy

mented, often through a relatively large middle management layer. The flow of communication is top-down and fairly formal. However, because an organization has to be able to function like a machine, its members tend to create numerous informal channels to make things run more smoothly and to keep the work enjoyable. The environment in which this type of organization operates tends to be relatively simple and stable because there is little change in the products and services they provide.

In the machine bureaucracy the internal and external processes tend to be highly structured. The ICT applications that are used are formal, standardized information systems such as centralized administration and management systems and collective customer and product databases. Integrated applications play an important role at the operational cores. They are the organization's main information channel, from the top down and back up again. Sometimes mistakes occur in this process due to difficulties in the shared system and a lack of co-operation on the part of specialized units. When integrated systems fail to perform adequately there is a tendency for informal communication channels – such as e-mail – to emerge. The ICT applications that are used at the base of the machine organization, in the operational cores, are a kind of administrative conveyor belt. In so-called workflow systems (see Chapter 2) each employee or department fills in part of, for example, the insurance form until the claim is completed. These systems are standardized to such an extent that they can continue outside the organization. There is an increasing tendency to let clients fill in part of the form on the Internet, making them carry out part of the work. Management and staff groups use ICT for unstructured processes. Integrated applications and knowledge management systems will, however, hardly be used at all.

The division structure, also known as the diversified organization, is originally a machine bureaucracy that has been split up into different divisions that each make their own products (Figure 3.6). An example of this is Philips, a company with divisions for household appliances, lamps, computer chips, and so on. Although the divisions operate relatively autonomously, they continuously have to report to company management concerning their output. Because the company's processes are highly structured, both at the operational and management levels, monitoring systems play a key role with regard to operational processes and management information. Permanent registration is one of the main applications of ICT. Management at

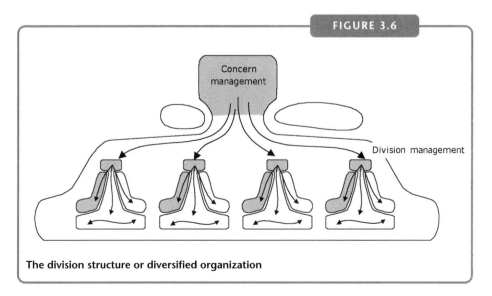

FIGURE 3.6

Concern management

Division management

The division structure or diversified organization

division level has a large responsibility. They are the company's axis and, together with the company's top management, play a role in the decision-making process. Work at division level is standardized and, as we mentioned above, its output (performance and yield) is continually monitored. Division management is free to choose a structure that matches the product, work and environment (sometimes the divisions operate in very different markets). The production of computer chips, for instance, implies a totally different organization from the production of software.

Another type of diversified organization is the matrix organization. In the matrix we may find the tasks of an organization on one side and the skills on the other. The employees are positioned in the cells. They can be placed in more than one cell because they may have several skills or be involved in a number of tasks. Here the matrix organization is a flexible type of organization that can adapt to changing tasks and individual capacities. The matrix organization is often used by organizations that handle projects that require varying combinations of skills. In light of the relatively unstructured and temporary nature of many processes, project groups tend use the Internet and various online databases to gather information. To exchange information they use all sorts of communication systems: (mobile) telephony, video-conferencing, e-mail, and so on. In addition, applications that facilitate co-operation and knowledge management-like systems are important as well. This way it is also possible to form so-called virtual teams within virtual organizations (see Chapter 7).

In the division structure, first, centralist information systems are used that enable the divisions, or project groups in matrix organizations, to account for their results to central management. The databases of company headquarters and of the divisions/groups are linked. Within these units there is a variety of ICT applications, depending on the relevant tasks and environment. Company management will discuss the desired strategy, using, among other things, decision support systems.

The fourth configuration is the professional bureaucracy, which Mintzberg later dubbed the professional organization (Figure 3.7). This kind of configuration is often found in the service sector, for instance in universities, hospitals and large software companies. It consists of largely separated operational cores with highly educated professionals. The level at which they operate requires a certain autonomy. Their work is complex and the environment stable, as there is little change with regard to type of clients (patients, students and other clients). The work itself is not standardized, although the skills are. Qualifications are of crucial importance. They are the basis on which the

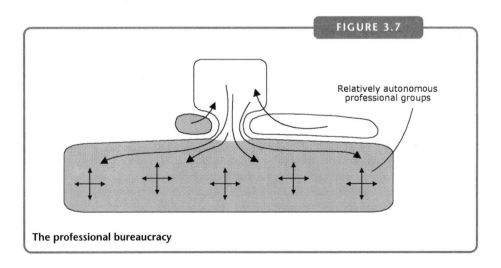

FIGURE 3.7

Relatively autonomous professional groups

The professional bureaucracy

professionals can do their jobs and the organization is decentralized both horizontally, in terms of specializations, and vertically, in terms of independent competencies. The decision-making process is expected to be bottom-up. When that is not the case, as can be seen in many schools, universities and healthcare institutions, there is likely to be friction between management and staff. The authorities of top-level management, which is supposed to make the organization as a bureaucracy more professional, will conflict with the independence of the professionals. The technological structure and supporting services also find it difficult to deal with this type of organization. Supporting services often use applications that facilitate processes that are often highly structured, such as patient, student or client administrations. These systems will not be used to their full potential due to the demands of the professionals or their refusal to use them. Information systems that are imposed from above are often mistrusted. The introduction and acceptance of hospital and general practitioner (GP) information systems, electronic patient files, care passes and so forth, is extremely problematic, to give but one example.

Professionals are interested in individual applications that support them in their work: high-quality systems that touch the boundaries of ICT and their profession, for instance advanced software, simulation and knowledge systems, computer-aided design–computer-aided manufacturing (CAD-CAM) systems for designers or architects, diagnostic systems and applications for physicians, in addition to word processors and Internet browsers. Due to the high level of independence, applications such as e-mail are an extremely important means of co-ordination.

The fifth and final configuration we will discuss here is the adhocracy, or innovative organization (Figure 3.8). This organization is characterized by the way project teams of experts are formed on an ad hoc basis. It resembles the matrix organization, but in a matrix organization the tasks, expertise and environment are more fixed or standardized. Organizations need the ad hoc formation of project teams to be innovative and to respond to a complex and constantly changing environment. Examples of adhocracies are IT companies, advertising agencies and research consultancies. Although the tasks and skills are not standardized, the project team approach is. In this relatively 'flat' type of organization the project teams operate with a large degree of autonomy, since they are responsible for the results of their project. There is, however, a great deal of competition within and between the project groups with regard to the collective resources. In the adhocracy a layer of professionals has replaced the former middle management layer.

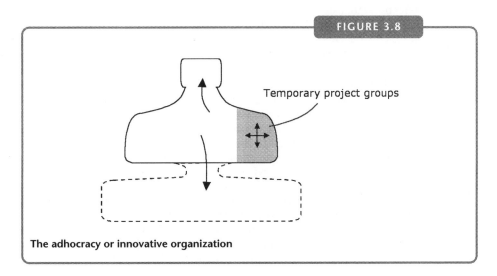

FIGURE 3.8

Temporary project groups

The adhocracy or innovative organization

The operational work that in other types of organization is carried out by operational cores is often outsourced. Much of the communication in adhocracies is informal, there are relatively few hierarchical relationships and internal and external processes are unstructured. Relevant ICT focuses especially on communication (e-mail, Internet, video-conferencing) and on project administration (customer requirements, goals, resources, time management and intermediate results). There are few collective standardized information systems. The systems that are used, such as intranets, CSCW (computer-supported collaborative work) and GDSS (group decision support systems) support the project and decision-making process.

The culture of an organization has an enormous influence on the possibilities of introducing ICT. There has to be a match between the features of the ICT applications, which are often new to the organization, and the characteristics of a culture that has existed much longer. Organizational cultures cannot change overnight. They are long-lasting shared values that are expressed in the way members of the organization behave. It is the values that determine whether or not the employees will accept an ICT application. Forms of expression reveal how they actually deal with the new technology, often in ways that are different from what the designers and decision-makers envisaged.

We will discuss the relationship between an organization's culture and ICT with the use of the concepts of the renowned Dutch culture sociologist Hofstede, who in his international comparative research has constructed a number of dimensions and organizational culture types (Hofstede, 1991). He distinguishes six cultural dimensions in organizations which to some extent overlap and which we will apply to the use of ICT.

1   The first dimension is that of the process-oriented versus the result-oriented organization. Examples of process-oriented organizations are factories and administrative organizations that perform the same tasks every day, whether it be assembling products or processing forms. Result-oriented organizations, for instance architectural firms, research organizations or website designers and healthcare and educational organizations, provide products or services on demand which are judged on the basis of their quality. In a process-oriented culture the behaviour is standardized, as are the information systems that are designed to make the work more efficient and effective. In a result-oriented culture people are expected to respond creatively to changing circumstances, and ICT is designed to facilitate rather than automate the work in a way that is seen in a process-oriented culture. Information and communication technology applications that do not add value to the work or that impose the values of others will be rejected. This is what often happens with the large-scale information systems for GPs and hospitals that have a hard time being accepted by the medical staff in question. The reason for this is that, although in some ways their work is a process, and can be organized and automated as such, they focus on the result: using their personal judgement to help individually different people.

2 and 3 Some organizations have a culture that emphasizes the role of people in the organization. In these organizations there will be a group culture based on the values and interests of the organization. Socio-emotional and informal communication is very important. In this type of culture there is an emphasis on consultations and meetings; one might call it a discussion culture. It is found, for example, in traditional service organizations and family businesses. In other organizations, on the other hand, the importance of the work and of professionalism is emphasized. Members of this type of organization identify with their profession rather than the organization, and are relatively individualistic and independent in their work. They are judged on the basis of their performance. Most of the communication that takes place is task related and formal. Everything is written down in reports and project plans. This can be

seen in professional agencies and IT organizations with highly skilled employees. In this kind of organization new ways to communicate and applications such as laptops and other mobile equipment, mobile Internet access and CSCW applications will receive a warm welcome. In a people-oriented culture, on the other hand, they will be considered a threat because they will individualize the work and make it more impersonal, or at any rate less enjoyable.

4 and 5 The culture of an organization is important to its environment as well. Some organizations have cultures that are open and customer oriented. New people are adopted quickly by existing teams and customers occupy a central position in every aspect of the organization. This can be seen, for example, in service and sales departments, information centres and media. On the other hand, there are organizations that interact with their environment in a relatively closed and procedural fashion, for example government departments such as the police and security services, and supervisory bodies. New employees have to meet special requirements, and there is a very specific culture. These organizations use their own highly secure ICT applications that can only be operated by experienced and authorized personnel. Open and customer-oriented organizations, on the other hand, use ICT applications that provide access to consumers and citizens, in particular communication-oriented applications of Internet voice response systems.

6 Finally we can distinguish between cultures where the activities of employees are strictly monitored, on the one hand, and cultures which favour looser forms of control, on the other. Some organizations are very formal and task oriented. Employees continuously have to adapt their behaviour and performance to the norm and are monitored by their superiors and by registration systems. This type of organization uses ICT applications that support structured and standardized processes, for instance databases, and uniform round-the-clock information systems. In organizations where monitoring practices are less strict, for example because people are only being judged on their results, there is a need for less structured and less standardized ICT applications that facilitate the individual creativity of employees. In such a culture ICT plays a facilitating rather than registering role.

TABLE 3.2

Frequent combinations of structures and cultures in organizations

Structures	Cultures
Simple structure	Process oriented
Machine bureaucracy	People oriented
Division structure	Organization related
	Closed
	Tight control
	Procedural
Professional bureaucracy	Result orientated
Adhocracy	Work oriented
Matrix organization (some)	Professional
	Open
	Loose control
	Customer oriented

TABLE 3.3		
Cultural typology of organizations according to Hofstede (1991) [in brackets: associated structures according to Mintzberg, 1983]		
	Egalitarian	Hierarchical
Few rules and procedures	'Village market' Advertising agency [Adhocracy]	'Family' Orchestra [Simple structure]
Many rules and procedures	'Well-oiled machine' Hospital [Professional]	'Pyramid' Bank [Machine bureaucracy]

These six cultural dimensions can be matched perfectly to the structural configurations we discussed in the previous paragraph. In Table 3.2 the combinations that occur frequently, though not exclusively, are presented.

Hofstede's cultural typology of organizations is also useful in this context. In a 2×2 table he distinguishes four recognizable types of organizations based on their internal distribution of power, which is expressed either in an egalitarian or hierarchical culture and in the relative need for certainty, which can lead to a culture with many rules and procedures or to one with few rules and mostly informal solutions (see Table 3.3).

Hierarchical organizations with many rules and procedures, for examples banks and government ministries, have a clear profile. The implementation of ICT is relatively simple: highly regulated, structured and standardized. Egalitarian organizations with few rules and procedures, such as service organizations, are fairly straightforward as well. They resemble a town market or loose networks where negotiations are continuously taking place. Information and communication technology has to support the information and communication processes without suffocating the employees' creativity. Other resources would not be accepted. Those types of organizations that combine an egalitarian culture with many rules or a hierarchical culture with few rules are more problematic. In those cases the implementation of ICT often goes awry. Hospitals, for example, have to carry out extremely complex and fragile activities – treating patients – and as a consequence they are highly regulated. At the same time there is an egalitarian and comradely atmosphere that emphasizes the human element. In addition, the professionals who work in hospitals can be extremely independent in their work. Any attempts to implement highly regulated (hospital) information systems will clash with the culture of professionalism and the informal and people-oriented atmosphere (patients and colleagues). Similarly, the more hierarchical entrepreneurial organization or family business will find it difficult to accept ICT applications that presuppose a high level of participation on the part of the (few) employees. Professional design applications or e-mail, which allow people to communicate in an open and direct way and as equals may put the role of 'orchestra director' to the test.

The assumption of the approach as discussed in this chapter is that ICT applications have to align with the structure and culture of an organization. In practice, however, we see that reality is more ambiguous than this assumption: ICT will influence structure and culture, while organizational structure and culture will also play a role in the type of applications that will be adopted, the way they are going to be implemented, the different ways of use of similar technologies and differences in impact. These topics will be our core focus in the chapters on adoption, implementation, use and effect.

PART II

4   Adoption: from exploration to decision-making

CASE STUDY

A WiFi world?

Wireless fidelity or Wi-Fi refers to networks that use radio technologies to provide wireless connectivity. It is basically a radio signal that beams Internet connections out 300 feet, and can be used to connect computers to each other, to the Internet, or to wired networks. The technology is defined in the IEEE 802.11 range of standards, and has been around for about five years. Since early 2001, the growth in WiFi products has been dramatic (WiFi Alliance, 2003). Over the last two years, the technology has also found increasing adoption in the corporate world. General Motors (GM), for instance, decided to adopt a Wireless LAN based on these standards, in order to develop an enterprise-wide technology architecture. By May 2003, GM had deployed WiFi in 90 of its manufacturing plants, but was still holding off on WiFi at headquarters because of security reasons. Other organizations have started to invest in the technology as well, such as UPS, Fidelity Investments and trucking company TRL Inc. For each of these companies, security risks are serious barriers in the full deployment of the technology, but they are all expecting that enhancements to the technology will be released later this year that can overcome these issues. (Business Week [28 April 2003]; Computerworld [5 May 2003] and Information Week [3 November 2003]).

In an analysis of this adoption process, Au and Kauffman (2003) note that this situation has created a kind of 'wait and see' stage, or an 'adoption inertia': a number of firms have made initial investments and have made the decision to adopt the technology, but are waiting for the technology to develop further (especially with regard to security) before they will fully deploy it. So these organizations do have the advantage of obtaining a first-hand learning experience, but they also run the risk of investing in a technology that may never live up to the current expectations. Other organizations, not wanting to take such risks, are waiting to see what the experiences of these 'first movers' will be – and how the technology will further develop, and how alternative technologies may further develop – before they decide whether or not to adopt this technology.

The case described above shows how complicated and crucial the decision whether or not to adopt a certain technology can be. Decision-makers are strongly influenced by what other organizations do – they may want to be the first to reap maximum benefits from a technology, or they may want to wait for others' experiences before they decide. They may also decide to adopt a technology so as not to be 'left behind' – the only one not on the 'bandwagon', so to speak. They are also faced with a high degree of technological uncertainty: will an emergent technology live up to its expectations, will the promised enhancements be implemented – or will the technology be surpassed by a new, superior one, causing all the investments to be lost?

All in all, the phase of *adoption* is a phase that is characterized by a high degree of uncertainty and complexity, and it is that phase in the innovation process that is the focal point of this chapter. In this chapter, we will first define the term 'adoption' and then discuss the role of the organization as well as the individual in this phase in detail. Subsequently we will address the interaction between supply and demand, between 'technology push' and 'organizational pull' in the adoption of ICT in organizations. Based on this we can identify a number of factors that influence the way the adoption phase develops with regard to ICT in organizations. These factors are discussed in detail in Section 4.3. Finally, we will present a conclusion in Section 4.4.

4.1 ADOPTION IN TWO STAGES

In the case of GM's decision to start using WiFi networks, it was of course the organization's management that made this decision. In the adoption phase, the organization's management functions as a gatekeeper, making the strategic decision whether or not to introduce a certain innovation into the organization. We call this decision the *adoption* decision and it is on this decision that we focus in this chapter.

The adoption decision

In chapter 1 we discussed the way Andriessen (1989) sees the process of adoption as an introduction and incorporation of ICT in organizations. In this chapter we will deal with the adoption phase, which Andriessen (1989: 19) defines this phase as: 'the phase of exploration, research, deliberation and decision-making to introduce a new system into the organization'. The result of the adoption phase thus is the decision whether or not to introduce the innovation to the members of the organization or, to put it differently, the decision whether or not to implement the innovation.

Rogers (1983) describes this phase as 'initiation', a phase that, according to him, consists of all activities concerning the gathering of information, outlining and planning that lead to the *decision* to adopt. Rogers' initiation phase therefore is almost identical to Andriessen's adoption phase. Both describe the phase as a phase in which an exploration is rounded off with a decision. This can also mean that the innovation is *not* implemented.

Two units of adoption

As we described in Chapter 1, Rogers (1983) emphasizes the specific character of diffusion in organizations. He refers to the adoption decision made in organizations as *contingent innovation decisions*: 'choices to adopt or reject that can be made only after a prior innovation-decision' (Rogers 1983: 347). The individual employee's decision to adopt or reject is such a contingent decision: it can only be made after the organization has decided whether or not to purchase a certain technology. This is especially relevant when this organizational decision can be characterized as an *authoritative innovation decision* at the top level of the organization (a decision made by a limited number of individuals who have either power, status and/or know-how): the individual decision depends on the decision made by the organization. If the organizational decision is a *collective decision* (a decision supported by the members of a social system), this dependency is different. If all the members of the organization have an equal vote in the organizational decision to adopt or reject the innovation, then the different individual decisions become the input leading to the final organizational decision.

Rogers argues that the diffusion of innovations in organizations always involves two 'units of adoption':

- the organization that decides whether or not to adopt on the basis of the goals and needs of the system as a whole; and
- the individual whose decision depends to a large extent on the organizational decision, but who has the freedom to see to what extent his individual decision conforms to the organizational decision.

Based on this we can describe the importance of the implementation phase (see chapter five) as the ability to translate the organizational decision into a large number of individual decisions. An organization failing to do this will have made an 'empty' decision, one that cannot be translated into the incorporation of the innovation into the organization.

BOX 4.1

Instant messaging (IM) instead of e-mail

An example of how an organizational adoption decision can be undermined by individual adoption decisions is provided by the increasing use of instant messaging by workers to get around restrictions placed on what they can do by e-mail. A survey by filtering firm Surf Control Survey indicated that more and more individuals in organizations are using instant messaging as they feel that too many restrictions are placed on their use of e-mail. Their study found that almost 40 per cent of staff in UK companies are using IM programs while in the office (BBC News, 8 January 2004). An IDC study found comparable results for the USA, although other analysts (from Gartner and Ferris Research) expected that a convergence between e-mail and IM was on the cards, rather than e-mail being threatened or replaced Instant Messaging (Internet Week, 30 October 2003).

Nevertheless, this tendency shows how an organization's policy towards ICT can lead to individual adoption decisions which can undermine that policy – and the organization's adoption decision, in this case the decision to adopt e-mail. As IM creates some important security problems, analysts warn that organizations should do more to limit those problems. Although the primary reason for using IM rather than e-mail is because it is a faster way of communicating, the second reason mentioned is the fact that it enables users to send the private messages they would rather not send via a corporate e-mail system. Viruses and offensive content can also cause a problem (BBC News, 8 January 2004).

This distinction between organizational and individual decisions matches the classification into different levels of analysis (organization, environment and individual) presented in Chapter 1. There we argued that adoption is a process that takes place especially at the level of organizations and their environment. What is important is to explore the environment, and to arrive at a decision on the basis of this exploration. This organizational decision eventually has to be translated into individual decisions, keeping in mind, as we have indicated earlier, that it is difficult to separate the individual decision whether or not to adopt from the actual use of the technology by that individual. After all, that decision implicitly manifests itself when the individual either starts using the application, or not, as the case may be. That is why in this chapter we will mainly focus on the organizational decision. For a more elaborate discussion of the individual decision and the factors that are of influence, we refer to Chapter 6, where we will discuss the use of ICT or media choice.

Innovativeness of organization and individual

The question is how to ascertain when an organization arrives at a positive decision. In other words, how quickly does an organization decide to adopt a technology during the diffusion process of that technology? Rogers uses the term *innovativeness*, which he defines as: 'the degree to which an individual or other unit of adoption is relatively earlier in adopting new ideas than the other members of a system' (Rogers, 1983: 22). In other words, the more innovative an organization is, the sooner a relatively new idea will be adopted. Referring to the case description concerning WiFi technology, we can conclude that GM and the other organizations already investing in the technology are more innovative than organizations that are postponing their decision. Based on variations in the level of innovativeness, Rogers distinguishes the five units of adoption we have described in Chapter 1: innovators, early adopters, early majority, late majority and laggards.

Although these adopter categories are commonly used to describe individuals, we are here focusing on the organization as unit of adoption. Consequently, it is possible to describe the innovativeness of organizations with the use of these categories as well. The 'system' of which these units of adoption are a part can be the economic system, the market or the society. It is relative to the other organizations in such a system that innovativeness can be described.

All in all, it is the organizational decision to adopt or reject a technology we are focusing on here. The question is, on the basis of which variables can we describe and explain this decision? Before answering this question, it is important to take a closer look at the specific case of the adoption of ICT applications.

 ADOPTION OF ICT: PUSH AND PULL, OPPORTUNITIES AND DEMANDS

Before describing the specific dynamics concerning the adoption of information and communication technologies, we have to answer the question of *why* an organization considers an ICT application; in other words, what is the justification to proceed with the adoption phase? Related to this are the following aspects:

- Changing requirements from the environment and the organization: the environments within which organizations operate are becoming increasingly complex (hard to understand) and turbulent (subject to constant change). If an organization is to function in this kind of environment, an accurate, fast, correct and complete exchange of information with the environment is vitally important. To a large extent this has to do with strategic management, (Henderson, 1984; Parker, 1996) and with the decisions that affect the organization's competitive position, customer relationships and the relationships with the environment. Needless to say, a changing environment and strategic choices in turn affect the way internal processes are shaped. Information and communication technology makes it possible to deal with this. We will take a closer look at this in Chapter 7, when discussing the effects of ICT.

- Availability of technology: the mere fact that ICT applications are available is also a reason to consider to what extent these applications have to be adopted by the organization. Even when there is no immediate demand from the environment, it may be wise to look at a new ICT application. One of the potential applications of the WiFi technology described at the beginning of this chapter, for instance, could be for companies to supply their customers with the latest stock information, regardless of the actual demand for such a service.

- The behaviour of others: the 'me-too', or 'bandwagon' phenomenon also plays an important part in justifying the adoption of ICT applications (see also Box 4.4). The fact that the competition switches to an ERP system to handle its internal logistics may be enough reason for an organization to do so as well. With externally oriented applications this becomes even more evident. An important supplier's switch to XML-based web services for data exchange, for instance, may be a very good reason for an organization to adopt this technology as well. This has nothing to do with any internal demands or technological possibilities, but much more with economically rational behaviour and 'network externalities' (which will be discussed in more detail in section 4.3).

Although our focus in this chapter is on the adopting organization, this organization's interaction with ICT suppliers is important as well. This is especially so when we consider that a similar interaction takes place again during the implementation phase (see next chapter) in which the organization's management (or ICT department) can more or less be considered the supplier and the potential users of the application become the customers.

The interaction between 'technology-push' and 'market-pull' is of great importance at the market level where innovations are developed and subsequently offered (Bouwman and Neijens, 1991; Frambach, 1993). We can compare this distinction with the one we made between 'technology push' and 'technology pull' in Chapter 2, although in that chapter we focused primarily on the process of *development* of the technology. When we look at adoption we are more concerned with the *distribution* of ICT applications. The examples described above of arguments in favour of adoption match this distinction: concrete needs are created by changing circumstances, on the one hand, whereas on the other hand the fact that the technology already exists is an important factor as well.

Frambach (1993) pays explicit attention to the perspective of the provider of innovations. Frambach criticizes much of the diffusion research for focusing predominantly on the adopter's point of view when trying to explain decisions regarding adoption – and thus ignoring the influence the supplier of the innovation has on

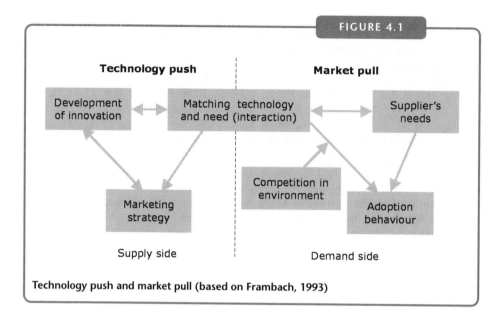

FIGURE 4.1

Technology push and market pull (based on Frambach, 1993)

those decisions. In his model Frambach sees the organization as a unit of adoption – the emphasis being on the organizational adoption of innovations, as it is in this book. Frambach integrates the principles of Rogers's diffusion theory and elements of industrial marketing and innovation management, presenting an integrated model of the organizational adoption of innovations. In Figure 4.1 we have presented a simplified version of this integrated model. In this chapter we are especially interested in the interaction between 'technology push' and 'market pull'.

The core of Frambach's argument is the match between technological supply, on the one hand, and the potential buyer's demand, on the other. According to Frambach, this match is a crucial factor in the diffusion process: the extent to which a supplier succeeds in matching his or her innovation to the needs of potential buyers is crucial for the success of the innovation. Based on this, suppliers are advised to involve potential buyers in the development of the innovation, to ensure an optimal match. This interactive development of innovations reflects modern ideas concerning new relationships between suppliers and buyers: early supplier involvement (Clark, 1989), network organizations (Monge and Fulk, 1999), customization (De Vries, 1998), and so on. Especially in the case of a technological innovation like an ICT application, we can define the development of the innovation (until a match is made) as technology push – keeping in mind that an interactive development is a good way of involving market pull in the development process.

This interaction between technology push and market pull can also be seen when we look at the considerations that play a role in the organizational adoption decision with regard to ICT applications. There is a link with the interaction between demands and possibilities presented in Chapter 1. In the adoption phase demands and possibilities will have to be weighed against each other as well: a decision based primarily on demand factors will result in ICT applications that support the way an organization is currently working and communicating. On the other hand, decisions that are only based on the technological possibilities will most likely lead to the adoption of ICT applications that will lead to far-reaching changes in the organization.

BOX 4.2

Technology push: you need this – you just don't know it yet

At Microsoft Research's annual Techfest, the software giant presented a lot of gadgets and projects that may never make it into a for-profit product – but also some that will. Regardless of any market demand or user need, the researchers at Microsoft develop new technologies – just because they are technologically possible. As the head of Microsoft Research put it, the researchers try to anticipate what Microsoft developers will want in several years.

The SenseCam, for instance (described by Microsoft as a 'visual diary of sorts') is a small camera designed to be worn around the neck. It responds to changes such as bright lights and sudden movements and can take up to 2,000 images in 12 hours without the wearer doing a thing. One day, SenseCam might even respond to other stimuli such as heart rate or skin temperature. And it could eventually link with other technology, such as face recognition, to remind wearers when they have seen someone before. Another project converts a regular webcam image into low-resolution animation – stripped of everything but the eyes, lips, nose, and eyebrows. It is easier to transmit than full video and can be used with instant messaging to convey emotion and nuance.

And the researchers are already thinking ahead. One item that may very well meet actual user needs is an alarm clock that figures out when to wake you based on current traffic conditions (Information Week, 4 March 2004).

As we argued in Chapter 1, it is important to find the right combination of the two perspectives. The decision to adopt an ICT application will not be taken (provided the organization is not in some sort of crisis) with the intention of using the application to bring about radical changes in the processes and structures. Normally speaking, the primary focus of an organization (especially a more traditional one) will be on the 'demands': what does my organization look like, what are the requirements with regard to communication and information supply, and how do these requirements translate into ICT applications? A drawback of a strict adherence to this approach is that an organization may not pay sufficient attention to the benefits applications offer in terms of process innovation, services and products. Therefore, it is important also to look at the possibilities of the technology, to assess beforehand what the benefits may be in terms of improving and changing existing processes and structures (a subject we will examine more closely in the chapter concerning the effects of ICT). However, a strict adherence to this approach carries the risk of technological determinism, which in turn can result in a poor match between technology and organization. In that case, organizations run the risk of making an 'empty' decision, as we described earlier, a decision that cannot be translated into a successful implementation.

In this paragraph we have specifically addressed the adoption of ICT in organizations, and in particular the question as to how a balance can be struck between the technological components and the organizational variables. This has added meaning to the adoption decision and we have a clear idea about what considerations play a role in that decision. In the next paragraph we will discuss the factors that influence the decision in more detail: both the timing (how innovative are the organization and its individual members?) and the decision itself (adoption or rejection).

4.3 A CLOSER ANALYSIS OF ADOPTION

In Chapter 1 we have indicated that this book examines the process of adoption, implementation, use and effects of ICT from a number of different perspectives: the organizational, technological, economic and user perspectives. In the following paragraphs we will address a number of important theories concerning factors that influence the adoption decision, and discuss the various perspectives.

Relative advantage

According to Rogers (1983), five characteristics of innovations influence the course of the diffusion process. What is especially important in the decision whether or not to adopt an application is the relative advantage, or: 'the degree to which an innovation is perceived as better than the idea it supersedes' (Rogers, 1983: 15). This is above all a matter of *perception*, and the extent to which the innovation offers a relative advantage in any 'objective' sense of the word is less important – and hard to establish in advance anyway. Rogers argues that the bigger the relative advantage of an innovation, the sooner it will be adopted. We argue that this perception is heavily influenced by two other features of innovation mentioned by Rogers: compatibility and complexity. Therefore, these features are discussed together in this section.

An application's relative advantage refers to the extent to which it offers a strategic advantage, is better, works more efficiently, is easier to manage, and so on, than the applications the organization used before. Is the application sufficiently advanced, user-friendly and integrated with other applications as to offer clear advantages over existing applications? The technology itself is considered a factor, but especially in combination with economic criteria. It is important to note that it is, above all, the *expected* advantage we are talking about here: the degree to which the organization, on the basis of a description of the technology and functionality, expects to benefit from the application. The extent to which an application really offers a relative advantage can only be established in the use and effect phases (see Chapters 6 and 7).

As we mentioned earlier an important influence on the perception of relative advantage is the *compatibility* of an ICT application: its compatibility with the infrastructure, transport service and other applications being used in the organization (for a discussion of these layers see Chapter 2). What is important here is to what extent the technological components of the ICT application match the components of the organization's existing ICT applications. To give an obvious example: when the organization's network uses Windows NT as its operating system, it makes little sense to introduce an application that uses Novell NetWare. And an organization that wants an e-mail system that is easy to use should not install an e-mail system that is entirely based on the X.400 standard. The capacity of the infrastructure is important too: when the physical infrastructure has a limited capacity and the network only contains light servers, an application that demands a high capacity (such as video-conferencing) is not compatible with this environment. The compatibility of the different versions of the same software is an important factor as well: the new version of a word processor, for example, has to be able to read texts that were made in the previous version (upward compatibility), as well as save texts in the format of that version (downward compatibility). Anybody who has ever used the standard office applications (word processors, spreadsheets, presentation software, and so on) knows that in everyday reality this kind of compatibility is far from self-evident.

It may be clear that compatibility is partly also an economic criterion: the costs in terms of money, effort, processing errors, and so on increase when compatibility is poorer. When an application is non-compatible an organization can always decide to change the existing infrastructure, but generally speaking this is so costly that it is hardly a viable option. On the other hand, existing systems that have to be adjusted time and again tend to get in the way of innovation.

The crucial role of compatibility underscores the importance of *standardization*: agreed standards of technology that allow systems and applications to be interoperable and compatible. It is important to distinguish between *de jure* and de facto standards. *De jure* standards have been set by standardization agencies like the International Standards Organization (ISO), the International Telecommunication Union (ITU) or the Institute of Electronics Engineers (IEEE). An example of a *de jure* standard is the Ethernet protocol for LANs. De facto standards more or less emerge in daily practice, and they are not officially set: one could say that Windows has by now almost become the de facto standard for desktops, and TCP/IP for networks. Although TCP/IP *is* an officially determined standard for data transmission and internetworking (in RFC791 and RFC793, respectively), the technology was first developed in a bottom-up manner, before being officially described as a standard in 1981. This is contrary to many *de jure* standards, which are first defined and described officially, and subsequently translated into actual technologies. For the adoption of ICT applications it is important that they match the generally accepted standards, to ensure compatibility with the other systems in the organization and interoperability with the systems that are used by customers, suppliers and other external parties.

At an individual level an important determinant of the perception of the relative advantage of an ICT application is its *complexity*. In particular the accessibility of the application is important: are the interface and operation of the ICT application user-friendly to such an extent that the expected benefits may be achieved with a relatively modest effort? This issue will be further addressed in Chapter 6.

All in all, in explaining the adoption of ICT in organizations it is the extent to which both the organization and the individual expect to benefit from the ICT application that is important, as well as the extent to which this is expected to be realized against low costs. Relative advantage is a combination of technological features (features of the ICT application itself) and economic criteria. In the following paragraphs we will address these economic criteria and elaborate on the term 'relative advantage'.

Critical mass

As has become clear in Chapter 2, ICT applications are to a large extent characterized by their 'networked' nature. Networks and 'interactive media' can be seen as a form of 'collective action', where the members of a social system (for instance the employees of an organization) face the dilemma of having to incur costs to realize a collective good without being certain that others will do the same. On the other hand, when the collective interest has been secured all members will benefit, including the ones that did not contribute. Basically, a few members of the social system have to make large investments in time, money and other resources to realize the common good. Whether or not that common good is realized in turn depends on the extent to which a good's production curve is characterized by diminishing or increasing returns (Oliver, Marwell and Teixeira, 1985):

- In a situation of *diminishing returns* it is attractive for a small group to invest, because the first investments will yield considerable results. As the process continues, the relative investment benefits will decrease, as will people's readiness to invest, making it unlikely that the collective good will actually be realized.

- In a situation of *increasing returns* large investments will have to be made at the beginning of the process, with very few benefits, while further on in the process investors will increasingly benefit from the relative advantages. Each new investment yields additional benefits (network externalities). In this case the role of the initial group of investors is very important: the critical mass.

For the success of a collective action it is imperative that a limited number of members of the social system invest without being certain of the outcome. When there are enough initial investors, at a certain point it becomes worthwhile for other members of the social system to invest, thus accelerating the process. The individual decision to use a medium depends on the decision made by others (Markus, 1990). This is called the critical mass. In Rogers's diffusion model, the critical mass can be described as the point where the diffusion process suddenly accelerates, where the S-curve suddenly becomes steeper and the number of 'adopters' quickly increases.

Bouwman and Christoffersen (1992) discuss the connection between a critical mass of (information and communication) services and users. Electronic information services can only emerge when there are enough users. On the other hand, electronic services are only developed when there are a sufficient number of users. The same goes for communication services, where there has to be a sufficient number of communication partners. A number of parties will have to invest in terms of time, effort and money to break the stalemate and provide the collective good (Olson, 1965; Bouwman and Slaa, 1992). Monge *et al.* (1998) describe how important the concept of collective action is in this context. They argue that ICT leads to two types of collective goods:

- *connectivity*, the possibility for people involved to communicate directly; and
- *communality*, the availability of a generally accessible supply of information.

Collective action is necessary both for connectivity (being able to reach all relevant contacts through the ICT application) and for communality (having access to all the relevant information): in both cases the value of the public good is highly dependent on the number of parties taking part. Consequently, the decision whether or not to adopt an ICT application is highly influenced by the decisions made by others in the organization's network of suppliers, customers, partners, competitors, and so on.

According to Fulk *et al.* (2000), the same applies to the introduction of an intranet: there, too, a critical mass of both users and content is required for an intranet to be successful. The individual decision whether or not to adopt, which manifests itself in the users' willingness to invest in the intranet by contributing individual information (communality) and by actively taking part in the communication network (connectivity), is to a large degree influenced by the individual decisions of others.

Since, in our definition, adoption is considered at the organizational level, we can conclude that the relative advantage of an ICT application to a large degree depends on the willingness of various organizations in a certain network to invest in that application. After all, a critical mass in terms of connectivity and content is important not only in the individual member's decision whether or not to use an ICT application, but is, of course, just as important at the organizational level. The study conducted by Monge et al. (1998) into interorganizational information and communication networks supports this claim: organizations having to decide whether or not to adopt an ICT application are influenced by the degree to which other organizations contribute to the collective action, just as we discussed in the WiFi case at the beginning of this chapter.

Costs and benefits

In this subsection we will focus on the value of ICT applications and on the balance that has to be struck between this value on the one hand, and the costs involved.

BOX 4.3

Costs and benefits: VWebXML?

Volkswagen AG (VW), the German automobile manufacturer, is planning to adopt ebXML (electronic business using Extensible Markup Language), a standard developed by the United Nations for Internet-based business collaborations. General Motors has similar plans. The ebXML standard, established in 2001, provides a comprehensive set of specifications for conducting secure, reliable data exchange over the Internet. The relative advantage expected from this innovation is the reduction of costs, but it is also expected to improve the transmission of large amounts of data compared to EDI.

VW is expecting to cut $1 million in annual EDI fees and software using ebXML-compliant software to transmit documents. The company also expects the system to be better than EDI at supporting large, graphics-intensive files such as engineering specifications. For dealers, cost savings are the most important expected relative advantage: 'The biggest motivation for going to a web-based process is to contain costs,' according to one of 1,000 dealers in the United States and Canada that VW hopes to pull into its ebXML network. This dealer estimates his $12,000 data-communications bill – spent each month on point-to-point EDI and satellite services – could drop by as much as $6,000.

The Automotive Industry Action Group, which automakers established to address supply-chain issues, is spearheading an ebXML project, called Inventory Visibility and Interoperability, for improving inventory views within supply chains. More than 30 technology companies are involved, including BCE Emergis, Covisint, IBM, Microsoft, QAD, SAP, Sterling Commerce, and SupplySolutions. The project will cost about $40 million and could save $255 million a year by reducing shipping and inventory costs, the group predicts. (Internet Week, 5 March 2004)

The decision whether or not to adopt an ICT application will often be influenced substantially by considerations concerning the costs and benefits of ICT – considerations that are related to the justification of the investments the organization makes in ICT. Concerning investment decisions, a number of review studies have been published (Oirsouw, Spaanderman and De Vries, 1993; Renkema, 1996; Demkes, 1999), in which various methods focus on financial criteria, such as multi-criteria approaches, ratio approaches or portfolio approaches (Renkema, 1996). Financial methods focus on the average productivity, recovery time, net cash worth, internal yield. Examples of multi-criteria methods are:

- Information economics (Parker, Benson and Trainor, 1988), which tries to structure group decision-making. It focuses on the assessment of investment alternatives which it compares on the basis of weighed criteria. Information economics also focuses on added value instead of cost savings.

- The Kobler unit framework (Hochstrasser, 1994), consisting of four modules for justifying ICT investments that concentrate on critical success factors, risk assessment, business performance indicators and strategic alignment. This method also compares investment alternatives on the basis of weighed criteria.
- The SIESTA method (van Irsel and Swinkels, 1992), which is partly based on the strategic alignment model we discuss in Chapter 5, and distinguishes five phases in an investment cycle: identification (investigating which ICT applications can be of interest to the organization), legitimization (determining which ICT investment has the highest added value), realization (realizing the desired quality of the application), management (ensuring that the organization will profit as planned) and evaluation (determining whether the investment has delivered as expected). It may be clear that on the basis of the evaluation a new identification phase can be entered, starting up the investment cycle all over again. When we look at the subject of this chapter, the adoption of ICT in organizations, the 'identification' and 'legitimization' phases in this cycle are of interest. In these phases the expected relative advantage (translated into the expected added value) of the ICT application plays an important role.

Ratio methods assess alternatives on the basis of the ratio between criteria, and compare these ratios to other organizations.

- Return-on-management (Strassmann, 1990) or ROM uses a database as a benchmark to compare the expected effects of investments (or other interventions) in information and communication technology.
- IT assessment (van der Zee and Koot, 1989), in which both financial and non-financial ratios of investments are compared to benchmarks and historical analyses.

Portfolio methods assess investment proposals on the basis of a graphical representation of proposals' consequences concerning a number of decision criteria. Examples of portfolio methods are:

- Bedell's method (Bedell, 1985), which aims at finding productive applications by first analysing the currently present applications, and then prioritizing the proposed applications. Alternatives are presented in matrices ('portfolios') and then compared, assessing both organizational and ICT alternatives.
- Investment portfolio (Berghout and Meertens, 1992), which compares various investment proposals simultaneously on the basis of their contribution to the business domain, contribution to the IT domain and their yield (in net cash value).

In addition, some methods look beyond the mere financial considerations, for instance the balanced score card and the option theory, and an elaboration of the net cash worth concept (Renkema, 1996; Demkes, 1999). The balanced score card (Kaplan and Norton, 1992) is a performance measurement method, based on four perspectives: (1) financial, (2) customers, (3) internal business processes and (4) learning and growth. It helps an organization set objectives and determine priorities, considering all important measures together. The option theory (Dos Santos, 1991) is aimed at the stage of investment assessment, indicating whether investment in a new technology is justified. Benefits of investments are not only determined in terms of financial returns per se, but also in terms of options to invest in future projects. It incorporates the time value of money, as well as the value derived from changing circumstances. Basically, option theory tries to account for the inherent uncertainties concerning the value of any investment proposal.

According to Renkema (1996), the expected value of an ICT application to an organization is the sum of the financial and non-financial costs and benefits related to the investment. The term 'value' that is used here is as essential as it is controversial, as indicated, for example, by Bannister and Remenyi (1999). The problem is that it is often hard to quantify the benefits – in particular the non-financial benefits are often more qualitative in nature (strategic advantage, improved quality of service, improved innovative capability, and so on.) and as such it is hard to translate them into a quantitative determination of the value of an application. We will address this problem in greater detail when discussing the economic effects of ICT. At any rate it is clear that there are financial risks involved in any adoption decision (Renkema, 1996): the consequences of an investment can only be determined to a certain degree in advance and there is always a level of uncertainty as to the real value of an investment proposal.

Finally, it is important to point out that there is a difference both in the size and term of investments in various kinds of ICT. It is, for instance, less drastic and extensive to replace certain subsystems while keeping the existing infrastructure intact, than it is to set up an entire new infrastructure. The Gartner Group (1998) draws the following distinction:

- End-user applications, such as word processors, spreadsheets, and so on. Investments here are relatively modest (possibly even limited to a few workstations) and short term: Gartner talks of a turnover of one year.
- Group applications, such as Groupware, Workflow, Desktop Video-conferencing, and so on. Investments here are more extensive (by definition several workstations, often entire departments or the entire organization), and the average turnover period according to Gartner is three years.
- Infrastructure, both physical (hardware and cables) and in terms of applications such as messaging, document sharing, shared directories, and so on. In general these are substantial, organization-wide investments with an average turnover of approximately ten years.

Economically speaking the decision whether or not to adopt an ICT application is an investment decision at the beginning of an investment cycle. As far as adoption is concerned, the identification and legitimization phases of this cycle (in terms of the SIESTA method) are important. One has to keep in mind that the consequences of an investment cannot be predicted with certainty and that there is a certain risk involved in any adoption decision. Especially when over time an ICT application is gradually being used in different ways from what was initially expected (the phenomenon of 'reinvention' that will be discussed in Chapter 6), the costs and benefits may well be different from what people anticipate in the adoption phase. Nevertheless, these expectations are all an organization has on which to base its decision whether or not to adopt.

The organizational context

The organization is the context in which the entire process of adoption, implementation, use and effect of ICT takes place. Adoption has been defined earlier as a primary organizational process, and it therefore makes sense that a number of the characteristics of this context have an impact on the course of this phase in the process. As far as adoption is concerned, it is especially the structure and culture of the organization that are important. In Chapter 3 the relationships between the structure and culture of organizations and ICT are described. Structure and culture to a large extent determine the way processes in organizations take place, and what resources are available to support them. On the basis of those characteristics an organization should be able to assess in advance to what extent a certain ICT application matches the organization's characteristics and decide whether or not to adopt the application.

Rogers (1983) distinguishes a number of structural and cultural characteristics that influence an organization's innovativeness (or its willingness to adopt in general): centralization (negative impact on innovativeness), formalization (negative), size (positive), complexity of the structure (positive), internal coherence (positive) and the degree to which the organization finds it easy to release and reallocate resources (positive). The characteristics of an organization also have an impact on the kind of decision that will be made. As we described above, using Rogers's terminology, there can either be an *authoritative* or a *collective* decision. An authoritative decision means that the power centre in the organization makes the decision and the users are faced with a fait accompli, whereas a collective decision involves (a large portion of) the members of an organization in the decision-making process. It is hard to tell which of these types of decision is better – there is no doubt, however, that there is a clear relationship between the size, structure and culture of an organization, on the one hand, and the kind of decision, on the other. In a large machine bureaucracy or a division organization an authoritative decision is more likely (and probably also more feasible), while in a professional bureaucracy or adhocracy the chances are that the decision will be a collective one. The following section will discuss the organizational decision-making process in some more detail.

The organizational decision-making process

It may be clear that the adoption of ICT in organizations is a decision-making process. It is often assumed that this kind of decision is a completely rational one based on an objective assessment of various clear (particularly economic) criteria. This *rational decision-making model* is sometimes referred to as 'homo economicus': man as decision-maker who (March and Simon, 1992) has an unequivocal goal, knows what that goal is, and all the options available to achieve that goal, knows what the costs and consequences of each option are, is capable of determining the 'maximum' outcome and has an infinite capacity to process information.

The idea that the decision-making process in organizations is basically a rational and economic affair was criticized in the 1950s by Simon, who argues that decision-makers are faced with a *bounded reality*: they do not have all the information in advance, and in general do not aim for a 'maximum' decision (should such a thing exist in the first place), but settle for a satisfactory solution. Simon (1957) calls this the 'satisficing principle': the goal of the decision-making process is not the maximum result, but a predefined notion as to how good an alternative must be – and any alternative that matches or even exceeds that notion is considered acceptable. This can be translated into the decision-making process concerning an ICT application: the circumstances in which decisions are usually made (uncertainty concerning fast technological developments, uncertainty concerning the expected benefits and actual costs, uncertainty concerning the match between organization and ICT, and so on.) will put the rationality of decisions being made under further pressure.

Simon sees the decision-making process as a way to solve a problem, and distinguishes three phases:

- *intelligence*: identifying and defining the problem;
- *design*: finding possible solutions; and
- *choice*: assessing the various possibilities and selecting one of the available alternatives.

These three elements are all part of our definition of the adoption phase: exploration and research to find out what ICT applications are available, assessing these applications in the light of the organizational needs in order to come to a possible 'solution' and, finally, the decision whether or not to use the application, the outcome of the adoption process.

Although in everyday practice it may be possible to reconstruct such a neatly phased process in retrospect, it often looks different during the decision-making process. Cohen, March and Olsen (1972) do not see the decision-making process as a sequential process, but more as a kind of garbage can where problems, solutions, participants and decision-makers come together. That does not mean that the decision-making process is completely random: an organization can match the various elements through structuring, specialization, consultation, and so on. The harder it is to regulate these elements, the more important the moments that certain issues are discussed become, as well as the participants in the decision-making process. In selecting these moments and participants, decision-makers with a feeling for the political element of the decision-making process can have a great deal of influence.

Another decision-making model is the *political decision-making model* (Miller Hickson and Wilson, 1996). According to this model, decision-making is a power struggle in which various stakeholders try to control the organizational resources, often against a background of conflicting interests. This approach, like the bounded rationality model, does not expect decision-makers to behave rationally all the time. It is unlikely that all the relevant information is available (after all, information is power), and usually the process of negotiation leads to compromises. This model recognizes the high level of subjectivity in the decision-making process and helps explain why the 'best' solution to a problem is rarely the one that is chosen.

The *chaos model*, finally, emphasizes the role of obscurity, mistakes, ignorance and subjectivity in the decision-making process. Objectives are often unclear and subject to change, individual behaviour is frequently based on incomplete or incorrect information and often serves the interest of the individual as much as that of the organization, and so on. The model in particular applies to situations where technologies are unclear, where there are strong fluctuations in the amount of time and effort that can be dedicated to the process, and where choices are inconsistent and ill-defined (Lahti, 1996, in Demkes, 1999). Decisions are made when problems, solutions and individuals are in agreement (Demkes, 1999).

Demkes (1999) specifically pays attention to the decision-making process surrounding ICT investments, and has developed (based on a decision-maker with a 'bounded rationality') a method to support decision-making processes of this kind. Demkes identifies a number of features of the decision-making process surrounding ICT that make the process of assessing and deciding extra difficult:

• the speed of technological developments, which means that technologies are quickly outdated;

• the fact that ICT investments are usually part of a complex of investments;

• the fact that ICT is an integrated part of business processes, and as such is hard to identify as an entity that can be evaluated separately;

• the often qualitative nature of the costs and benefits of ICT; and

• the fact that ICT investments often transcend the boundaries of individual organizations.

These factors cause a great deal of uncertainty with regard to the decision-making process surrounding ICT applications, making it hard to explain the process using rational models. Trends seem to have an equally big influence as scientific cost–benefit analyses – assuming that such analyses can be made scientifically, which, considering the uncertainties described above, is by no means certain.

Au and Kauffman (2003) argue that the Rational Expectations Hypothesis (or REH) and adaptive learning theory, both based on a model of an economically rational decision-maker, do have an explanatory value in analysing ICT adoption and investment decisions. These theories assume that decision-makers are able to utilize all available information efficiently and can learn the true value of a prospective investment over time. Even seemingly 'irrational' behaviour as fad-like behaviour or the 'bandwagon' effect (see also Box 4.4) can be explained in economically rational terms, according to these authors. On the other hand, their view of rationality is not the old-fashioned one, but much more one of bounded rationality, and they emphasize the importance of learning and adaptation of such rational assumptions over time.

BOX 4.4

Decision-making: me too, me too

In an analysis of decision-making processes surrounding the adoption of information technology, Walden and Browne (2002) focus on the 'fad-like' nature of such processes. In other words, on the tendency of decision-makers to ignore their own private opinions about the value of a technology and instead focus on the observed actions of others – comparable to what we previously described as the 'me too' phenomenon. Such decision-making can become very problematic if the observed behaviour in question is based on still other observed actions. Examples of such fad-like behaviour are found in the rise of outsourcing, the implementation of ERP systems, the establishment of a chief technology officer in organizations, and in e-commerce.

Walden and Browne use the 'information cascade theory' to explain this phenomenon. This theory states that, in the course of a diffusion process, later adopters are more likely to rely on observed actions over their own private opinions. This suggests that in many cases, firms may indeed follow leads from other firms in spite of private information contradicting those leads. According to this theory, this results in firms making better decisions overall, but may occasionally lead to an incorrect cascade, wherein all firms follow the wrong course of action. Such a course of action, however, will tend to disappear relatively quickly as more public information about its detrimental results becomes available.

Bannister and Remenyi (1999) also address the organizational decision-making process surrounding ICT, and explicitly include its non-rational elements in their model. Decisions, they argue, are not based exclusively on an objective analysis of figures, results, profit, costs, and so on, but on cultural, political, personal and other 'subliminal' factors as well. In their model we recognize the principles of bounded reality, garbage can, political decision-making and the chaos model. The decision whether or not to adopt an ICT application is hard to rationalize, and according to Bannister and Remenyi there is one important factor that is often overlooked: instinct, trust, intuition – an approach that is based on the environment in which people and organizations actually operate, rather than on 'what the spreadsheets say'.

Although the decision whether or not to adopt an ICT application may primarily be an assessment of the costs and benefits, Bannister and Remenyi argue that there are many other factors involved in the decision-making process. The psychology of the individual decision-makers (and the interaction between them), for instance, as well as their values, skills, and so on, has an important impact on the decision-making process. The culture of an organization (its shared values), in other words the 'psychological disposition of the organization', plays an important role as well – for instance, how innovative is the organization, how willing is it to take risks, to what extent is it influenced by what other organizations do ('me too' decision-making), and so on?

We can conclude that the role of rational, economic criteria (relative advantage in cost–benefit terms) in the decision-making process surrounding ICT adoption may be an important one, but that this role is certainly not unequivocal. Research (for instance by Au and Kauffman [2003], but also the IT investment research cited in the previous section) does support the importance of such criteria, but there is also much evidence that other factors are of considerable importance as well. So the central formal criteria in such decision-making may be economic, but the assessment of such criteria is strongly influenced by organizational and individual factors surrounding the decision-makers. Besides, it is questionable to what extent such criteria are as rational and quantitative as they are sometimes assumed to be. Many of the investment assessment methods discussed in the previous section are aimed at qualitative as well as quantitative assessments – that is, not only financial costs and benefits, but also all kinds of 'soft' contributions (both positive and negative) of ICT to organizations. The rationality of evaluating such criteria is by definition very limited, since 'objective' measures are hardly available.

CONCLUSION

In this chapter we have discussed the first phase in our model: the adoption phase. It has become clear that this phase consists of two stages: in the first stage the organization, after gathering and assessing information, decides to 'adopt' an ICT application, and in the second stage it is up to the potential users, the members of the organization, to support or reject that decision. That is the reason why in this book we have drawn a distinction between adoption as an *organizational* process, and use as an *individual* process. Building on this distinction, we have defined individual adoption as ICT use, which is discussed in Chapter 6. In our view, adoption is an organizational decision process.

Ideally, the final decision to adopt (or reject) an ICT application is made after a careful assessment of technology and organization, considering the demands made by organizational processes and structures with regard to the means of communication and the possibilities ICT offers to change and improve these processes and structures. As we discussed in Chapter 1, in the adoption phase the interaction between organization and technology plays an important role. Information and communication technology suppliers have to be aware of the need to match the technology to the organizational demands of potential users.

Technology and organizations are, however, only two of the factors that influence the speed and outcome of the decision-making process discussed in this chapter. First, the relative advantage of the ICT application to the organization is important: expectations concerning improvements in processes, structures and market position, related to the expected efforts required to realize those improvements. To determine this relative advantage, a number of *economic criteria* in terms of costs and benefits are central, but a number of *technological* features of the ICT application play a role as well. We have specifically paid attention in this chapter to the fact that ICT can be seen as a kind of 'collective action', making the element of achieving critical in terms of connections, and content an important variable in the assessment an organization makes with regard to the costs and benefits. The organizational decision-making process with regard to this assessment is an issue in itself, and it turns out that, although the formal focus of such decision processes is often on economic (and, to a lesser degree technical) criteria, *organizational* variables and the specific *psychological* characteristics, both of the individual decision-makers and of the organization as a whole, play an important part as well.

It has become clear that in the adoption process described in this chapter not much is certain even with regard to the 'objective' factors of technology and economy (costs and benefits): technological developments take place at a breathtaking pace, and it is extremely complicated to determine which technologies are essential to the organization, and in the adoption phase (prior to the actual implementation) the costs and benefits of ICT applications are extremely difficult to assess. In short, the decision whether or not to adopt a certain ICT application is based on rational considerations only to a limited extent, depending to a large degree on intuition and experience – and perhaps even coincidence.

Despite all this, the adoption phase does lead to a decision. If this decision means that the organization wants to implement the ICT application, the organizational decision to adopt has to be translated into a series of individual decision-making processes: the members of the organization have to be persuaded to integrate the application into their daily activities. Which brings us to the implementation phase, the subject of the next chapter of this book.

5 Implementation

Implementation of a new benefit system

For some considerable time the Amsterdam Municipal Social Services Department has been developing a new benefit system (NBS). Eventually it appeared in the media that the development of this new system had encountered substantial problems. This case study focuses on the events surrounding the implementation of the system. The case shows that both from a technical and from an organizational point of view many things can go wrong when a new system is implemented. It would appear that all the rules of a successful implementation have been violated.

MISTAKE 1: NOT A MOMENT'S REST

Generally speaking stagnation means decline. A constant stream of information can, however, have an adverse effect. In the case of the Amsterdam Municipal Social Services Department four different reorganizations took place in a ten-year period. With each change it is important to build in various phases. In the first phase it has to become clear why the organization needs to change. People need to become aware of the change, understand why it has to take place and be able to picture it in their minds. The next phase focuses on the actual implementation of the change. Finally, the change has to be consolidated and evaluated. In the Amsterdam case the organization was given no time at all to familiarize itself with a certain situation. As a result it is difficult to determine the outcome of an implementation process from the outset. Consequently, it becomes difficult to establish a basis of support for the new system.

MISTAKE 2: IGNORING THE USERS

Another mistake that is often made is a failure to pay sufficient attention to the needs and wishes of the people who will be using the system. For the technical implementation of the system (the actual development of the software) it is important to make a good analysis of the tasks the system has to perform. In many cases that involves more than simply describing those tasks. Most of the time the difference in level of abstraction on which users (day-to-day activities) and developers (Universal Modelling Language [UML] diagrams) conceptualize reality has to be taken in account. Furthermore it may be the case, for instance, that as a result of the implementation of a new system there is a change in the way certain tasks are performed. In cases were the building of new

CONTINUED

systems are combined with restructuring operations, extra complexity is built into the project. New processes are hard to conceptualize and to understand, procedures how to deal with errors are neglected. A second obstacle is ignoring user feedback in the test stages. Not only are the end-users in a position to offer valuable information, using that information may help them accept the new system. In the case of the Amsterdam Municipal Social Services Department little attention was paid to what the users had to say, both in terms of describing the tasks that had to be performed and with regard to the feedback offered by the users. Communication is key in any implementation process.

MISTAKE 3: UNRELIABILITY OF THE SYSTEM

Whereas the second mistake had to do with the fact that the system does not do what it is supposed to do, the third mistake involves the reliability of the system. The Amsterdam system 'went down' all too frequently (van Mierlo, 1999). Although all software programs contain bugs, the system that was introduced in Amsterdam was extremely unstable. Taking into account the poor level of support, this meant that the system performed very poorly indeed, which did little to help acceptance of the system within the organization. Failure of an immature system can reduce trust to such a level that even updates of the system will not be used by the individual user.

MISTAKE 4: USER-(UN)FRIENDLINESS

A remark made by one of the employees, that 'the logic of the people who thought up the NBS did not always match the logic used by the employees' (van Mierlo, 1999), is an indication that it is not always easy to understand the system. The problem is that all too often systems are being developed on the basis of technological possibilities rather than the needs and wishes of the people for whom they are designed.

MISTAKE 5: INSUFFICIENT SUPPORT

There is a direct link between the previous two points and the level of support. This is another area where a great deal went wrong. Whenever any failures in the system occurred there should have been excellent support, possibly in the form of a good helpdesk. Another way to increase the likelihood of a successful implementation is to provide the employees with training. The Amsterdam Social Services Department, however, failed to do either. Employees cannot go on when they are stuck.

MISTAKE 6: POOR PROJECT MANAGEMENT

The Standish study shows that, on average, projects exceed the original budget by 189 per cent. The main reason why many ICT projects turn into financial fiascos has to do with poor project management. Poor project management can mean a failure to involve the employees or obtain management support, that the boundaries of the project are poorly indicated or that the expectations that are being created are unrealistic (Standish, 2000). In the case of the Amsterdam Social Services Department it would appear that these problems also played a role. Miscommunication and confusion appear to be the main causes of the problems. Furthermore, one has to be aware that governance of IT systems

CONTINUED

takes about 70 per cent of the budget. Updates will be made starting from the moment that the system is implemented. New releases have to be built and so on. The shift from project management towards governance of the IT system is important. In many cases the building of a governance body is forgotten and knowledge about the system is not transferred from system developers to the people responsible for the day-to-day governance of the system. It is important that, starting from the moment of implementation, user communities are established to discuss priorities with regard to problems to be dealt with and to define additional or new user requirements.

MISTAKE 7: EXODUS

As a result of the problems described above, many employees decided to 'throw in the towel'. Because the implementation process took place at a time when the economic climate was favourable, there was no reason for the employees to stay and weather a poorly working system. As employees abandon ship, they take with them what knowledge has been accumulated over time, which reinforces the problems surrounding the implementation of a new system.

This case shows that implementation is a crucial phase following the decision to acquire or develop a system and before the system is being used. Research indicates that a mere 15 per cent of ICT projects is implemented successfully. Over 50 per cent of the projects, although successful in terms of implementation, either goes over budget, takes longer than planned or is implemented with diminished functionality. The remainder of the projects is cancelled before reaching the actual implementation stage (Standish, 2000).

5.1 INTRODUCTION

In Chapter 1 we defined the implementation phase as follows: 'the phase of internal strategy formation, project definitions and activities in which the adopted application is introduced within the organization, with the aim of removing reservations and stimulating the optimum use of the application'. We immediately have to add that, with regard to the application being adopted, organizations can rarely implement existing applications without any further changes. Those cases where that is possible often involve relatively limited systems with few structural implications for the organization, for instance the implementation of a video-conferencing system or the creation of a group decision support room. With the implementation of large systems, often designed to support heavily structured internal processes, the problem is that the system has to be 'built' according to the functional specifications provided by (ICT) management. The process of determining specifications from within the organization, but also from the users, up to the eventual introduction on the work floor is also considered part of the implementation process. This is more to do with systems implementation, the implementation of the technology. As is clear from the introduction to this chapter, a correct and successful technical implementation is of great economic importance. In this chapter we address the technical as well as the social implementation, in other words, the organizational and user aspects and the tension that exists between the two. We want to stress that the implementation process should be not be taken lightly. McDonagh (2001) argues that 50 per cent of the projects either fail or are cancelled completely, while in 40 per cent of all cases implementation is either late or over budget. In Box 5.1 some examples are provided.

BOX 5.1

Failure of implementation

- A project for the California Department of Motor Vehicles with the objective to revitalize its driver's licence and registration application process. At the moment that the project was stopped $45 million had been spent (McDonagh, 2001).
- The failed implementation of SAP at FoxMeyer, a US-based drugs company. The implementation not only cost $65 million, twice the amount it was originally supposed to cost, it could only handle a small fraction of the orders. FoxMeyer spiralled towards bankruptcy in 1994, blaming the failed implementation of the ERP system, and the company sued both the providers of the application and the consultancy firm responsible for its implementation (Aron and Sampler, 2003).
- The PATHWAY initiative of the UK government, where £878 million was spent on a magnetic stripe card (McDonagh, 2001).

But there are also numerous cases where the implementation of ICT in the business environment was a success, for instance the implementation of ICT at Cisco's, after a major failure of its legacy system had shut down the company for two days (Simons, 2001; McAfee, 2003). Another successful example is the introduction of a flight information system on Schiphol airport, one of the major hubs in Europe. This central information system is built on a proprietary basis of components for message exchange, proprietary software to be used on an XML server and specific systems developed for application servers. One hundred and thirty project team members built the total system in 18 months. The system is capable of processing more than 2 million messages a day, equivalent to 4 gigabyte of daily data. The system comprises 38 totally automated interfaces to connected systems. Twenty thousand people a day use the system. Development costs amounted to €13 million. The new system replaces a system that has been operational for 17 years. (AG, 2 April 2004)

In Chapter 1 we discussed demands and possibilities and how they play a role in the interaction between the organizational domain and the ICT domain. In this chapter we shall see that a further distinction can be drawn between the two domains: on the one hand we can distinguish between management processes and operational processes and, on the other hand, between ICT management and operations. It is, therefore, not just a matter of organization versus ICT, but between strategy versus operations as well. Each of these four elements plays its own role in the implementation of new ICT systems and applications.

The implementation of new technological systems and applications affects the way the organization and organizational processes are given shape. At the same time changes in the organization require new technologies. In such cases ICT is viewed as a technological miracle to solve all kinds of organizational problems because the implementation of new systems often leads to organizational changes (see Chapter 7). Consequently, not all implementation processes take place on a planned basis, and often they will be the result of 'emergent change' (Orlikowski and Hofman, 1997). When that is the case, technology leads to adjustments that are often not anticipated. Because of this, not all ICT projects are successful, and nor are they executed as planned. On the contrary, many projects are terminated prematurely or turn out to be more costly than expected. These increased costs are the product of bad planning and a failure to finish on time. Often, the failure of projects is blamed on poor user participation, incorrect, incomplete or insufficient user specifications, insufficient support from responsible management, unclear or unrealistic objectives, faulty planning, an unclear definition of intermediate results, and so on. This chapter focuses on all these aspects. Below, we begin by discussing what it is exactly that we mean by implementation. After that we address *business IT alignment*. Those of us familiar with business IT alignment will associate it with the strategic alignment model presented by Henderson and Venkatraman (1993), but at present new variations are available. Business IT alignment is a tool that helps gain insight into the various roles and communication processes that play a role in implementation. Next, we address the more technical aspects, followed by the organizational aspects. We conclude by providing some practical guidelines that are of importance in the implementation of ICT projects.

DESIGN AND IMPLEMENTATION OF ICT SYSTEMS AND APPLICATIONS

Technological innovations, which include innovations in the area of ICT, are seen as an impulse to reinforce the competitive position of companies and innovation (see previous chapter). In spite of this, as we have seen, all kinds of innovations often do not have the desired outcome. The reason for this is a faulty implementation of the new technologies or of updates of existing technologies. In many situations there is not a situation where one has to start from scratch (a 'green field' situation) and one has to be aware of the way new systems are integrated with existing, legacy systems. But even in cases where the implementation is fairly successful, a complete realization of the expected strategic and other benefits is not guaranteed. Sometimes the implementation of a new system does not have the expected benefits. Research into the importance of implementation, differences in implementation strategies and the realization of the desired goals, especially with regard to the implementation of ICT systems, is limited. Although general theory formation surrounding organizational change is abundantly available, it does not focus much on ICT as such. This restriction is both quantitative (there are few studies available) and qualitative (there is a great deal of attention to case studies, but there are relatively few overview studies, survey studies or longitudinal studies) in nature (Linton, 2002). In addition, the research findings are not unequivocal or consistent, and there is a low level of explanation. To summarize, theory formation surrounding the implementation of ICT systems and applications is limited. Often all that is done is to identify a number of critical factors, such as a clear definition of strategic objectives, commitment on the part of management, excellent project management, organizational commitment, an excellent implementation team and extensive training (Umble, Haft and Umble, 2003).

What do we mean by implementation? In its simplest formulation, implementation can be seen as the step between the adoption phase – the decision to acquire a new technology – and the phase in which the new technology is either (routinely) used or rejected. Implementation is an extraordinarily critical step between the decision to adopt a technology and its routine use. People change their behaviour with regard to the innovation, ranging from a refusal to use it, ignoring or avoiding it, via a less than enthusiastic or even forced use, to a professional and consistent use.

Andriessen (1989) uses both the term introduction and implementation (Andriessen, 1994). In his view (Andriessen, 1989), a successful implementation depends on having the right project structure and strategy, and on the existing organizational structure. As part of the project strategy, Andriessen mentions an adequate systems development method, which includes good planning and monitoring of progress. Systems development above all has to do with the technology and the way it matches the functional requirements. Questions that need to be asked are: do the technology and business processes match? In what way do these applications support the organization's (strategic) goals? What hardware and software do we need? Will there be increased network requirements? But also, how will the systems and applications be imbedded in the existing ICT structure? What interfaces need to be developed? In addition to the design criteria, other more user-related and organizational factors also play a role, such as in what way the users will be involved in the implementation process, how the pilot results will be translated into the way the system or application will be implemented or users will be trained, and whether or not research will be conducted into if and in what way the system or application is used.

Generally speaking, the first group of questions is seen above all as design related, whereas the second group is considered more an approach to the development of a system or application (Limburg, 2002). The traditional design approach is characterized by a systematic and methodical approach. A current situation (as is, IST) is compared to the desired (should be, SOLL) situation. The discrepancy between the two is considered to be the problem. To solve this problem alternatives are generated and the best alternative is selected, based on a number of more or less explicit criteria. Design methods are used to translate requirements that will lead to the desired situation, which are formulated in everyday language, into formal specifications. Most system development techniques are predominantly geared towards building process and data models and focus on the technical aspects of the information systems. The most promising design is implemented and evaluated.

In the chapter on technology we have already argued that we see technology above all as the result of a process in which many factors and actors play a role, and as such we have argued against deterministic visions regarding technology. However, as described above, many of the technical development methods and tools for the development of information systems used in the ICT community still resemble the traditional deterministic approach to technology design (Peiro and Prieto, 1994), as is reflected in the way information systems and applications are implemented in organizations. This has to do with system development methods. Broadly speaking we can divide these methods into (1) methods that follow a more or less linear path (cascading methods) and (2) methods that are more cyclical in nature (prototyping) and (3) have feedback loops (Wigand, Picot and Reichswald, 1997). In the case of the linear methods, project management perspective is usually leading. The underlying suggestion is that there is an irreversible process, with one phase almost automatically following another until the end-product is delivered to the user, who then has to learn to use it. In the case of the second group of methods the process is divided on the basis of software development stages. This approach leaves more room for feedback loops, although the user is more involved in the testing stages than as an active provider of input for the development of the software, application or system. We will discuss each of these methods in greater detail.

Cascading methods

The name cascading method derives from the way it is usually visualized, namely as a number of consecutive steps that follow one another like the cascades in a waterfall. The model distinguishes various phases that focus on specific elements, in line with the best that project management has to offer. The various phases are planning, analysis, design, implementation, and acceptance and introduction.

BOX 5.2

Prince2

A well-known example of a project management methodology is *Prince2*. This methodology manages the whole product life cycle from idea, via project to delivery and use. *Prince2* is a typical example of a modern top-down approach. The starting point is a business case, which summarizes the strategic objectives and advantages. In the business case the investment decisions are discussed. *Prince2* is based on the following principles:

- justification of investment (business case);
- fixed organizational structure;
- product based planning;
- flexible phasing; and
- flexible methodology.

It is more or less assumed that the analysis of the situation that has to be improved will certainly lead to the right solutions – the design – and that all that has to be done is to implement the design. It is also assumed that the analysis takes into account the competences within the organization and the way responsibilities are assigned. In other words, design and use are separated. Remarkably enough, in the design phase the automation department plays an important part in the realization and technical implementation of the design. All the user has to do is operate the new software, application or information system designed (or purchased and/or adapted to the organization) by the automation department in the correct and proscribed manner, whenever necessary, after receiving proper training. Examples or variations of these methods are Information Systems and Analysis of Changes, Information Modelling, System Development Method (SDM) and Linear Application Development (LAD) (van 't Veld, 1990; Bemelmans, 1991; Fokkinga, Glastra and Huizinga, 1996).

The SDM is a method that is often used and that includes a zero phase at which an information plan is drawn up, followed by the phases of: definition study, basic design, detailed design, realization, implementation and, finally, use and management. If a project fails it is not analysed in terms of a limited participation on the part of the users in the organization, but is instead described in terms of the 'inability to transform a strategic plan into action and insufficient budget (and therefore low priority!) for the implementation' (Bemelmans, 1991: 99). In order to improve the quality of the design, various validation steps and feedback loops have been added to the original cascading model. However, a conscious decision to involve the user in the design process has not been made, making it virtually impossible to adapt the man–machine interface of ERP systems to the preferences of individual users. Another drawback is that the system requirements can change because of the system itself or a changing environment. A linear development strategy makes it impossible to make substantial modifications. An additional disadvantage is that it is hard to keep visualizing the final result when concrete results are not forthcoming. Thus, the development runs the risk of being sidetracked and, as a consequence, the original objectives are not realized. To circumvent these drawbacks methods are used that are based on prototyping.

Prototyping

One example of a method that distinguishes software development stages is proto-typing (Wigand, Picot and Reichwald, 1997). This method presents a model of the intended software to the end users at an early stage. Users have a hard time making their needs and requirements explicit. Prototypes can help users to understand the possibilities of systems. By offering multiple versions the usability of possible versions can be assessed. There are exploratory, experimental and evolutionary prototypes. The exploratory prototype serves as a way of determining the full extent of system specifi-cations. When an experimental prototype is used the software is tested on the basis of partial specifications to investigate the feasibility of certain objectives. The evolution-ary approach involves a step-by-step development from prototype to final product. Although prototypes use the same phases that are used in the cascading method, they do so on the basis of small-scale subprojects. These subprojects are completed when a prototype is produced. Project management makes sure that the various prototypes contribute to the collective system. After the prototypes are tested the applications are implemented throughout the organization. Using prototypes makes it possible to adjust the process in mid-course, although here too the end-user is more a source of information than an actual participant in the development process.

Integration cascading and prototyping methods

The two methods described above have been integrated in the Spiraling model designed by Boehm (1988). In his model the project phases are embedded in an itera-tive process, in which prototypes in various stages of development are evaluated by end-users. This makes it possible to modify and/or further elaborate specifications. Various iterations will result in a better functioning prototype. This model includes planning, analysis and design phases, but an evaluation phase (review by users) has also been added. The project is completed by an acceptance phase. An example of this type of development method is Iterative Application Design (IAD). Within IAD an important role is played by workshops, for instance in involving not only developers and management, but the end-users as well. In addition, prototypes play an important role in all phases of the system development process (Tolido, 1996). Nevertheless, active participation on the part of employees rarely goes beyond taking part in work-shops and taking courses that will train them to become ideal users as envisaged by the developers of the ICT system of application.

System and application development aimed at supporting various functions within different types of organizations does not stop once the system or application has been introduced to the end-users and maintenance team. More often than not, the soft-ware has to be adjusted and redesigned on a continuous basis. Not only does this involve adapting the software to meet user requirements, it is also a matter of main-taining, upgrading, adjusting and perfecting the existing software (Quintas, 1996).

Although one would imagine that at that stage end-users would be in a position to have the software adapted to meet their requirements, that all depends on the degree to which the development of the software has been completed. A system or application that has been developed more fully will not allow for changes at a later stage. In addition, systems that have various development stages, such as systems supporting the operational activities of large organizations like banks, insurance companies and travel organizations, increasingly become a burden because often various systems and applications have been linked on an ad hoc basis. As a result, a change in one particular system or application may have huge unforeseen consequences elsewhere. Consequently, there is less flexibility and replacing entire systems and applications becomes even more complicated. So-called *legacy* systems (systems that have been developed over time and are deeply rooted in an organization because they are inter-linked with the existing structure and processes of the organization) are often so costly to replace as a result of the large investments that have to be earned back (*sunk costs*), that they stand in the way of the development of new systems and applications. In that sense some people talk of new forms of technological determinism.

5.3 DESIGN AND IMPLEMENTATION OF ICT SYSTEMS AND APPLICATIONS: ORGANIZATIONAL INTEGRATION

An important aspect of the technical design is that technical solutions should be contingent with organizational requirements. This contingency perspective assumes that managers try to balance strategy, organizational structures and processes to fit contingencies of environment, technology and other relevant organizational factors.

This contingency perspective is mentioned explicitly in the Strategic Alignment Model (Henderson and Venkatraman, 1993; Parker, 1996). The strategic alignment model (SAM) above all has analytical value and it is less valuable as a model on which to base research: the model has little to offer by way of causality, nor does it contain concepts that can readily be made operational. As a consequence, existing research using this model displays a high level of diversity and offers few unequivocal practical tools (Schepers, 2002). The model above all illustrates the relationship that exists between the organizational domain on the one hand and the technology (ICT domain) on the other (see Figure 5.1). We will discuss the model from this perspective in particular.

Within the organizational and technology domain a distinction is drawn between more strategic aspects – aimed at the organization's environment – and the more operational issues. The model describes how strategic decisions, both with regard to business strategy and ICT strategy, can be adapted to internal processes and structures. Vertical arrows indicate the flow from strategic processes towards operational processes. Horizontal arrows indicate functional integration: the business domain and the ICT domain have to viewed in an integrated way.

Henderson and Venkatraman (1993) suggest four ways to move through the model and thus assess the potential consequences for an organization.

- The introduction of new ICT systems and applications can lead to new strategic co-operation, which in turn affects the organization's structures and processes. The authors also call this form of strategy *competitive potential*. New ICT applications lead to new products or strategies which in turn lead to changes in business processes. This approach is closely related to the one used in *business process redesign*, where processes are 'optimized' on the basis of the possibilities of ICT.

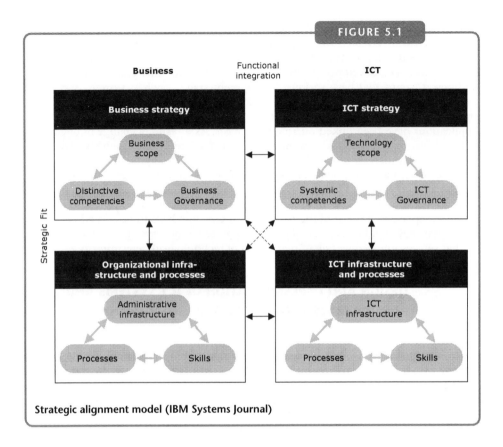

FIGURE 5.1

Strategic alignment model (IBM Systems Journal)

- On the other hand the initiative for strategic changes can also come from management: *technology transformation* as Henderson and Venkatraman (1993) call it. This involves a choice in favour of transformation of the technology, for example the introduction of an ERP system to improve the quality of management information, or the implementation of e-commerce. The implementation of such a system has a direct impact on the ICT strategy as well as on the ICT infrastructure and processes.
- A third perspective is called *strategy execution*. Here, the focus is on the question of what effect strategic changes in the business domain have on the ICT infrastructure and processes. Information and communication technology is seen mainly as a supporting activitiy.
- The final perspective identified by Henderson and Venkatraman (1993) is the one where the ICT strategy is aimed at improving the *service level* of the organization by making better use of the ICT infrastructure and processes.

In our view the strategic alignment model is useful above all to shed light on communication processes and on the role the various parties involved play in the implementation process (van Gurchom, de Wit and Franken, 1996). By looking at the process from the point of view of (1) the organizational and ICT domains, (2) strategy and operations, and (3) requirements and possibilities, it is possible to map and solve various problems and uncertainties in the implementation of new information systems and applications. Co-ordination between the various parties involved will improve. Communication between the actors involved is the core variable in explaining a successful implementation. Many ICT projects fail due to the absence of one of the parties involved, poor communication, uncertainty about the objectives and decisions based on assumptions rather than clearly stated principles. Combining perspectives and iterative co-ordination of requirements and possibilities has to result in a clear vision leading to a feasible project.

BOX 5.3

Case Younglife

In a small-scale project for an intermediary firm in the insurance branch (approximately 100 employees, a strong emphasis on customer intimacy, selling a financial product) the strategic alignment model was used to gain insight into the implementation of e-business solutions. On the basis of strategic statements and a required return on investment within a year, priorities were set using the four different perspectives: strategy, ICT strategy, operations and ICT operations. Although initially the focus was on the development of a website with an online calculator and the possibility to offer after-sales services, the main problems appeared to be related to the development and implementation of a marketing information system and the redesigning of one of the operational processes, in which ICT could only play a limited role. As a tool the strategic alignment model proved very useful in structuring communication processes, involving various parties in the projects and starting discussions. Ultimately, this led to (1) a shift in priorities, (2) a better integration and use of the marketing information system and (3) a redesign of one of the operational processes in order to prevent unnecessary loss of clients. The alignment model proved especially suitable for large vertically integrated companies and in situations where large business systems are implemented, although in practice it is also useful in defining different roles within a small organization and starting from there on assessing and organizing the communication process surrounding the implementation of various applications.

The strategic alignment model has been continuously adapted to present-day demands. Maes (1999) has added an extra layer to the model. He draws a distinction between strategy, culture and operations. He feels this nuance is relevant because there has to be a distinction between structure and process at an internal, operational level. Furthermore, he adds an extra column for information management, where he establishes a link with applications. In his model the ICT column is reserved for the technical organization in terms of networks, systems and databases.

Increasingly, ideas regarding alignment are linked to an architectural way of thinking. This involves the alignment between business architecture, application architecture and technical architecture. Business architecture defines the embedding of the business strategy within the organization. Translating adaptations in the strategy to the ICT domain is a slow and difficult process. Business architecture can play a significant role in translating the business strategy to the information and ICT domain as well as the design of the organization. Business architectures are the blueprints that help (re)design the organization (Presley et al., 2001) and translate external strategy into internal design. It describes the way the responsibilities regarding the most important functions and business processes are organized (Versteeg and Bouwman,

2004). Business architecture sheds light on the structure of, and overlap between, various business domains, making it possible to identify the value chain within the organization more clearly and to reassign the responsibilities accordingly. Furthermore, business architecture helps distinguish the activities within an organization according to technical support by ICT, production-related and commercial activities. This distinction makes it possible to use other co-ordination mechanisms, for instance by building in internal and external market mechanisms, both within the primary value chain and with regard to the supporting ICT processes (supply and demand, outsourcing of activities). As a result, the relationship between the various subdomains becomes explicit. Business architecture is an important tool to gain insight into the complexity and structure of an organization. The ICT architecture describes the long-term vision on ICT and on the embedding of development tracks within this vision. It makes explicit which standards are to be used, for instance Extensible Markup Language (XML) for documents and Extensible Style sheet Language Transformations (XSLT) for document presentation, and which principles have to be followed, for instance a three-tier architecture. The application architecture details the software application components and their interaction. Its details can be described using object or component models, or application frameworks. At this moment application architecture is based on client-server applications, moving from the expansion and integration of applications to the integration applications based on different architectures. Communication between components is asynchronous. Middleware enables the integration into a common environment. The user interface moves from graphical towards object oriented, enabling users to manipulate objects on the screen. Objects and components are promoted by the integrated development environments, in which applications are constructed by the configuration of templates.

Modern architecture-based development methods are aimed at standard, reusable components and at web services that are the basis for the design of flexible software. These component-based or service-based development methods offer organizations greater flexibility, are easier to manage and allow for a more flexible response to user requirements in a cost-effective way and within limited time frames (Stojanovic, Dathanayake and Sol, 2001). Business logic and application functionality converge and reuse makes integration in new systems less complex. By using these components the development of ICT systems and applications increasingly becomes a matter of the selection, reconfiguration, adaptation, construction and application of replaceable and reusable system and application elements. The technical side is increasingly characterized by flexibility and even commodification. Future application architecture will become highly distributed, consisting of interoperable components that encapsulate standard functionalities. Flexibility made possible by modularity is a key element for the application layer (Janssen and Wagenaar, 2003; Aerts et al., 2004: 8). Information and communication technology platform architecture describes the computer, networks and peripherals, operating systems, database management systems, user interface networks, system services and middleware, and so on, that will be used as a platform for the construction of the systems of the organization (Aerts et al., 2004: 8). All three architectures have to be aligned, with a strong focus on the increasing demand for flexibility and agility. Modularity is an important principle supporting the upgrading and reuse of existing components, while at the same time reducing the costs of system development and maintenance. A system that consists of moderately complex components with maximum cohesion, minimal coupling and well-defined interfaces restricts the impact of changes to a few components (Aerts et al., in press: 11). This way of thinking can contribute to increasing flexibility, then, and thus to a more flexible alignment between strategy, business processes and ICT.

5.4 CRITICISM OF EXISTING DESIGN AND IMPLEMENTATION METHODS

There is a great deal of criticism regarding the existing design methods that are inspired by systems technology, including the contingency and architecture approaches, both from a theoretical and a practical point of view. Limburg (2002: 58) summarizes the criticism as follows:

- Different parties and people involved have different interests and ideas about reality.

- Organizations and their environments change continuously, often in an unpredictable and uncontrollable way (Orlikowski *et al.*, 1999) and, as a result, the usage also changes. Furthermore, the nature of a problem can change over time and there is a realistic risk that at the moment the solution is provided the problem has changed or no longer exists.

- It is impossible to specify a design in detail, the design itself can be attribute to changes and lead to unexpected use. Users reinvent the application and systems to fit into their behaviour, which can lead to a very innovative and creative use of applications and information systems, but also to disasters. Users are quite capable of giving technologies a function other than the intended ones (Rice and Rogers, 1980) and of manipulating technology (Orlikowsky, 1992; Flichy, 1995) or rejecting it. Only the actual use provides insights into the way applications and information systems are (or are not) used.

As a result, implementations, which are often accompanied by change, fail. Many attempts have been made to improve the various phases in the design process, for example by putting greater emphasis on problem analysis, increasing user participation, emphasizing the socio-technical aspects of the design and implementation process, and by increasing flexibility through the use of architectural concepts. Besides the more traditional technologically deterministic system approaches there are approaches that focus more on the concepts of organizational development and social constructivism. In these approaches the assumption is that the organizational reality as such does not exist, but is continually being created through the interactions of people within an organizational context. These approaches focus on users and social relationships rather than on the tasks and processes in the organization or on the technologies. According to some (Peiro and Prieto, 1994; Qvortrup, 1994; Quintas, 1996) the design and implementation methods described above are fundamentally unsuitable for capturing the human and social aspects of communication. These methods focus not on social relationships, but on data flows as determined by heavily structured business processes. These data flows can be described, analysed and automated, at least that is the assumption. With regard to the development methods it makes no difference whether these data flows are handled by systems or by humans. Brown and Duguid (2000) have pointed out that this is certainly not the case with all organizational processes. Some organizational processes can only be carried out successfully because humans are capable of interpreting the information and translating it to a concrete situation. There are only certain types of relatively well-defined, linear and limited processes that can really be supported by ICT. Brown and Duguid argue that in many cases information flows acquire meaning only in a specific context. It is often the unwritten rules and consensus between everyone involved that determine what information is meaningful, when it is meaningful and to whom. These rules and insights emerge in a continuous process that is part of people's daily activities. Interaction is a central element of organizations (Qvortrup, 1994).

From the perspective of *social shaping of technology*, all kinds of alternative development methods are being suggested. Eason and Harker (1994), for instance, outline a development method whereby minimal specifications are provided for socio-technical criteria and various actors are actively involved in the design process. The method contains three design levels – individual, group and organization – and it has various consecutive phases: general design, applied design and local adaptations. Qvortrup (1994) champions the concept of social experiment. Social experiments have to be seen as learning processes of specific target groups with regard to how to deal with new technologies. The results are in the knowledge that is acquired concerning the preconditions for such learning processes (Lieshout and Mol, 1989). Methods that are more development oriented can best be illustrated by juxtaposing them with the traditional system-oriented design methods. This comparison is based on Boonstra (1992: 69).

TABLE 5.1

Comparing traditional implementation method to a development approach

Characteristics	Traditional implementation and design methodology	Development approach
Perception of organization	Formal system and reservoir of grown ficiencies	Integral system and source of knowledge, insight and experience
Problem orientation	Directed to solution	Directed to problems
Objective	Stable end situation	Increase ability to change
Process	One time linear process	Iterative, ongoing process
Rationality behind process	Economic technical	Social-political
Process control	Initiated, co-ordinated and controlled from the top. Tight norms and planning	Initiative in one of the power centres. Control is appointed after consultation with parties involved
Decision-making	Structured and formalized, with much influence from the top	Negotiation and consultation with all parties involved
Difference in opinion	Denied or ignored	Openly discussed
Change method	Task structure	Combination of process, negotiation and task structure
Work method	From abstract model and descriptions of organizations to concrete way of working	From concrete ways of working and problems to general objectives and abstract models
Role of outside consultant	Expert who uses empirical-rational strategy	Changing roles with several strategies
Implementation	Division between design and introduction. Implementation is aimed at making the new situation acceptable	Fluid transition from problem diagnosis to goal-setting and change
Participation	Difficult	Good possibilities

Technology is given shape in a specific, 'natural', ever-changing social context, for instance a business environment, which is not by definition a context that allows for all kinds of experiments. This context is by no means stable and is in continuous flux. Traditional implementation approaches usually assume that there is a stable organizational form as well as a technology that is suitable in particular to that context (Table 5.1). This makes implementation a very diffuse process, which culminates in the use and eventually a redefining of technology. We will come back to this in the chapter on the effects of ICT.

In addition to assumptions regarding the stable context in which ICT is introduced, there are also implicit assumptions concerning the nature of technology. In approaches surrounding the implementation of ICT systems it is more or less taken for granted that they are large-scale, relatively inflexible and company-wide systems. Although it is undoubtedly true that administrative and transaction-processing systems are relatively inflexible, ICT technology is subject to change as well. We have illustrated earlier that there is a transition from large, traditional, complex business systems towards more modular and flexible solutions based on open standards and architectures. Information and communication technology is also subject to change, then, and the way technology is used is shaped in the course of the implementation process and afterwards. An important role is played by the way new information systems and applications that are innovating fast and evolving are implemented within changing and learning organizations.

ORGANIZATIONAL IMPLEMENTATION

Organizations are constantly subject to change and they are influenced by all sorts of interventions. Over the past decades ICT has become an important trigger for organizational change. Although social systems cannot be designed and imposed, attempts can be made to influence and realize the way organizational objectives are achieved through clever interventions and strategies. To do so, it is important to have a knowledge of processes of change. The focus is on human behaviour, organizational culture, the stimulation of change, hierarchies and an awareness that organizational change is a continuous process.

Lewin (1947) defined planned organizational change in three phases: 'unfreeze' the current situation so that people are aware of the need to change and the change can occur, then 'move' to make changes, and finally 'refreeze' the new situation in place. Within this basic framework several authors have developed frameworks that relate the type of organizational change to the implementation strategy that should be used to realize that change.

Before we describe two of these frameworks in more detail, we will first lay out the dimensions on which the frameworks are built. The choice of an implementation strategy is largely based upon three factors: first, the degree to which the end situation is clear; secondly, the size of the planned change; and; thirdly, the degree to which management and organizational members have an equal say in the change. Together, these three factors will influence the amount of resistance against a change that is to be executed and the choice for a specific implementation strategy (Figure 5.2).

First, the size of the planned change. Technical changes, including changes surrounding ICT, are not accepted at face value in organizations. Generally speaking, changes evoke both enthusiastic reactions and resistance. Positive reactions usually do not present a problem, but changes that are expected to have a negative effect or whose consequences are unclear, or changes in organizations that are associated with

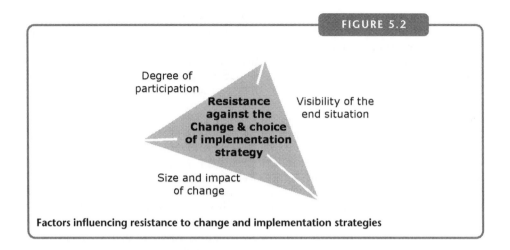

FIGURE 5.2

Degree of
participation

**Resistance
against the
Change & choice
of implementation
strategy**

Visibility of the
end situation

Size and impact
of change

Factors influencing resistance to change and implementation strategies

past negative experiences, will meet with resistance. Such changes are seen as a threat to the culture of the organization or to the position of groups or individual employees. Resistance to change is stronger if the members of an organization are not prepared or attempts are made to implement a change too quickly (van den Hooff, 1997).

The second factor is the visibility of the end situation. Partly depending on the size of the change is the visibility of the end situation. When organizational members are faced with an insecure future they are likely to resist the change. The risk of losing a powerful position, or maybe even losing a job, for many people is a daunting prospect.

The third factor that influences resistance to a change and choice for an implementation strategy is the direction in which the change is started and the way in which it is managed. In other words, the third factor relates to the degree of participation in the decision and design process. The choice facing a manager is one between obtaining full participation from his employees in the decision-making process and implementation (participative) and a directive approach whereby employees are confronted with the decision to implement a new technology. This choice involves the question of whether to implement from the top down, whereby the process is managed by a centralized project team, task force or individual manager, or from the bottom up, placing responsibility as low in the organization as possible. Both approaches have advantages and disadvantages. In the case of a top-down approach, commitment on the part of middle and lower management can be low, but it does offer the possibility to use experienced managers and there is a high level of control by management, which helps safeguard continuity. In the case of a bottom-up approach, the people who actually have to work with the new technology are directly involved in its implementation, which means that the technology will better meet user requirements. A drawback of this approach is that there is a lower level of management control, which makes it more difficult to safeguard continuity.

Taking these three dimensions into account, we will present two frameworks that describe implementation strategies. First, Kim and Lee (1991) point to the barriers that can exist between departments, especially when it comes to co-operation and communication between system developers – those responsible for the technical implementation described earlier – and the intended users.

- *The empirical, rational strategy*: this strategy is based on the assumption that the members of an organization act rationally and make their decisions on the basis of rational considerations, taking their own interests into account. Methods that play a role in a rational strategy are user training and education, selection and deployment of the right people, effective communication between system developers and users, the use of external experts, and the use of methods and procedures aimed at creating realistic expectations.

- *The normative, re-educative strategy*: this strategy is based on the notion that people are primarily geared towards satisfying needs and that these needs depend on the context within which people find themselves. To realize changes one has to focus both on the structures within the organization, such as roles and relationships, and on personal attitudes, behaviour and values. Methods that play a role in this strategy are facilitating and promoting user participation, re-education aimed at creating a climate in which a system can be implemented, activating learning processes to help people get acquainted with the system, applying techniques to influence personal attitudes, values and setting up an implementation team within an organizational structure.

- *The power/coercive strategy*: in this strategy authority and sanctions play an important role. These tools become more effective when there is a certain positive reward. Methods that play a role in this strategy are appointing a project leader with authority, acquiring support from people who (will) offer resistance, assigning a certain level of authority to the project team, setting up a reward system related to the system that is to be implemented, setting up a steering committee, realizing coherence between system development and power structure that exists within the organization, and defining explicit objectives the system has to realize.

Van der Zee (1995) presents a framework in which four implementation strategies are presented:

- *Diffusion approach*: the innovation is made available to the employees who can decide on their own whether or not to adopt the change. This strategy is most suited when the change involves a clear improvement.

- *Directive approach*: the end situation is clear and the change is implemented by the force of power. This approach is needed when the situation is getting out of hand an intervention is needed to save the organization.

- *Interactive approach*: this approach is well suited to professional organizations in which the members are capable of providing meaning to the planned change. This strategy is suggested when the new situation is not clear and has a significant impact.

- *Development approach*: this approach is aimed at increasing the competences of organizational members. The strategy should be applied when the organization is going though a fundamental change.

In everyday practice one is likely to encounter these strategies in hybrid rather than pure forms, and a choice in favour of one of these strategies may very well be the outcome of negotiations with the parties involved instead of being the kind of rational choice suggested by the contingency approach. In three case studies McLoughlin and Clark (1995) found examples of a top-down directive approach, while they also found elements of participation. Another case involved a mixture of a top-down and a bottom-up approach with a blend of a participative approach whereby responsibilities were assigned at a low level within the organization. A third case involved a top-down approach, whereby a manager was responsible for the introduction of the new technology, and a participative approach. In short, no clear-cut image emerges.

The decision as to which specific implementation strategy to adopt depends on the characteristics of an organization. On the one hand, this involves characteristics that have to do with the organization and its integration in a certain context and, on the other hand, it concerns the tasks that have to be carried out by the system being implemented. From a contingency perspective there is no standard solution available.

We started this section with a short description of Lewins's unfreeze, move, refreeze model. Here we will examine this process in more detail. Vinkenburg (1995) provides five steps in the actual process of changing an organization. In this process the change agent fulfils an important role:

- *Direct attention*: a change agent should create a situation in which others can focus on the intended change.
- *Provide perspective*: a change agent should be able to show the added value of a change not only for the top management, but also for the individuals on the work floor.
- *Create a change climate*: a change agent should be directly accessible for organizational members and create support for the change, for example by influencing opinion leaders within the organization.
- *Plan the intervention*: a change agent should plan how the actual change will take place. Interventions can be gradual or immediate. In some cases the change will take place person by person, in other situations the change is group by group or department by department. In many cases a quiet period, for example a weekend or the period between Christmas and the new year is used to actually change the systems so that employees, returning on Monday or in the new year can work with the new system.

5.6 CONCLUSION

Implementation can be interpreted in a broad as well as a narrow sense. A broad definition takes into account everything that takes place between the decision to adopt and the actual use. It is possible to make a further distinction between the more technical implementation of the ICT system and application on the one hand, and the organizational implementation, on the other. Information and communication technology systems and applications are usually introduced within organizations in a fairly linear way, without paying a great deal of attention to the way these systems and applications will be incorporated into existing behaviour. As a rule, users are consulted primarily to formulate user requirements, and the systems and applications are built according to these specifications. Not much attention is paid to implementation in a narrow sense. Implementation in a narrow sense above all has to do with learning how to work with the new ICT systems, in other words, with the steps that are needed for the transformation of the use of an existing system towards a new system. In this sense, implementation involves the behaviour of employees, expectations with regard to the changes, hierarchies and organizational change made possible by ICT systems and applications. Management has to make sure that the organizational changes take place as smoothly as possible and is responsible for a change in strategy.

It is remarkable that, in general, relatively little attention is paid to the economic or psychological aspects of implementation. The primary focus is on how technology can be applied, taking into account organizational and technical aspects.

6 Use: individual, group and organization

The electronic calendar

An electronic calendar is an application that serves the same purpose as a regular (paper) calendar. The advantage of an electronic calendar is that it allows people to share their calendar with others, making is easier, for instance, to schedule a group meeting. These two functions are represented in Figures 6.1a and b.

FIGURE 6.1

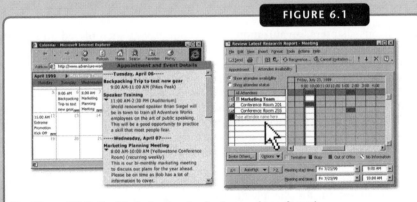

The Microsoft® Outlook® electronic calendar (www.microsoft.com)

Research (van den Hooff, 2004) indicates that over time a shift took place in the way the electronic calendar was used at a Dutch Ministry: from an improvement of individual efficiency and effectiveness as a result of easier individual calendar management towards improved co-ordination due to a collective use of the calendar. In this context 'collective' refers to the use of the application as a kind of 'groupware', with colleagues being able to access and modify each other's calendars. It would seem that (people within) organizations have to go through a learning process when they start using new technology.

CONTINUED

This study indicates that individual differences, such as the degree to which a person is willing to open up to others, affect the speed with which this process takes place. Within the organization mentioned above there were some people who systematically refused to give others access to their calendars. As a result, they benefited less from the use of the electronic calendar.

In addition, it turned out that some people benefited more than others from the electronic calendar. Managers and consultants have more appointments, for example, so they benefit more from the use of the electronic calendar than, say, administrative staff or policy-makers. The tasks these various groups have to perform vary to such an extent that it affects the way the technology is being used. The group to which the individual belongs also plays an important role.

To summarize, the use of a new technology depends on the interaction between the technology, the user (and his or her tasks) and the organizational environment.

6.1 INTRODUCTION

In the previous chapters, organizations and technology as such played an important role. In this chapter we will treat them as a given context. Within that context the organization's employees use an information and communication technology to perform their tasks. We will therefore focus primarily on the *individual* level of analysis in our model. In other words, the use phase is *the phase in which the members of an organization use the ICT application in their daily activities*. Within each organization it is possible to identify a large number of activities, depending, among other things, on the kinds of products and/or services it offers. A mission statement is the core summary of the activities an organization performs. From this mission statement many tasks and subtasks can be derived. Each task can have practical (for example manufacturing a product), as well as information (for example seeking information on competitors, checking output levels), communication (for example discuss a strategy or attend a meeting) or transactional (for example paying a bill, changing someone's salary scale) aspects. Information and communication technology primarily supports these information, communication and transactional aspects of a task. Although in this chapter we focus primarily on the individual level, to get a complete picture of the use of ICT in organizations it is important to look at the group and organizational level as well.

As we indicated earlier, however, the individual is our focal point when we discuss use of ICT: for many tasks it is the individual who decides whether or not to use a certain ICT application in the performance of his or her tasks. Therefore, we begin this chapter with an overview of theories concerning *media choice and use*. The actual use of an ICT application often takes place through interaction with others (particularly when referring to what we have described in Chapter 2 as *communication services*). Since there are often specific group dynamics at work in this process, we will address the use of ICT in groups in section 6.3. In section 6.4 we will discuss some aspects of the use of ICT at the organizational level. The conclusion to this chapter is presented in section 6.5.

6.2 INDIVIDUAL AND USE: MEDIA CHOICE AND USE

Our central focus in the study of ICT use in organizations consists of the users' information and communication tasks, and the tools (such as, for example, ICT) they use to perform those tasks. Our focus is not on the use of ICT as it is more or less prescribed in structured processes and, consequently, we will not discuss the use of applications such as workflow management and administrative or personnel management systems. Instead, we want to address the use of ICT systems and applications in processes where users have a choice. The assumption is that people do have access to these systems and applications.

Accessibility

Based on an extensive literature research McCreadie and Rice (1999) distinguish six types of accessibility: physical, economic, political, cognitive, affective and social. Physical accessibility has to do with the question of whether or not a potential user has direct access to a service. Three aspects are important here. First, the technology: what technology is needed to use a service or application? In an environment where the technology is still being developed that question is certainly not insignificant. What is important as well is how advanced the technology is: is it an entirely new system or a new (software) application that can be implemented in a specific system? The context is also important. Does a user have access to an application at his or her desk, or does he or she have to go to a special room or computer? At that point, other users play a role as well: when there is only a single computer with an Internet connection, and that computer is occupied, other users have to wait. The concept of physical accessibility involves more than the simple question whether or not people have the right technology. It is also about the likelihood of people getting acquainted with the technology, and about how easily it can be reached.

Affective accessibility refers to the question of whether or not the medium matches the user's daily activities. Again, this form of accessibility depends both on supply and demand. The likelihood of a particular medium being used depends on the user's knowledge and behaviour. People who are accustomed to using the telephone for various activities are more likely to do so when confronted with a new question. It is simply one of their daily activities.

User friendliness is often considered a prerequisite for successful services, for instance in Davis's (1989) technology acceptance model, which will be discussed in more detail later in this section. This variable is an important determinant of the degree to which affective accessibility serves as an obstacle. Rather than being crucially important to the success of a technology, however, it must be seen as a precondition. An essential variable is the user's level of experience – not just in terms of estimating the suitability of a medium for a specific task (see the following paragraphs), but also in terms of the extent to which the user is *capable* of using a specific technology. A system like UNIX, for instance, which can hardly be accused of being user-friendly to a novice user, is perfectly accessible to an experienced user. It is, therefore, not the level of user-friendliness itself that is important, but rather the right match between the user's experience and the complexity of the system. Poor accessibility can even be seen as a challenge: computer games, where reaching the next level is made difficult on purpose, are a case in point. In addition, people derive a certain status from their ability to operate complex systems.

The question as to why people use or do not use certain applications that match their needs and behaviours, is the frequent focus of communication research studies. Many of those studies are based on theories that are known as *media choice (and use) theories*. In the next sections we will discuss these theories and the various trends that can be distinguished.

Objectivist or contingency theories: social presence and media richness

The most important premise of these theories is the contingency paradigm, which assumes that things that have a good match or fit will be able to function effectively and efficiently. This paradigm has been used in organization theory for quite some time. On the basis of various studies, Galbraith (1973) argues that there is no optimum way to organize things, and that a successful organization adjusts its organizational form to the level of uncertainty it faces and the diversity of the tasks it performs. In other words, it is not so much a matter of finding the ideal organizational form, but rather of establishing an (optimal) fit between the organization and its environment.

This notion can be applied to media choice as well: there is no single medium that is uniquely suited for all tasks. Effective communication depends on choosing a medium that is compatible with the task at hand. Various theories, such as *hot and cold media*, (McLuhan, 1964), *social presence theory* (Short, Williams and Christie, 1976) and *media richness theory* (Trevino, Daft and Lengel, 1990) are based on this idea, and take a somewhat rational and objectivist approach.

McLuhan (1964) distinguished hot from cold media based on whether they provide information in respectively high or low definition. Hot media consequently elicit less involvement from the user whereas cool media require increased involvement. Social presence not only examines media characteristics but also relates these to task performance. *Social presence theory* is based on the assumption that media vary in the degree to which the user experiences the psychological proximity of other individuals (Short, Williams and Christie, 1976). Social presence is conveyed by features that are deemed important in interpersonal communication, such as *non-verbal signals, proximity and orientation* (physical distance and relative positions), and *physical appearance.* According to Short, Williams and Christie a higher degree of social presence leads to a richer, less ambiguous perception of the persons one is communicating with, and consequently to more social communication. The empirical support for this theory is mixed at best – even Short *et al.*'s own early findings suggest that media low in social presence (for example auditory channel only) resulted in greater social influence between communication partners than those higher in social presence (see also the SIDE theory discussed below).

Building on these insights, *media richness theory* (Daft and Lengel, 1984) proposes that not all communication media are equally suited for the different information requirements that different tasks create. Daft and Lengel distinguish two different information requirements: *uncertainty*, the lack of information, which creates the need for *more* information, and *equivocality*, the absence of clear definitions of situations, which does not require more information as much as it requires *richer* information, information with a higher ability 'to change understanding within a time interval. Communication transactions that can overcome different frames of reference or clarify ambiguous issues to change understanding in a timely interval are considered rich' (Daft and Lengel, 1986: 560).

An announcement that a meeting has been rescheduled, for example, can only be interpreted one way. A discussion concerning (an organization's) strategy, whereby managers have to agree on a solution based on a wealth of information, on the other hand, has a higher level of equivocality.

Media are more suitable for equivocal information tasks, or have a higher degree of *media richness*, if they score higher on the following four criteria: (1) the possibility of *instant feedback*, (2) the medium's ability to convey *multiple cues*, such as body language, facial expressions, tone of voice and so on, (3) the use of *natural language* to convey subtleties and nuances, and (4) the *personal focus* of the medium. Based on these criteria, face-to-face communication is the richest form of communicating, followed by media forms like the telephone and e-mail. Lean media like brochures and reports are at the bottom of the list. As far as the World Wide Web is concerned, the level of richness depends on the way pages are designed.

BOX 6.1

Inappropriate use of ICT according to media richness theory

In October 2001, employees of the high-tech firm Ubinetics exploded in anger as management had used e-mail to lay off their colleagues. One of the company's divisions was called to a meeting by boss Bjorn Krylander to be told of the 15 job losses. He then said if there was an e-mail waiting for them when they returned to their desk, then they had lost their job. In spite of the fact that this was combined with a face-to-face meeting, employees felt that this was a very inappropriate way of communicating such a sensitive message to them. (Ananova, October 2001)

Considerably more inappropriate (and conflicting with media richness principles) is the use of mobile phone text messages or e-mail messages by Malaysian men – in order to divorce their wives! Under the Islamic laws of the country, such a message announcing the intention to divorce is sufficient for a man to divorce his wife. Not the other way around, of course – for a woman to divorce her husband is much more complicated. In 2003, this custom had become such a nuisance to the Malaysian authorities, that the laws concerning the subject would be amended to explicitly exclude the possibility of divorcing through electronic messages. (Ananova, September 2003)

With regard to the matching of tasks and media, the assumption is that in order to communicate effectively a lean medium should be used for tasks low in equivocality, and a rich medium for tasks with a higher level of equivocality. In order to reschedule a seminar, (low equivocality) e-mail is an appropriate medium. The seminar itself (high equivocality) is face-to-face. If a message low in equivocality is communicated via a rich medium, this can possibly lead to confusion and inefficient communication – for instance, when a financial controller reports the organization's year results to his superior in a face-to-face conversation. Conversely, the use of a lean medium for a message high in equivocality may lead to misunderstandings and incorrect interpretations of the message – for instance, a psychiatrist who communicates his diagnosis of a complicated case to his colleague with the help of a standardized form with only closed answering categories. In sum, according to the media richness theory effective communication is all about finding the right fit between task equivocality and media richness, rather than using the richest medium. In Figure 6.2 this principle is presented graphically.

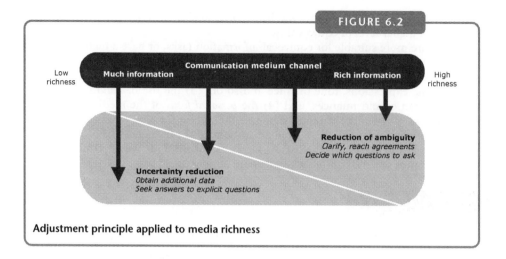

Adjustment principle applied to media richness

Media richness theory is frequently used, but, like social presence theory, there is little consistent empirical evidence to support it. The theory is also subject to considerable criticism, aimed especially at the following assumptions ascribed to the media richness theory (Fulk, Schmitz and Steinfield, 1990):

- *Media*: each medium has its own fixed characteristics – the richness of a medium is *non-variable*, regardless who uses the medium and in what context it is being used. The characteristics of the task are objective as well.
- All users know the differences between media in terms of their objective character- istics. People are aware of the inherent differences between the various media and tasks. Variations between tasks as well as their level of equivocality are fixed and equally salient to everybody.
- *Media choice processes*: individuals make *independent choices*. The social environment in which these choices are made have no immediate impact on that process. The only possible exception occurs when the sender wants to add a symbolic sign, indi- cating, for instance, authority or commitment, to the message – see the *symbolic interactionist* approach below.
- Media choice is a *cognitive process*. Attitudes and behaviour are the outcome of cog- nitive evaluations of media characteristics and message requirements. The choice process is forward-looking – the choice depends on an assessment of current needs and future goals.
- Media choice is *objectively rational*. The user evaluates the characteristics of the task and medium and chooses the medium best suited to the task, as 'prescribed' by the media richness theory. Rational choices are based on the inherent characteristics of the task and medium. There is little room for individual variation.
- Behavior is *motivated by efficiency*. The use of rich media to perform tasks with a low level of equivocality often leads to inefficient communication.

In a later publication, Trevino, Daft and Lengel (1990) present an addition to media richness theory (their *symbolic interactionist perspective*), in which they acknowledge that media characteristics are not entirely objective: media also have a symbolic value, and this symbolic value can lead to media choices which are not optimal in terms of the 'fit' between task and medium. Users can perceive a medium as 'cool' or 'sexy', dull or impersonal, as a threat to their jobs or as an opportunity to 'score' (see also Sitkin, Sutcliffe and Barrios-Choplin, 1992). Face-to-face communication, for instance, symbolizes commitment and personal interest, and this symbolic value was found often to be an important reason for communicating face to face where another medium would have been more optimal in terms of this 'fit'. Still, the central premise of this theory is that there is an optimal possible fit between task and medium, and that users aim to achieve this fit.

Subjectivistic approaches

There are several subjective approaches towards the study of media choice: for example social influence, technology acceptance, channel expansion, and social information processing theory. In this section we well elaborate on these subjectivist approaches.

The *social influence model* (Schmitz and Fulk, 1991) argues that media richness cannot be determined objectively. What is important is the way various media are perceived. The perception depends on the user's attitude as well as the opinions and behaviour of others. Furthermore, different people may have different perceptions. The same holds true with regard to tasks. A second set of factors that may influence the choice of media is the (lack of) experience people have both with the task and with the technology.

The basic principles of this approach are (Fulk, Schmitz and Steinfield, 1990):

- Media evaluations (perceptions and attitudes) are a function of (a) the objective characteristics of the media, (b) media experiences and skills, (c) social influence in the shape of overt opinions of employees, behaviour imitation, group values, social definitions of rationality, and (d) previous media-related behaviour.
- Task evaluations are a function of (a) objective characteristics of the task, (b) experiences and skills related to the task, and (c) social influence in the shape of overt opinions of employees, behaviour imitation, group values and social definitions of rationality.
- The media used by an individual are a function of (a) media evaluations, (b) media experiences and skills, (c) social influence, (d) task evaluations, and (e) situational factors like individual differences, facilitating factors and direct restrictions.

This leads to the graphical representation of this model in (Figure 6.3).

According to this model, the use of ICT is not a purely rational matter of matching media and tasks. The opinions people have concerning their task, and the media they can use to perform these tasks, and the social context are equally important. To a large extent the use of ICT is determined by personal preferences, user styles and organizational cultures. In other words, according to such subjectivistic approaches, the individual user's social environment is an important influence in their media choice and use.

The assumption that media richness cannot be determined objectively is also the central premise of the *channel expansion theory* developed by Carlson and Zmud (1999). Their theory identifies certain experiences as important in shaping how an individual perceives a medium's richness. These experiences include experience with the channel, experience with the messaging topic, experience with the organizational context and experience with other communication participants. Through these experiences communication participants develop associated knowledge bases that may be used more effectively to encode and decode rich messages on a channel. In this way an 'objectively' lean channel can become increasingly appropriate and usable for rich communication.

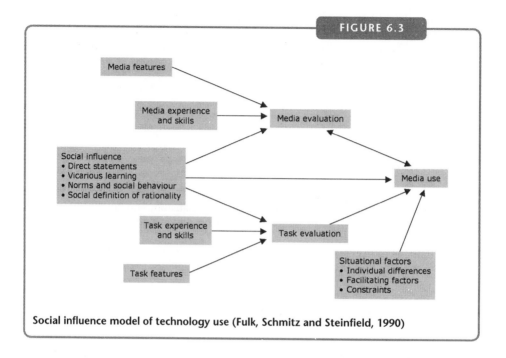

FIGURE 6.3

Social influence model of technology use (Fulk, Schmitz and Steinfield, 1990)

In a study concerning the use of e-mail, Markus (1994a; 1994b) also indicates that prior experience with an ICT application has a clear influence on the perceived richness of that application. Markus (1994b) applies a *social definition* perspective, which argues that a medium's 'appropriateness' for a certain task evolves from the experience the organization has with that medium, and such 'social definitions' of appropriateness may not conform to objective definitions. Walther (1992) reports similar findings. In his *social information processing theory* (SIP), he contends that social presence does not automatically disappear as a result of reduced media capacity to convey cues. According to SIP, participants in a communication process using any medium, have similar needs for uncertainty reduction and social relations. So, regardless of the medium used, communicators will want to establish meaningful social relationships. In order to realize such needs in an ICT setting users will adapt their linguistic and textual behaviours in order to be able to communicate socially relational signals via text only. In a later study, Walther (1996) argues convincingly that ICT possesses certain characteristics which make it very well suited for interpersonal communication (traditionally the domain of 'rich' media) – and even facilitate communication that surpasses normal interpersonal levels, what Walther calls 'hyperpersonal' communication. Walther's argument is that 'cues filtered out' approaches, like media richness theory, have always had a blind spot for these characteristics, and that they pay insufficient attention to the influence of time in the process. Time, Walther concludes on the basis of a considerable number of studies, is an important factor in determining the degree to which computer-mediated communication (CMC) media are used for interpersonal (that is, rich) communication. The perception of a medium's richness, in other words, changes with time, and with the experience and expertise that users have with using that medium.

In their research into the use of e-mail, Dimmick, Kline and Stafford (2000) conclude that the richness of that medium is very relative: richness is only one of the criteria being used when people choose a particular medium, and their study indicates that the fact that e-mail makes the limitations imposed by time and geography irrelevant is more important than the degree in which the medium is suitable – 'objectively speaking' – for rich communication. As Dimmick, Kline and Stafford (2000: 241) put it: 'e-mail is used to obviate the barriers posed by time zones and work schedules even though it may not be the optimal medium for conveying or expressing feelings'.

BOX 6.2

Competing video-conferencing systems: the role of social influence

Kraut *et al.* (1998) report a study concerning two competing desktop video systems (Cruiser and MTS), introduced into the same company. Technologically and qualitatively the two systems were virtually identical. Still, at the end of the 18-month research period, Cruiser had 80 active users, whereas MTS had zero (although both had started with about 18 users). The explanation for this difference, Kraut et al. contend, is not in the technology or in differing matches between task and technology, but in social influence mechanisms. People used a particular system more when more of their co-workers used it, and less when more people were switching to the other system. Kraut et al. identify two related, yet different, ways in which social influence operates:

* The *normative* dimension: when the majority of co-workers start using one of the two systems, and report positively on it, a set of socially shared beliefs about the system's value is developed and reinforced. Hence, the organizational norm concerning Cruiser became a positive one, whereas that concerning MTS became negative through social influence mechanisms.
* The *utility* dimension: with more co-workers using Cruiser, this system's utility rapidly surpassed that of MTS. The number of people with whom one could communicate via Cruiser increased significantly as it declined for MTS, creating a critical mass for Cruiser – a point that MTS never reached.

As both mechanisms are self-reinforcing, their combination created a situation in which one system became a success, while the other one became a total failure.

Thus, subjectivist approaches to media choice are based on the assumption that task and medium characteristics cannot be determined objectively, and are subjective perceptions. The same goes for matching medium and task: different users will make different choices based on their personal perception. Research indicates that their social environment can mould the attitudes, values and behaviour of people.

As Kraut *et al.* (1998) argue, this social environment plays two roles: on the one hand, it constitutes the 'normative' environment (in terms of co-workers' attitude towards, and use of, a new medium – in line with social influence theory), on the other hand, it also strongly determines the medium's utility (its added value in terms of communication tasks). This utility is, of course, strongly dependent on the number of useful contacts who use a certain medium. This is related to the concept of a 'critical mass' (Markus, 1987; 1990). In order for any 'collective action' to become valuable to the members of a social system, a sufficient amount of these members need to take part in this action (Oliver, Marwell and Teixeira, 1985). Thus, for a new technology to become truly useful, it is necessary that enough members of a social system accept it to make it worthwhile for all the others to use it. The fact that we are dealing with an 'interactive' medium here increases the importance of a 'critical mass'. Theoretically, if only one member accepted an interactive medium, it would be of absolutely no use to him or her, because there would be nobody for him or her to communicate with. Once enough members start using the medium, it becomes interesting enough for the majority of the members of the social system to start using it. This is the point where the rate of adoption rises sharply, where the 'critical mass' occurs. So, the number of co-workers using an ICT application is not only an influence in terms of social influence as such, but also in terms of enhanced utility of the medium – the higher the relative number of co-workers using it, the more useful the medium becomes to a user.

The variable of 'utility' strongly resembles what Davis (1989) calls the 'perceived usefulness' of an information and communication technology. This perceived usefulness is a key variable in Davis's *technology acceptance model* (TAM), which seeks to explain the use of ICT by focusing on the users' *attitude* towards the technology, and their subsequent *intention* to use it. This model is an adaptation of the theory of reasoned action (TRA) proposed by Fishbein and Ajzen (1975) to explain and predict the behaviours of people in a specific situation. Two key variables are central in this technology acceptance model: the technology's *perceived usefulness* and its *perceived ease of use*. These perceived system characteristics are expected to influence an individual's attitude towards the system, which influences their intention to use it, which in turn ultimately leads to their use (or non-use) of the system. Figure 6.4 gives a graphical representation of the TAM.

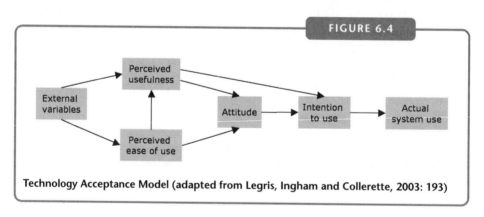

FIGURE 6.4

Technology Acceptance Model (adapted from Legris, Ingham and Collerette, 2003: 193)

The perceived usefulness of an information and communication technology is defined as 'the degree to which a person believes that using a particular system would enhance his or her job performance' (Davis, 1989: 320). Perceived usefulness has a number of different dimensions, such as usefulness for job effectiveness and efficiency, and for the job as a whole.

The other key variable, 'perceived ease of use', is defined as 'the degree to which a person believes that using a particular system would be free of effort' (Davis, 1989: 320). This relates to the physical effort of using the system (its 'physical accessibility', so to speak), as well as the mental efforts necessary to use it and the ease of learning to use the system (its 'affective accessibility'). Perceived ease of use is hypothesized not only to influence attitude and subsequent intentions and behaviour, but also perceived usefulness: such usefulness is expected to increase, as its ease of use is higher.

The TAM has received considerable empirical support over the years (Adams, Nelson and Todd, 1992; Davis and Venkatesh, 1996; Chau and Hu, 2002; Legris,

Ingham and Collerette, 2003). An important finding is that perceived usefulness is often found to be a more important determinant of system use than perceived ease of use – and that perceived ease of use is, indeed, often found to be a determinant of perceived usefulness. This empirical testing has also led to the model being extended with a number of variables – especially concerning the 'external variables' in the model. There is a wide range of such variables, as Legris, Ingram and Collerette's (2003) meta-analysis of TAM research shows: from intrinsic involvement to prior use and experiences, from level of education to task technology fit and from gender to job relevance.

An external variable that was consistently found to be of relevance is one also identified in the social influence model: a user's prior experience with the technology in question, with ICT in general or with comparable technologies (Legris, Ingham and Collerette, 2003). In many other studies (that is, not TAM based) concerning the use of ICT, experience with the application is identified as an important determinant of the way in which, and tasks for which, ICT is used. Despite the considerable empirical support that TAM has received some critical remarks should also be made. Methodological issues are that many of the validations were performed among students. Moreover, the research is based on self-reports. Consequently, it is not system use that is measured but, rather, variance in self reported use. A more fundamental issue is that one can wonder to what degree TAM really explains behaviour. One can argue that media use is nothing more than a logical consequence of perceived usefulness and perceived ease of use. If we compare this to the notion that someone who is tired goes to sleep and someone who is hungry will eat, the TAM model becomes rather obsolete. The central question, of course, is how a certain kind of hunger relates to the consumption of a certain kind of food or, with respect to TAM, to explain how specific uses are related to the use of specific technologies. Despite the many shortcomings of the media richness model, it does attempt to explain technology use based on the characteristics of both tasks and technologies.

Finally, Venkatesh *et al.*, (2003) test and integrate no less than eight different models concerning ICT use in their unified theory of acceptance and use of technology (UTAUT), presented in Figure 6.5. Among these models are Rogers's diffusion model (see Chapter 1), TAM and the theory of planned behaviour. In UTAUT, social influence is an important variable, together with performance expectancy and effort expectancy (related to TAM's perceived usefulness and perceived ease of use,

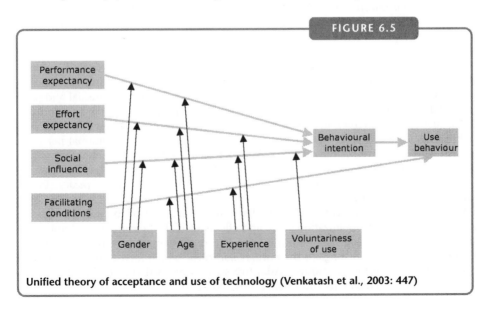

FIGURE 6.5

Unified theory of acceptance and use of technology (Venkatash et al., 2003: 447)

respectively). Experience is found to be an important moderating variable in this model, which, according to Venkatesh et al.'s analysis, has a significantly stronger explanatory power than each of the separate models.

The approaches we have discussed so far have in common that they focus on the subjective perception of the characteristics of tasks and media forms. They recognize that the technology has a number of inherent, objective characteristics – it is the perception of those characteristics that varies. Research in this context focuses, for example, on the relationship between characteristics (individual characteristics, differences in function and position in the hierarchy) and tasks of participants in a communication process, on the one hand, and the choice of ICT applications, on the other (see, for example, Hinds and Kiesler, 1999). Such studies often ignore communication content, have a blind spot for other 'competing' forms of communication and pay little attention to the context in which the communication takes place. This context refers to the organization, unit or group within which the communication takes place and to the user's everyday reality (routines, values, social relationships and shared history, visions, opinions, and so on). In the next section we will discuss approaches that do take this context into account: approaches that argue that technology only acquires form and meaning when it is being used – 'socially constructed' – in the interaction with users and organizations.

Structurationalist approaches

The third kind of approach to media choice in organizations consists of integrated theories that try to include the objective and (inter-subjective characteristics of ICT applications as well as the context in which these characteristics are shaped. These theories focus on the actual *interaction* between users, their organizational environment and the technology. One such theory is Orlikowski's (1992) 'structural model of technology', which is based on two principles:

- the duality of technology: technology is both the result of human action (technological innovation) and a tool for humans to accomplish some action (organizational innovation);
- technology is interpretively flexible: the interaction between technology and organizations is a function of the different actors and socio-historical contexts implicated in its development and use.

These principles lead to the model in Figure 6.6. In this model arrow (a) designates the technological innovation process (technology as the outcome of human action), whereas (b) stands for the effects of technology on users. The organizational and professional constraints influencing this interaction are signified by arrow (c), and the consequences this interaction has on this context can be found in arrow (d). In a later publication Orlikowski (2000) proposes an extension to this structurational perspective, in which she stresses the dynamic character of this interaction: technology is not the stable result of this process, but a dynamic element of it.

Another theory focusing on this interaction is *adaptive structuration theory* (Poole and DeSanctis, 1990; DeSanctis and Poole, 1994). According to DeSanctis and Poole, 'traditional' perspectives like media richness are part of the *decision-making school* in the study of organizational use and effects of ICT, focusing on technological structures and technologically determinist in nature. Orlikowski's work, according to DeSanctis and Poole, belongs to the *institutional school,* which focuses on social structures and non-determinist models. Adaptive structuration theory (AST) integrates such perspectives, DeSanctis and Poole (1994) contend.

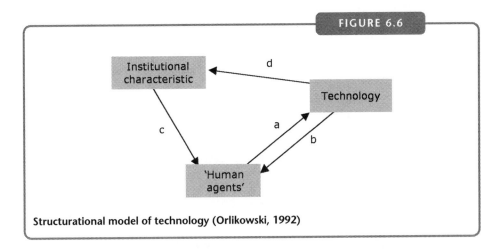

FIGURE 6.6

Structurational model of technology (Orlikowski, 1992)

Adaptive structuration theory belongs to what DeSanctis and Poole call the *social technology* perspective. This perspective acknowledges that technologies do have structures in their own right, but that social practices moderate their effects on behaviour. Structures exist in organizations, regardless of technology – for instance, reporting hierarchies, standard procedures, and so on. Some of these structures are incorporated into technology design, for instance in a work flow application or a group decision support system. In terms of AST, these structures provided by the technology itself are called its *structural potential*. Other sources of structure are the tasks (which can be highly structured or unstructured) and the organizational environment (for instance, cultural beliefs or spending cuts).

Then there are the *structures in action*: social structures which emerge in human action as people interact with these technologies. This is called *structuration*, 'the process by which social structures (whatever their source) are produced and reproduced in social life' (DeSanctis and Poole, 1994: 128). To illustrate this, DeSanctis and Poole use the example of a GDSS with a highly restrictive structural potential, in which decision processes are restrictively designed, limiting participation and informal exchanges. Such a system would lead to a decision process in which the formal agenda and procedures are closely followed, leaving little room for decision structures other than those embedded in the system. So, the restrictive structures embedded in the technology are translated into restrictive structures in the actual decision making process. This is called *appropriation*: through the appropriation of rules and resources embedded in a technology, social structures are brought to life. Such appropriations are not automatically determined by technology designs, they are shaped as users interact with the technology.

At the centre of AST is the social interaction between participants in a communication process, and their interaction with the technology. These interactions are determined by the structures embedded in the technology, tasks and organizational environment, as well as a number of characteristics of the participants themselves (the group's internal system, in DeSanctis and Poole's terms). These interactions themselves produce potential new sources of structure (the results of the task, for instance), as well as new social structures and a number of outcomes. Figure 6.7 summarizes the central propositions of adaptive structuration theory. This is a somewhat adapted version of DeSanctis and Poole's original model: where they explicitly focus on decision processes (since they also focus on GDSS), we use 'communication processes' and 'communication outcomes' here to emphasize the broader applicability of the model.

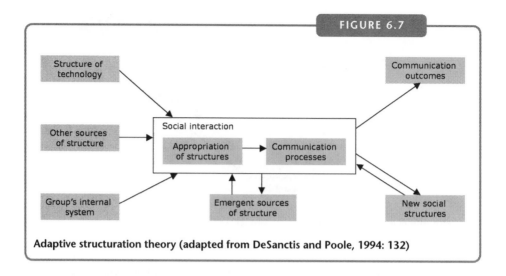

FIGURE 6.7

Adaptive structuration theory (adapted from DeSanctis and Poole, 1994: 132)

Contractor and Eisenberg (1990) also focus on the interaction between technology and social structures, which, they argue, are mutually influential 'in an emergent pattern of mediated and non-mediated social interaction' (ibid.:147). Fulk (1993) also argues that the use of technology is a process of social definition that is strongly influenced by a shared experience with a technology, as well as by shared meanings, values and behavioural patterns in organizations. This in turn is related to the concept of *reinvention* we discussed in Chapter 1: the (perceived) characteristics of a technology are affected by its daily use, and as a result it may end up being used for something entirely different than was originally intended.

A clear example of a *reinvention* process is the telephone. Its inventor, Alexander Graham Bell, initially had no clear idea of what the function of his new invention should be, but it was expected to be used for cable broadcasts. The first demonstrations of the telephone involved music and drama being performed for an audience (de Wit, 1994). It was only later that transferring the human voice became more important, but even then people saw the telephone in terms of the unilateral exchange of business or informative messages – certainly not in terms of social communication – that surely required people to see one another! By now it may be clear that the fact that telephony has freed communication of the restrictions of time and place far outweighs the fact that people cannot see each other.

We can see this process of *reinvention* (or *adaptation*, see Tyre and Orlikowski, 1994) in the use of ICT in organizations as well, especially in applications that are used for richer tasks than the ones for which they were originally designed. When we look at the use of ICT then, it is above all the process of social definition of a medium (and all factors influencing that definition) that is interesting. Lee (1994) argues that, instead of being an inherent property of the medium itself, the richness or leanness of an ICT application is an emergent property of the interaction between the technology, the users, and their social and organizational context. In Lee's *hermeneutic* perspective, the receivers of e-mail messages are active producers of meaning, not passive recipients of data. In this view, both message content and a medium's appropriateness for conveying such content are socially defined over time by members of the organization. Ngwenyama and Lee (1997) offer a *critical social* theory approach towards media richness, based on Habermas's theory of communicative action, which illustrates how communication richness *emerges* during the communicative actions studied, as a result of the interaction between people, medium and social or organizational context.

In short, the approaches discussed above argue that the use of ICT implies that technology, user and organization influence each other. This is in line with the views we expressed earlier on the interaction between organization and technology. In addition, this implies that the use of ICT affects individual users and their organizational context, as well the technology itself, in a number of ways. It also implies that, when studying use and effects of ICT, we should not rely on deterministic models but must really investigate the ways in which people use these technologies – and the effects this use has on the technology itself. This also means that longitudinal studies are called for, focusing on the mutual influences of social and technological structures. We will get back to this in Chapter 7.

Conclusion

This section has shown that the choice and use of ICT applications by individuals in organizations is determined by a complex interaction between technology, organization and individual users. A large number of factors affect the degree and way in which an individual employee uses ICT to perform his or her tasks: technological (accessibility, richness, symbolic meaning, complexity, and so on), organizational (as the social environment with its values and examples, as the context within which tasks are determined and carried out, as a source of structures) and individual factors (experiences, tasks and skills, perceptions and behaviour).

Studies that use conjoint measurement could be very helpful to elaborate on the relation between tasks, technologies and context. Conjoint measurement is a method of investigating in what way individuals combine information to reach decisions. Respondents are presented with fictitious cases. These cases are brief descriptions of a situation that contains information describing the situation accurately. The differences between cases in relation to respondents' preferences provide insight into which task and context characteristics influence ICT use. This opportunity, to obtain insight into the multidimensional space of ICT use, can be very helpful in the development of a more elaborate theoretical framework that underlies the use of ICT. For an extensive review of conjoint measurement, methods and applications, see Gustafsson, Herrmann and Huber (2003).

ICT AND COMMUNICATION AT THE GROUP LEVEL

As we have explained at the beginning of this book, ICT has a number of functions: (re)producing and storing documents, accounting, calculating and processing data, and communicating. In this section we will discuss the use of ICT at the group level, focusing on the communication function. A group consists of two or more people who interact and influence one another. Dividing lines between groups can be caused by differences in time and distance. ICT is often seen as a way to transcend these differences. As a result, electronic groups can emerge from an existing (physical) group. Examples of this are video-conferencing, which allows people from different continents to meet 'face to face', a worldwide team using a shared design system (for instance CAD – computer-aided design) or a group decision support system (GDSS), which allows people to reach a decision on the basis of, for instance, brainstorm sessions. In addition, people may form new groups (or 'communities') on the basis of shared interests, for example a discussion forum on interactive policy-making, a news-group discussing a certain product or an e-mail to an organization requesting information. Information and communication technology supported communities play an increasingly important role in organizations. A well-known example is Xerox's discovery that informal meetings by maintenance mechanics play an important role in solving the problems that these mechanics face (Brown and Duguid, 2000; van der Sluijs, 2001). Xerox's example has led various organizations to try and support com-munities (of practice) themselves, not only by physical means, but also by using ICT to facilitate the sharing of knowledge and the development of social capital (Huysman and De Wit, 2000; Huysman and Van Baalen, 2001).

The concept of community is not only used within, but between organizations as well, often referring to virtual communities, digital cities, and so on (Jankowski and Van Selm, 2001). Thus, ICT makes it possible to blur boundaries and create a 'global village'. Groups can also be connected by various social values. The central question of this section is whether or not there are differences between physical and electronic groups and, if there are, what these differences are. In other words, is there a difference in the way group processes develop in these two types of commu-nity? To answer this question we need two concepts that are related to the way group processes develop:

- Conformation: people like to belong to a group and they are prepared to go far in conforming to the prevailing group values. A large number of experiments have shown that people are prepared to face highly dangerous situations to avoid contra-dicting group values.

- De-individuation: this theory (first developed at the end of the nineteenth cen-tury) argues that people in a group (electronic or otherwise) are less aware of themselves as individuals than people who function as individuals. Because of this de-individuation, people are less inclined to conform to the prevailing social values within their group.

The importance of group values in the electronic situation

When we discussed media richness theory we saw that it is harder to convey, for example, social cues in an electronic environment than it is when people meet face to face. A positive effect could be that people feel less inhibited because they cannot be immediately identified. For many people this offers a welcome opportunity to share experiences with other people. A negative effect of de-individuation could be 'flaming' (escalating conflicts in electronic communication).

Generally speaking, ICT based communication offers fewer possibilities of ascer-taining who the other person taking part in the communication is. In the physical world a person's clothes, accent or looks provide social cues, which in computer-mediated communication are absent. The *reduced social cues approach* (Kiesler, Siegel and McGuire, 1984; Sproull and Kiesler, 1986) for instance, states that the fact that ICT reduces the social cues communicated leads to decreased awareness of both self and others, resulting in uninhibited and anti-normative behaviour. As people lose their individuality and are submerged in the group, social and normative influences are assumed to be undermined.

Such assumptions are challenged by the *social identification model of de-individuation effects,* also known as the SIDE model (Reicher, Spears and Lea, 1994) Spears and Postmes, 1995; . This approach argues that typical characteristics of ICT communication, such as de-individuation, group immersion and the limited transfer of social cues, lead to strong and consistent social effects and normative influences. The SIDE model proposes that social cues can facilitate the individuation of communication partners – in other words, forming impressions of them as idiosyncratic individuals. In computer-mediated conditions, where social cues are relatively scarce, *group* characteristics are likely to be attributed to individuals – that is, their *social identity* is likely to become more salient than their individual identity. Thus, provided that the relevant social group and its attributes are known, the lack of social cues in ICT can 'accentuate the unity of the group and cause persons to be perceived as group members rather than as idiosyncratic individuals' (Tanis and Postmes, 2003: 679). So, SIDE theory argues that group interests become group members' primary focus when ICT is their primary means of communication. This, in turn, could lead group members themselves to conform to group norms more readily in ICT conditions than they would in face-to-face conditions.

The role of conforming and group values in communication

Research has identified a number of ways in which ICT, conforming behaviour and group values influence the nature of electronic communication. This relates to the way newcomers are treated, the way ideas and opinions are expressed, the role played by power, status and leadership and, finally, the way trust is created. In the remainder of this section we will discuss these phenomena in further detail.

A newcomer in an electronic situation does not know the values of a group and he or she will have to learn what they are. In the real world we use past experience and observation to adapt quickly to a new situation. The fact that, in the case of the Internet, experience and social cues are not available (especially for novices) has given rise to 'netiquette', an abbreviation of the words 'network' and 'etiquette', which describes the dos and don'ts of online communication. There are general rules regarding politeness (for instance treating others the way you want to be treated), and rules that especially refer to the online situation (it is against 'netiquette', for instance, to use too much bandwidth by sending an e-mail to everybody rather than just the people for whom the message is intended) (Shea, 1994). Frequently asked questions (FAQs) are another source of information for newcomers regarding the desired behaviour.

BOX 6.3

Spam can endanger your health

One of the most prominent (and arguably most annoying) breaches of netiquette is spamming – sending unsolicited e-mail messages to as many recipients as possible, mostly of a commercial nature. The origin of the term 'spam' is allegedly related to a Monty Python sketch on the canned meat, in which the name 'spam' is repeated ad infinitum.

In 1994, the Arizona law firm 'Canter and Siegel' was the first to commit the sin of spamming. The two lawyers (Laurence Canter and Martha Siegel) posted an advertisement to about 6,000 of the estimated 9,000 or so newsgroups that comprised Usenet (a collection of discussion groups that once formed the heart of the Internet), promoting their services in obtaining a Green Card. The Usenet community reacted with fury, and sent such a volume of replies ('mail

CONTINUED

bombs') that the firm's providers' servers crashed. Ultimately, provider PSI agreed to give back Canter and Siegel their access on the condition that they would never use it again for such purposes.

Sanford Wallace was the self-proclaimed 'king of spam'. Owner of Cyber Promotions Company, he sent out unsolicited e-mails on every possible subject for any client who asked him to. Ultimately, he suffered the same fate as Canter and Siegel, as his provider, after incessant attacks from anti-spammers, decided to discontinue service to Cyber Promotions. Another 'spam king', Alan Ralsky, suffered a similar fate – after an article on his practices was published, activists gathered on the slashdot.org website and saw to it that a deluge of catalogues, advertisements and brochures was delivered to his mailbox. Not his e-mail box, this time, but his 'snail mail'. Although this motivated him to sue those responsible, it has not stopped him from continuing his practices.

And for each spam king down, another one rises: by now, Bill Waggoner is the new target for anti-spammers worldwide, flooding mailboxes with messages on penis enlargers, low interest mortgages and easy weight-loss plans. And as long as regulations concerning this behaviour are insufficient and there is money to be made, spam will continue to be a menace to e-mail users worldwide, and a threat to the medium's effective use.

What is the meaning of spam for organizations? Estimates vary from 25 per cent (Radicati and Khmartseva, 2003) to more than 80 per cent of all e-mail messages is spam and that worldwide billions of dollars are lost as a consequence of deleting spam (Krim, 2004). At this moment several countries are working on legislation that helps to temper unsolicited e-mail. Sending lewd e-mail messages and deception will be forbidden. Also the possibilities of filtering spam and do-not-spam-registration will be enhanced. Violators risk a maximum one-year prison penalty. However, the international character of the Internet makes prosecution of violators very difficult.

Another difference between electronic and physical communication is the role played by power, status and leadership. A relatively poor social situation and/or anonymity can lead people to change the way they communicate their ideas. It can mean that people are more willing to share those ideas. An example is provided by electronic meetings (GDSS), where the best ideas are sometimes provided by people who are not primarily expected to offer those ideas, since they are 'juniors' – in age or in hierarchy. The absence of status information can thus lead to more productive decision-making processes. Other studies indicate, however, that anonymous discussions are less productive because, according to the SIDE model, people are not identified as individuals, but in terms of the social identity salient in the group. The uniformity caused by this process (every group member is related to the 'prototypical member' or the social identity) can frustrate a fruitful exchange.

A third characteristic of electronic communication has to do with communication outcomes. Because taking part in group discussions involves not only formulating one's own point of view, but also paying attention to the online discussion itself, it becomes harder to express one's opinions. In addition, electronic discussions are often polarized. Because in electronic situations like-minded people often cling together (for instance in the case of a newsgroup), the chances are that nuances lose out to extreme opinions.

Trust, in other words knowing what to expect from other parties, is a significant ingredient of effective interaction. An important way of creating trust in an online world is by showing commitment. An example of this is an agreement between members of a team to make sure everybody hands in their contribution in time to meet the deadline. Thus far, there is not much difference between online trust and trust in the real world. The big difference is that in the electronic world agreements are written down, for example in an e-mail or electronic calendar.

Conclusion

In summary, we can say that, although there are some differences between online and physical communication and group processes, the human factor and human values play an important role in both cases. We might even argue that human values are even more crucial in online communication. On the one hand, the use of ICT in groups could be related to a diminished social consciousness (cf. *reduced social cues approach*), on the other hand, under certain conditions, it could be related to a stronger 'group feeling' (cf. *SIDE*). Both arguments find some empirical support but, as we have discussed before, experience with a medium leads users to get used to its limitations and possibilities – and, thus to the fact that less social cues may be communicated via ICT, and how to deal with that.

TRENDS AND DEVELOPMENTS IN THE USE OF ICT IN ORGANIZATIONS

In the previous sections, we have elaborately discussed theories concerning the use of ICT on the individual and group level. This section has more of a practical focus, as it sketches the developments in ICT use at the organizational level. As we have indicated earlier, since the beginning of the 1990s ICT has increasingly been used to support external processes. The focus is no longer only on internal processes, but much more on the relationships between organizations and their environment. Although electronic data interchange (EDI), used for formalized communication and transaction processes within various sectors (the transport sector is leading the way) was developed in the 1980s, it was the arrival of the Internet in the early 1990s that provided the breakthrough. Organizations increasingly use ICT to communicate with their environment. They provide information concerning their organization and the products and services they provide on the Internet. Many websites are little more than electronic brochures.

As a next step in the use of ICT, various possibilities for communication, personalization and intelligent searching methods can be added, as well as developing communities, for example by offering links to related organizations. This development is aimed at reinforcing the interaction between organizations and their environment. Internally, organizations offer a variety of information and communication possibilities through, for example, intranets and workflow systems. Increasingly, a distinction has to be drawn between highly formalized processes in organizations and processes that are relatively open and unstructured (Brown and Duguid, 2000). Above, we have briefly discussed the phenomenon of business process redesign (BPR), which is especially important in routine tasks and processes. Leaning too heavily on ICT, however, carries the risk of ignoring various forms of co-operation and improvisation, leaving valuable expertise untapped. There is, therefore, an increasing need for ICT applications that support systems aimed at sharing knowledge and co-operating.

The transfer of interaction and communication to transaction applications characterizes a third phase. This concerns actually realizing and closing transactions between various companies and between companies and consumers. Over the past couple of years, many organizations have taken steps to realize this phase, as indicated by the increasing sales of CDs, books, airline travel, vacations, theatre tickets and so on (cf. Box 6.4). The central problem in this respect is the integration of the front office and back office. The front office is the organization's interface with its environment, for example a shop, counter, call centre or website – activities that have been developed over time in the two previous phases. The back office consists of all kinds of internal processes, together with all sorts of existing computer systems and applications. This integration is not limited to the organization itself. Many organizations work together with, and depend on, other organizations. The integration of front and back office processes transcends the boundaries of the organization. Many organizations are in fact hampered when they have to work together with other organizations that use antiquated business systems and applications, and are unable to develop interfaces. It must be possible to exchange information about and from suppliers in an easy and reliable way.

BOX 6.4

Facts and figures e-commerce

Although publicity surrounding electronic commerce has been sceptical at best lately, the statistics show that this line of trade is still of increasing importance.

The US Department of Commerce, for instance, reports that retail e-commerce sales in the third quarter of 2003 were $13.3 billion, up 27 per cent from the third quarter of 2002, and up 6.6 per cent from the preceding quarter (http://www.census.gov/mrts/www/current.html, February 2004). Although e-commerce sales amount to a modest 1.5 per cent of all sales, this proportion is gradually increasing. Also, amazon.com reported their first profit – for the year 2003 – after having first been heralded as the prime example of 'new economy' success, and subsequently as the prime example of the 'dot com bust'.

For the UK, the most recent statistics are from 2002, and these show a similar trend: total sales over the Internet by UK business amounted to £23.3 billion in 2002 – a rise of 39 per cent on the previous year's £16.82 billion. This represents 1.2 per cent of total sales both online and offline. Of this £23.3 billion sold online, £6.4 billion was sold to households (and could probably be counted as 'retail sales). (http://www.statistics.gov.uk/pdfdir/ecom1203.pdf)

Finally, in the Netherlands, online spending by households amounted to bought for €937 in 2002, a growth of 78 per cent compared to 2001's €527 million. In the first half of 2003, spending amounted to €575 million, a 36 per cent increase compared to the first half of 2002. Travel is responsible for the largest proportion in spendings (39 per cent in 2002), followed by hardware and software (15 per cent) (http://www.thuiswinkel.org/onderdeel/welkomstpagina/home_shopping_netherlands).

The final phase is the transformation of organizations. Processes between organizations become transparent and are based on Internet technology: e-business. Companies work together to maximize customer value. Increasingly, they will do so in so-called value-webs. Core concepts in this respect are data-mining, mass communication, agent technologies and sector-specific business models. We will discuss these developments in greater detail in Chapter 8.

Although the four-phase development is fairly generally recognized and has been described by many authors, in reality we see that companies find themselves in very different phases. In addition to companies that are developing into network companies – examples often quoted are Cisco and Nokia – we also see companies that offer their information on the Internet for the first time. Also, to give another example, some government organizations use ICT to provide the taxpayer with active support on filling out tax forms, whereas other government services limit themselves to offering basic information on the Internet. To some degree this is due to the orientation of organizations with regard to innovation. This orientation varies across sectors and also depends on the size of organizations.

In practice, small and medium-sized enterprises (SMEs) are lagging behind in the use of ICT. Having said that, we must emphasize that these businesses, companies with up to 200 employees, are very diverse in terms of size, innovativeness and strategic vision. The relatively slow adoption and incorporation of ICT within SMEs is caused by a complex set of factors. One of the main factors doubtless is the fact that the existing technological solutions hardly meet the needs of SMEs, in terms of functionality, costs and knowledge as well as personnel. Add to that the short-term behaviour, the lack of opportunities to experiment and the absence of a strategic vision often displayed by SMEs, and it becomes clear why they find it difficult to adopt ICT. Small- and medium-sized enterprises focus on realizing immediate profits and solving specific problems, such as shortening delivery times, finding new customers and improving the quality of their products. In cases where SMEs do use ICT, suppliers and customers have often forced them to do so.

6.5 CONCLUSION

In the past few decades ICT has experienced a tremendous development. Increasingly complex, network-like structures have emerged from simple stand-alone applications. The main conclusion of this chapter is that the use of ICT is not simply the result of the introduction of a new application in an organization. As far as individual users are concerned the choice of communication medium is strongly related to the nature of the task they are performing. This does not mean that it is simply a matter of matching the characteristics of medium and task in an objective and rational way: the use of ICT involves a complex interaction between individuals, organization and technology. The degree to, and way in, which technology is actually being used is to a large extent determined by technological, organizational and user-related factors.

At the group level ICT is especially used in communication processes. Increasingly, ICT is used to facilitate co-operation within teams and/or communities independent of time or place. It turns out that there are a number of similarities between computer-mediated communication and physical communication. There are, however, a number of striking differences as well: under some conditions, group values are even more important in electronic communication than they are in the physical world, while power, status and leadership become less important. In addition, in electronic discussions and decision-making processes there tends to be a polarization of opinions.

At the organizational level the use of ICT is largely determined by the nature of the organizational processes. Certain demands are made by the characteristics of business processes on the communication tools, and ICT offers certain possibilities to meet these demands (for instance time and place related) and to improve certain processes (especially interorganizational ones, as we have seen). We have established that organizational processes increasingly transcend organizational boundaries (interorganizational business and communication processes) and that, as a result, the same applies to the use of ICT.

This is in accordance with the trend we have described here. Initially, ICT was predominantly used in structured, internally oriented administrative processes, but as time goes by we see that ICT increasingly plays a role in external – structured and unstructured – transaction- and transformation-oriented processes. In this respect the use of ICT is developing along the same path as the technological developments outlined in Chapter 2. Based on this, we may assume that ICT will have an increasingly important impact on the strategic position of organizations. Before we can say more about that, however, we will have to examine the effects that ICT has on organizations – which are the subject of the next chapter.

7 Effects: tasks, processes and structures

Organization-wide knowledge-sharing or electronic fences

In a study of the effects of intranet use on knowledge management within a European bank, Newell, Scarbrough and Swan (2001) found some remarkable consequences of this ICT application. With the implementation of an intranet, the bank aimed to realize its ambition to become a truly global, networked bank. This ambition was formulated after clients left the bank because they felt they were not getting an integrated service across the 70 different countries in which the bank was located. In the realization of this vision, an important contribution was expected from its newly developed worldwide communications infrastructure, connecting all of its businesses. The bank aimed to develop a global network in order to integrate the knowledge existing within the bank, in which a central role was ascribed to intranet technology.

The original intranet project was a centrally resourced one, and created an internal network across the various divisions within the bank, aiming to get knowledge used and shared at an organization-wide level. An unexpected outcome of this project was a sort of 'centrifugal force', which caused different groups within the organization to create their own intranets. These different independent intranets were generally quite successful, whereas the central intranet (the actual infrastructure for organization-wide knowledge-sharing) never really lifted off. So, rather than actually integrating individuals across the different parts of the organization, the intranet project helped to reinforce the existing functional and national boundaries with what Newell, Scarbrough and Swan call 'electronic fences'.

A first explanation is provided by the organizational context within which the application was developed, implemented and used. The bank had a history of decentralized development, with a relatively hands-off approach from central management. Since the current organization largely stemmed from a series of acquisitions of various organizations, each with their own histories, technologies and cultures, this was a logical (and broadly supported) way of working. Among others, this manifested itself in the fact that each division was judged on its own performance against agreed targets. While a global intranet might very well have contributed to improved performance in the long term, the short-term interest for each division was in spending its resources in a way that would improve efficiency and effectiveness at the individual level.

CONTINUED

A second explanation stems from the nature of intranet technology: an inter-active, decentred and flexible technology, which therefore has the potential for multiple interpretations and effects. In that sense, Newell, Scarbrough and Swan refer to intranet as an 'open-ended' or 'equivocal' technology (Weick, 1990; Orlikowski, 1992). This flexible and equivocal nature of the technology matched the organizational context characterized by decentralization and local autonomy, but it was at odds with the central vision of integrated knowledge management. So, the unexpected effects of intranet in this case are the result of an interaction between organizational context and technological characteris-tics, reinforced by a lack of central management control.

7.1 INTRODUCTION

The case outlined above clearly illustrates that the effects of ICT in organizations are not a simple matter of cause and effect, but part of a complicated interplay between organizations, users and technology. This is our central premise throughout this book, and it is specifically salient in this chapter, as we focus on the effects of ICT use in organizations. The *effects* of ICT on both organizational processes as well as communi-cation within and between organizations will, in the final analysis, determine whether the decision to invest in a certain ICT application is justified (see Chapter 4). It is in the effect phase that it becomes clear what exactly the value of ICT is for an organiza-tion and what contribution the technology can make to improving the performance of an organization. In Chapter 1 the 'effect' phase is defined as follows: the phase in which the consequences of the use of an ICT application for an organization become manifest: consequences for the individual performance within the organization, for the communication processes and structures within and between organizations, and for the position of an organization within its environment.

This definition makes clear that, in our discussion of ICT effects, we focus on differ-ent levels of analysis. Coleman (1990) argues that such a distinction between different levels of analysis is essential in the discussion of these effects. According to Coleman, one of the central problems in social science is that of accounting for the functioning of some kind of social system. In relation to this book, the goal is to obtain insight into the consequences of the application of ICT for the functioning of organizations. Yet, Coleman argues that in most social research, observations are not made on the system as a whole, but on some part of it. More specifically, empirical studies take place at the micro or individual level. Similarly, in this book research takes place on the individual level rather than a comparison of organizations or societies. One of the problems of social sciences is that somehow we need to aggregate the effects on the micro or indi-vidual level to the effects on the meso (organizational) or macro (societal) levels.

Figure 7.1 is a graphical representation of this micro-to-macro problem. We want to obtain insight of the effects on the functioning of organizations on the meso level and of technical and social developments on the macro level. The dotted lines repre-sent these goals. However, the instruments we mostly use measure implementation, use and effects on the micro level: we interview managers, implement systems on the work floor and design questionnaires that are posted to co-workers. The question is how these changes on the micro level influence changes on the meso and macro levels.

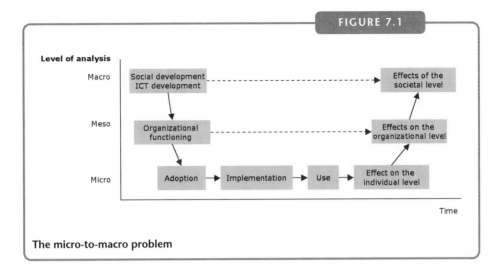

FIGURE 7.1

The micro-to-macro problem

There are two reasons that cause the difficulties of translating the results that are found on the micro level to the meso and macro levels. First, there is the problem of aggregating the results. Although (statistical) analysis is helpful, the result is always a generalization based on a limited number of observations. The second problem is that not only ICT developments and adoption decisions influence the final outcomes. Other factors (ranging from political, economical, social and technological development) influence the way in which organizations and societies are developing.

Having said this, we will try to provide an analysis of the effects of ICT in this chapter. To map these consequences we will begin by re-emphasizing our position that such effects (just as adoption, use and effects) are part of a dynamic and complex interplay between users, organizations and technology, before discussing a number of ways to categorize ICT effects. Secondly, we will specifically discuss which effects can be described for individual users and their tasks, for processes and structures in organizations, and finally for the relationships between organizations and their environment.

7.2 ICT EFFECTS: NO SIMPLE MATTER

Throughout this book, we have emphasized that the adoption, implementation, use and effects of ICT constitute an interplay between user, organization and technology. In the previous chapter, we discussed approaches such as adaptive structuration theory (DeSanctis and Poole, 1994) and the structurational model of technology use (Orlikowski, 1992), which have as their central premise that technologies in themselves have no autonomous effects. These effects are part of a dynamic and complicated interplay between actors, institutions and technologies, and as such are hard to determine – as illustrated by the case outlined at the beginning of this chapter. Although such structurationalist approaches are sometimes criticized for their somewhat vague and indeterminate nature, and because they make it hard to analytically distinguish causes and effects, the core of these approaches is in line with much of the discussion concerning ICT effects. This discussion tends to focus on the fact that such effects are hard to determine, that they can 'go both ways' (either positive or negative), are strongly determined by all kinds of contextual variables (such as organizational culture, user experience, innovativeness, tasks and so on) and tend to differ over time.

In other terms, perspectives on the effects of ICT can be both 'utopian' (stressing the various benefits of ICT for organizations) or 'dystopian' (maintaining a pessimistic view of the consequences ICT use has) (Kling, 1996; Katz and Rice, 2003). Our primary starting point in the discussion of ICT effects is neither utopian nor dystopian. Our central premise is that this is no simple matter, that such effects sometimes seem contradictory, impossible to determine without knowing the context in which ICT is used and that, in any case, they are never unambiguous.

Still, the effects of ICT are crucial in determining the value of such technologies. When an organization decides to adopt and implement an ICT application, there is generally a certain level of expectation as to the improvements this application will bring about in the organization:

- An organization wants to reduce its storage costs, and adapt its production to changing market requirements. It is therefore important that information regarding these requirements be processed quickly and accurately within the production process. The company decides to create a website where customers can place orders, and a back office system that translates these orders into production specifications.

- Knowledge within a software company is located in various places (the programmers are located in India, the marketing people in the USA and the research department in Amsterdam), and all these people have to work together in teams that have to develop a product in a short period. An ICT application that supports long-distance collaboration (computer-supported collaborative work) can help enable this.

- Employees of a home-care organization spend two hours a day collecting their work schedules and handing in their daily reports at the head office. The organization arranges for their work schedule to be sent to their personal digital assistants (PDAs) or mobile (general pocket radio service – GPRS) devices, and for the employees to be able to send back their reports after each visit.

Needless to say, these are but a few examples of the reasons for which an organization can decide to adopt a certain ICT application. The extent to which such expected effects as described above are actually realized depends, again, on the context in which they are used. In addition to these intended and predicted effects, however, there are also often unforeseen effects, as the case discussed before clearly illustrates. Concerning the examples listed above, the following unexpected effects can be imagined:

- The website in the first example can lead to a situation whereby the production department communicates directly with customers, which used to be done by the account managers. This means that the position of the account managers changes considerably.

- The CSCW application from the second example may lead not only to an improvement in efficiency within the organization, but also to a higher level of commitment to the geographically dispersed team than with the department that the people involved are a part of, thus putting pressure on the original departments within the organization.

- The time that the home-care employees gain may not be translated into more time per customer, but rather into more customers per day. In addition, the fact that the employees hardly pay a visit to the head office may put pressure on their commitment to the organization.

Of course, the observation that ICT effects are ambiguous, contradictory and hard to determine does not help us much analytically when discussing such effects. Therefore, we will now discuss some classifications of these effects, culminating in our own classification which is derived from the different levels of analysis discussed in Chapter 1.

First-level and second-level effects

A first classification is the distinction between first-level and second-level effects that was introduced by Sproull and Kiesler (1991). *First-level effects* of ICT are effects that have a direct impact on the individual performance: changes in efficiency of this performance and in the productivity of individual employees (and thus the organization as a whole). Thanks to ICT, time and distance are becoming less of a barrier to communication, and it becomes easier for people to exchange and share information across organizational and geographical boundaries. These effects are operational, and are, in Sproull and Kiesler's view, usually the effects that are intended when a communication system is being introduced: 'First-level effects of communication technology are the anticipated technical ones – the planned efficiency gains or productivity gains that justify an investment in new technology' (Sproull and Kiesler, 1991: 4).

Sproull and Kiesler argue that such a system also leads to *second-level effects*: changes in the social structure of the organization. This has to do with changing and new communication patterns, new roles within social networks, new patterns of dependence between actors, and so on.

There are, for example, new communication patterns that are less restricted by formal organizational boundaries, and geared towards functional needs – the R&D employee working on the development of a certain product may well feel the need to communicate intensively with someone at the university rather than with his or her R&D colleagues. As a result, communication becomes more external.

In addition, ICT can lead to a less formal communication climate. As we discussed in Chapter 6, ICT transfers fewer 'social cues' – it is of less importance whether the person at the other end is sitting behind a large desk in a grey suit, or a 16-year-old whizkid sitting in his parents' attic. What matters is the information this person can provide.

Although this classification has its charms, there are some problems with the distinction between first- and second-level effects. Different issues are confounded in this distinction – for instance, first-level effects are assumed to be intended, direct as well as operational, whereas second-level effects are described as unintended, indirect and more strategic in nature. In practice, of course, many effects can be direct as well as unintended, operational as well indirect, and strategic as well as intended. Organizations may well aim to achieve second-level effects (collaborative technologies such as groupware, for instance), and find (possibly even negative) first-level effects (longer meetings, less efficient communication) as an 'indirect' result of the use of the application. Also, the distinction between task-related and social effects is problematic – in the case of a GDSS, for instance, the social process is the task.

Time, distance and relationships: from efficiency to innovation

A different classification of ICT effects, focusing more on the nature of the effects themselves than on the level on which they emerge, is found in the 'impact–value framework' created by Hammer and Mangurian (1987). This analytical framework was presented in Chapter 3 to indicate in what way ICT can help achieve an organization's objectives. The impact–value framework is a matrix that helps identify changes in management as a result of the use of new communication technologies.

Using this framework (see Table 3.1) it becomes clear that the use of modern ICT applications has an impact in various areas. Since ICT nowadays plays a role in virtually all processes within an organization (Porter, 1985), we can witness these effects in various areas within the organization. The central issue here is that all these effects combined can improve an organization's competitive position (see also: Porter and Millar, 1985).

When comparing the impact–value framework with the distinction between first- and second-level effects, we can argue that the first-level effects can be found most of all in the top left-hand corner of the framework, where speed and efficiency hold a central position. The second-level effects are to be found in the bottom right-hand corner, where the emphasis is on innovation and relationships – and thus, for example, on new patterns of communication. The latter effects, those to do, for example, with the way an organization interacts with its environment, are of more strategic importance than the more operational effects in the areas of speed and efficiency. When new relationships and networks with suppliers, customers, competitors and strategic partners emerge, the impact on the strategic position of an organization can be far-reaching.

Although the impact–value framework provides more insight into the actual possible consequences of ICT for organizations, this classification is not without its problems either (see also Tiggelaar, 2001). Here, the dimensions are somewhat confounded – time and distance can be seen as somewhat separate dimensions, but what about relationships? Time and distance have certain objective values, but what is the value of a relationship? A comparable observation can be made for the value dimensions efficiency, effectiveness and innovation. The first two have to do with the relationship between means and ends, whereas innovation in itself is hardly a value. Finally, there is a pro-technology bias in this framework: all consequences are explained in terms of benefits. Although it is not difficult to find the flipside for each of these benefits, the terminology in this model is very much focused on positive effects.

A closer look at the effects of ICT

So, although the classifications described above are enlightening in some respects, they are confusing or limiting in others. We propose a somewhat less restrictive classification of ICT effects, which is more in line with our central premise of ambiguity, hard to determine and contradiction. We follow the levels of analysis presented in the first chapter, and will discuss possible ICT effects on each of these levels:

- effects at an *individual* level: the individual employee and his task, the degree to which the tasks of individual members of an organization can be made more (or perhaps less) efficient thanks to the possibilities ICT has to offer;
- effects at an *organizational* level, the significance of ICT to the organizational structure, the design and implementation of business processes (both within and between organizations), in terms of efficiency, effectiveness and innovation; and
- effects at the level of the *environment* within which organizations operate and the relationships between organizations and their environment.

In discussing each of these categories we will again use all of the perspectives presented in Chapter 1: the effects of ICT will be discussed in technological, organizational and economic, as well as user and psychological terms.

THE INDIVIDUAL: FROM PRODUCTIVITY TO SATISFACTION

When we talk about the effects on individual tasks, this has to do with the degree to which the individual employee notices the changes as a result of the use of ICT in his or her own work. In both distinctions discussed before (first- and second-level as well as the impact–value framework), such effects would be considered to be primarily task related, concerning productivity, efficiency and effectiveness of individuals' task performance. Benefits in these areas certainly are important effects of ICT at this level, and there is a considerable body of research that identifies such benefits. E-mail, for instance, would appear to have a consistent and reasonably convincing positive impact on the level of individual performance (van den Hooff, 1997).

However, and in line with our central premises of ambiguity and contradiction, there has been an ongoing discussion for some years concerning ICT's actual contribution to productivity and efficiency. Contrary to the research findings mentioned above, there is also a considerable body of research that at least sheds doubt on such contributions of ICT. 'Productivity' can be defined as the amount of output produced per unit (Brynjolfsson and Hitt, 1998: 1). This also means that productivity is not increased by working *harder* (which would mean an increase in input as well), but by working *smarter* – using new technologies in the production process. Information and communication technology is one of the technologies that could play a part here, but that does not mean that its contribution is without controversies.

A famous statement by Robert Solow in *The New York Times Book Review* (12 July 1987) was, 'We see the computer age everywhere except in the productivity statistics'. This is known as the 'productivity paradox' (Brynjolfsson, 1993). This paradox was first noted in the 1970s: although the capacity of and investment in computers showed a remarkable increase, the average productivity fell during this period – and most importantly in the ICT intensive service sector and among ICT workers. Morrison and Berndt (1990) for instance, on the basis of extensive analysis of economic data, contend that every dollar spent on ICT yields 80 cents in return – that is, a structural overinvestment in ICT. Baily and Chakrabarti (1988) report that growing investments in ICT in certain sectors has coincided with lower productivity figures. Roach (1991) argues how, especially in the service industry, investments in ICT were followed by a notable decrease in production figures. Brynjolfsson (1993), however, argues that these negative evaluations of the contribution of ICT to productivity are based on faulty assumptions. He suggests four explanations for this paradox:

1 Measurement errors: there are various indicators to measure output, but these are especially unreliable in the service sector (where the paradox is at its most pronounced).
2 Delayed impact: it takes some time (several years) before the benefits of ICT are translated into the solid statistics of productivity measurements.
3 Redistribution: this explanation assumes a different distribution of the benefits – ICT divides the pie differently, without making it bigger.
4 Mismanagement: this is the most pessimistic explanation, based on the assumption that managers take the wrong decisions when it comes to the use of ICT and deploy the wrong systems, as a result of which they will never reach any efficiency gains.

According to Brynjolfsson, the first explanation is the most important, which would mean that there is no real productivity paradox – but a measuring problem with regard to the output criteria in the service sector. Other authors (for instance, Yorukoglu, 1998; Anderson, Banker and Ravindran, 2003) argue that positive relations between ICT investments and productivity do exist. Crafts (2001) even argues that the contribution of ICT to productivity has exceeded that of steam technology and at least matched that of electricity – while, on the other hand, Gordon (2000) contends that ICT's contribution is in no way comparable to 'the great inventions of the past', such as electricity and the internal combustion engine. In less economic terms ICT's contribution to efficiency and effectiveness of individual employees is sometimes found to be a negative one as well, as a consequence of miscommunication, information overload, technical failures and so on. In short, the effects of ICT on productivity and efficiency are to an extent controversial, and as yet no coherent picture has emerged.

When we look at the effects of ICT in terms of the organizational position of ICT users, the picture is hardly less ambiguous. Ducatel (1994) provides an overview of the knowledge concerning the complex relationship between work and ICT users in organizations. The result is a considerable list of negative effects, such as:

• increased work pressure;
• lower job satisfaction;
• a fall in participation;
• isolation;
• fear of equipment; and
• cognitive overload.

BOX 7.1

Any key?

A clear example of how the use of ICT can lead to the exclusion of, or at least to a disadvantage for, people in organizations is provided by a British report on workers' knowledge of ICT. Although knowledge of how to use ICT has become a prerequisite to be able to function in modern organizations, a study by 'City and Guilds' (which awards work-related qualifications in England), found that one in seven workers needs help turning their office computers on or off because of their dismal knowledge of new technology. The research showed that about a fifth of staff asked for help to save or print a document and could not create a table on their screens to make it easier to write data. Firms were paying out an average of £49,000 a year for additional computer support because of the 'skills shortfall' of their staff, it was claimed. One in five firms admitted their workers only had basic computer skills, while some said employees had no information technology qualifications at all (Ananova, 5 September 2003).

It has to be added that these are effects that occur in the early stages – immediately after the implementation. In addition, Ducatel provides a more nuanced picture when he indicates that it is ultimately the individual user who determines the degree to which technology is being used in such a way as to either produce positive or negative effects. Walton (1989) also argues that technology has 'dual potentialities': it can produce one effect, but also the exact opposite, which brings us back to our central argument that effects of ICT cannot be isolated from the interplay between users, technology and context.

An important *positive* effect that ICT can have for individual employees is *empowerment*. As we shall see below (in section 7.4), ICT can either lead to an increase or to a reduction in vertical control in the organization. Empowerment has to do with the latter, the degree to which ICT helps employees gain control over their own work and are given broader and easier access to essential information in the organization (see, for example, Mogard, 2000).

An important *negative* effect of ICT is *information overload* (indicated rather cryptically as 'cognitive overload' in the list above). This effect, in turn, can be an important cause for a negative contribution of ICT to task efficiency and productivity. We speak of information overload when an employee receives more information than he or she can process (Schick, Gordon and Haka, 1990). In addition to the amount of information one has to process, the time available is also important (Snowball, 1980). On the one hand, ICT can easily increase the amount of information (in light of the various benefits with regard to the fast and large-scale distribution of information and the provision of access to all kinds of information, regardless of time and place) while, on the other hand, it can reduce the time available to process the information, as a result of the fact that ICT makes it so easy to bridge time and distance. In short, it is hard to prevent an increase in the use of ICT from leading to a growing sense of information overload. In a longitudinal study into the use of e-mail (van den Hooff, 2000) this was clearly confirmed: the longer people use e-mail, the more they use it, and the stronger the feeling that they receive more information than they can process. On the other hand, human beings have always had a limited capacity to process information, and the contribution of ICT can also be a positive one (as argued before).

To summarize, research concerning the effects of ICT at the individual level provides support for our central premise that such effects are ambiguous, sometimes contradictory and hard to determine. On the one hand, ICT can result in an increase in efficiency and effectiveness and in empowerment of the individual employee; on the other hand it can lead to a fall in productivity, feelings of uncertainty, dissatisfaction and information overload. The degree to which either of the two sides will be stronger than the other is to a large extent determined in the earlier phases of our model: adoption, implementation and use.

The extent to which ICT use results in productivity gains or declines, in empowerment or isolation and so on, is not determined by ICT as such. Therefore, the question underlying the discussion concerning the productivity paradox (whether 'computers enhance productivity') may be the wrong question – the question should be 'what is it that makes ICT contribute positively or negatively to each of these dimensions?' For instance, to what degree are users technologically inclined? To what degree is the technology reliable? Is software user-friendly enough (hearing users complain about Microsoft products, one would guess not)? Does the organization provide a stable environment for users to learn to use the technology? Hence, research concerning the contribution of ICT to such individual effects should look much further than investments versus returns.

ORGANIZATION: PROCESSES AND STRUCTURES

Following up on the productivity paradox argument made before, Brynjolfsson and Hitt (1998) argue that the question as to what extent ICT leads to more productive employees and organizations, is really obsolete. They argue that ICT may not automatically lead to an increase in productivity, but that it is part of a wider range of organizational changes that does. In this section we will place ICT within this wider range, as we investigate the possible consequences of ICT use on the organizational level. First, we discuss the consequences for processes in the organization, and then, we look at structural changes related to ICT use.

Processes: faster, better, different, more knowledge-intensive

The impact–value framework discussed previously is a typical example of a process view of ICT effects: it charts the consequences of ICT use for processes in the organization – whether these are completed in less time, more easily co-ordinated across distances, include other parties and roles, or are completely redesigned. The first contributions of these technologies were expected in terms of internal efficiency, but also both techno-logical developments and changing market conditions caused a shift in such consequences to include external effectiveness – the effectiveness of the interaction between customer and organization, which especially in the service sector determines the success of the organization (De Jong, 1993; Brynjolfsson and Hitt, 1998).

Of course, the wording used to describe these effects here again carries a certain pro-technology bias, as if ICT effects concerning organizational processes were unambiguously positive. They are not, as Box 7.2 illustrates. More importantly, much lit-erature seems to be too keen on ascribing such effects to the technologies themselves. As Winter and Taylor (1996) argue, there is no direct causal link between technology and the transformation of work – social, economical, political and cultural changes should be incorporated in such analyses as well. This argument will be further elaborated.

BOX 7.2

No e-mail 4u

In September 2003, the British high street retailer Phones 4u announced a ban on the use of e-mail by its staff. John Caudwell, the multi-millionaire owner of the chain (and a non-user of e-mail himself) explained this measure by the fact that his people spent far too much time on handling their internal e-mail, and that communication quality was suffering.

'Management and staff at HQ and in the stores were beginning to show signs of being constrained by e-mail proliferation – the ban brought an instant, dra-matic and positive effect,' Caudwell claims. 'Phones 4u staff have been told to get off the keyboards, get face to face or on the phone to colleagues. The quality and efficiency of communication have been increased tremendously in one fell swoop – things are getting done and people are not tied to their PCs. The net result is that the business has been dramatically liberated, leaving the typical Phones 4u person with an extra three hours a day to concentrate fully and with-out distraction on sales and customer service.'

Customers will still be able to contact the company via e-mail, since only internal e-mail has been banned (CNN, September 2003).

One example of such a non-technological shift that is related to the contribution of ICT to organizational processes is the increasing importance of knowledge as an organizational resource. Processes have become much more knowledge-intensive. In the 'resource-based' view of the firm, knowledge is considered to be the most strate-gically important resource (for example, Pettigrew and Whipp, 1993; Nahapiet and Ghoshal, 1998; Conner and Prahalad, 1996; Grant, 1996). Weggeman (1997; 2000) in this context speaks of the *knowledge-intensive organization*, an organization where knowledge is a crucial production factor and knowledge-workers are directly involved in the production process. In our economy, which has been described as the *knowledge economy*, the knowledge-intensive organization plays a central role. This development is not the result of ICT, but ICT is a tool that plays a significant role. Information and communication technology has an impact on various knowledge processes: the creation of, access to, distribution of and application of knowledge. The case discussed at the beginning of this chapter provides a clear example of the role ICT can play in such processes.

In Chapter 4 we have discussed an example of how the use of ICT leads to two kinds of collective goods (Monge *et al.*, 1998): *connectivity*, the possibility on the part of the parties involved to communicate directly with one another, and *communality*, the availability of a generally accessible collection of information. The connection to benefits for the knowledge-intensive organization is clear here. Communality refers to the creation of a generally accessible store of codified or explicit knowledge (knowledge that has been stored), in other words, access to knowledge. The realization of connectivity has added value particularly in terms of the sharing of knowledge (both stored knowledge – *explicit knowledge* – and knowledge that is in people's heads – *tacit knowledge*). For the distinction and interaction between tact and explicit knowledge, see Nonaka and Takeuchi (1995). The growing importance of knowledge is a typical example of a process change that was far from caused by ICT, but in which ICT does play a role.

Structures: horizontal, vertical, central, decentralized

In this section we will discuss the consequences of ICT for organizational structures using a model provided by Fulk and DeSanctis (1999). Organizational structures are aimed at increasing co-ordination and control across time and distance, and as will have become clear from the previous section, ICT offers new possibilities for this: a high increase both in terms of speed (time) and in reach (distance). It is logical that ICT facilitates other co-ordination mechanisms. Fulk and DeSanctis integrate the developments in the area of organizational structure in a model that, much like the one presented in Chapter 1, emphasizes the interaction between ICT and organization. In line with our own argument and Winter and Taylor's argument discussed in the previous section, they emphasize that this is not a simple matter of cause and effect, ICT being only one of the factors facilitating organizational change. This is presented in Figure 7.2.

The new organizational forms that, according to Fulk and DeSanctis, emerge in interaction with the ICT possibilities, are related to the influence that this technology has on the four 'key dimensions' of organizational structure that they distinguish:

1 Size, scope and product domain: changes in the size of the organization, in the scope of tasks and processes with which the organization occupies itself and in the products and services the organization is offering.

2 Vertical control: changes in the degree to which hierarchical, top-down control is exerted on the tasks and processes in the organization.

3 Horizontal co-ordination: changes in the level of and way in which lateral relationships between organizational departments and entire organizations emerge.

4 Kinds of connections: changes in the kinds of relationships that exist within and between organizations.

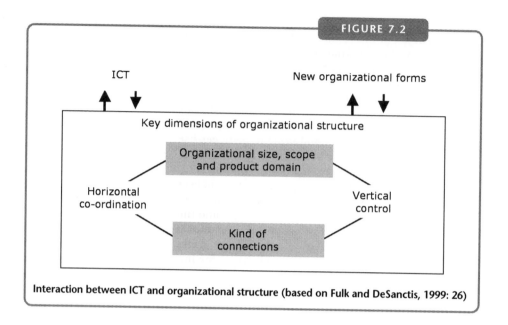

FIGURE 7.2

Interaction between ICT and organizational structure (based on Fulk and DeSanctis, 1999: 26)

Size, scope and product domain

The *size* both of organizations and of units within organizations is influenced fundamentally by the emergence of ICT. The reduction of overhead costs and of the numbers of 'layers' in the organization, right sizing, 'do more with less' are all ways to describe the trend towards slimmer organizations and units. The automation of various tasks helps here, as does the fact that ICT increasingly supports the co-ordination of tasks and processes. Thanks to a well-functioning ERP system, for example, the number of people involved in internal logistics could be reduced considerably. A workflow application containing the detailed 'routing' of products or documents within a business process would seriously reduce the co-ordination efforts required. At the same time this means, however, that organizations have become increasingly dependent on ICT – when systems take over a part of the human co-ordination tasks, the impact of a technological failure is far-reaching.

In addition, the general trend is for organizations to reduce their *scope* as well: organizations increasingly concentrate on their core business, hiving off or outsourcing secondary tasks. A bank's personnel restaurant, for instance, is not part of the primary process, but would traditionally be run by one of its own departments. Today it is the rule rather than the exception to contract to an external party (and the same goes for other facilities). Using this kind of agreement rather than the traditional hierarchical control provides a much greater degree of flexibility (rather than having its own division with a large number of employees that it cannot fire at will, an organization can now hire the capacity it needs) and clarity (it is possible to strike a hard deal with them, which is often more difficult when it comes to one's own employees). The main role of ICT in this process is that, according to many authors, it reduces the 'transaction costs': the costs of looking for suitable contract partners, of negotiating, closing the contracts co-ordinating the activities of the various parties and ensuring that the agreements are respected. These are all communication-oriented, information-intensive activities where ICT plays a facilitating role. On the other hand, the contributions of ICT in this respect are quite minimal (the technology facilitates the extra co-ordination, but does not in any way alter processes), and this trend creates problems concerning the loss of control, (again) a stronger dependence on technology, extra overhead and co-ordination in the sense that much has to be negotiated which used to be a matter of hierarchical control, and so on.

In the *product domain*, finally, Fulk and DeSanctis see a development whereby a growing number of organizations present themselves less and less as production organizations, and increasingly as information suppliers. Even a traditionally product-oriented organization like General Electric now sees itself mainly as a player in the 'information business'. The information that is collected during production and sales processes is becoming an increasingly important product domain for various organizations. Major travel agencies, for example, collect large amounts of information regarding the travel habits of various market segments and store the information in their data-warehouses, they combine this information and sell it to third parties such as airline and car rental companies (Fulk and DeSanctis, 1999: 13). Such combinations also enable firms to offer 'packets of services' – a financial service provider offering not only a mortgage, for instance, but also insurance, healthcare and even daycare.

Vertical control

Above we have discussed the phenomenon of outsourcing, a phenomenon that is symbolic for one of the developments regarding the vertical control in organizations that can be partly attributed to the use of ICT. This has to do with the fact that vertical (central, top-down) control of tasks and processes could increasingly be replaced by horizontal co-ordination – in other words, the hierarchical methods of organization can be replaced by market mechanisms. This is one of the visions concerning the consequences of ICT for vertical control in organizations: ICT leads to decentralization, to a flattening of the hierarchy. In this vision, in addition to market forces replacing a hierarchical control of activities, there is an increasing number of direct connections bypassing the formal structure. Information and communication technology facilitates the emergence of this type of connections, as we discussed in the paragraphs concerning the second-level effects. In addition, ICT provides empowerment to the employees through the wide availability of all sorts of information – these days it is hardly possible to keep one's employees 'ignorant' or to keep information from being distributed throughout the organization. As a result of these developments the vertical control of tasks and processes is increasingly eroding.

At the same time there are those who argue that ICT causes organizations to become more centralized. This particularly has to do with the use of ICT to control and monitor employees and their activities, and with the above-mentioned ICT based (rather than human) co-ordination of activities.

With regard to the first issue: the extent to which employers are allowed to monitor (and act on) their employees' e-mail and Internet behaviour, is an important issue in the Netherlands as well as in the USA . Particularly in the USA, 'electronic surveillance' has been a hot issue for some time (see, for example, Botan and Vorvoreanu, 2000). This whole discussion at least makes it clear that ICT offers employers unprecedented possibilities to monitor and control their employees' activities – to what extent they are *allowed* to do this, and act upon the information they have, is still subject to debate – but both in the USA and the UK there have been numerous cases where people were fired as a result of e-mail they sent or received, and as a result of the amount of time they have spent on 'non-work-related' websites.

BOX 7.3

Honour bound?

An infamous case of a private e-mail exchange that almost cost two profession-als their jobs is the exchange by two employees of the London law firm Norton Rose. A woman sent her boyfriend a lewd joke, to which he replied referring to their own intimacies of the night before. In her reply, she made him a compli-ment concerning his performance, which he chose to forward to a number of his co-workers, commenting 'Now that's a nice compliment from a lass isn't it?' One of his colleagues thought it would be a good idea to forward it to as many of his own contacts as possible, claiming 'I feel honor bound to circulate this.' Ultimately, Internet experts estimate that the message reached over a million mailboxes, and created a true news hype, including web pages on which the complete exchange was published, and including photos and personal informa-tion about those involved.

Of course, Norton Rose was far from amused by this considerable damage to its image as a serious and reliable law firm. Although it considered firing those involved, the firm ultimately chose not to. It did announce it would take unspec-ified 'disciplinary action', though. The damage was not limited to Norton Rose – the English Financial Services Authority suspended nine of its employees for forwarding the message to outside contacts, saying 'As a regulator anything we send out can be construed as a regulating document therefore our e-mails have to be watertight.'

In addition, there is an increase in vertical control through a stricter management of tasks and processes using ICT applications. In workflow applications computer rou-tines determine what happens, and they are usually less flexible than human managers. We also see this in call centres, for example: there, computers register how many calls are being processed per time unit, how many people are on hold, how long people have to wait before their call is answered, how fast their questions were answered, and so on. It is possible to display a kind of 'hit list' on a central screen, listing the names of the people with the best – or worst – performance based on these criteria.

Horizontal co-ordination

When there is less hierarchical management of tasks and processes, naturally it has to be replaced by something if the organization is to continue functioning – hence a shift from vertical control towards more horizontal co-ordination. In other words, the gen-eral trends is towards less hierarchy and more market forces.

Information and communication technology facilitates horizontal co-ordination mechanisms. Where geographical concentration (physical and organizational proxim-ity) used to be the primary co-ordination mechanism in organizations, we now have the possibility of 'electronic proximity'. Fulk and DeSanctis give as an example the changes in the area of logistics, where mobile systems for the processing of orders, the accessing of stock-related information, route planning and other logistical issues 'reduce the need for physical proximity to achieve horizontal co-ordination. Increasingly, distribution systems are changing from centralized warehousing facilities to many smaller, local storage units co-ordinated through information and communi-cation technology' (Fulk and DeSanctis, 1999: 19).

We can see the growing importance of horizontal co-ordination in processes surrounding product design. Here, we often encounter the phenomenon of 'concurrent engineering', where the traditionally serial design process has turned into a parallel process. Designers, engineers, suppliers and customers work together simultaneously on the design process, supported by CAD-CAM and assorted applications.

New organizational methods that are associated with increasing horizontal coordination are cross-functional teams and 'stockless production'. In cross-functional teams employees from different disciplines (for example production, marketing, R&D) are put together in a team working together towards a common goal (for instance a new service). Thus, small, multidisciplinary units are created that are responsible for the result and often work across geographical and organizational boundaries. Relational databases, knowledge systems and groupware play an important role here. 'Stockless production' concerns with the phenomenon of 'just-in-time' delivery. The idea is to avoid having to maintain large-scale stocks of spare parts and so on, and to make sure that materials that are needed for a certain task are delivered to the right place at the right time. Needless to say, this requires minute and up-to-date information on the process and the materials needed, which is where ICT (workflow systems, databases, and so on) plays an important role. Generally speaking, collaboration technologies (groupware, group decision support systems) fit this increased need for horizontal coordination.

Types of connection

In a time when bureaucratic methods of organizing are increasingly under pressure, the shape of an organization depends more and more on the actual relationships that exist between organizations and people, according to Fulk and DeSanctis. This brings us to the point where the organization and its environment meet, a subject we will discuss in the next section.

ENVIRONMENT: NETWORK ORGANIZATIONS AND INFORMATION ECONOMY

The relationship between an organization and its environment is a complex one, and it is often hard to indicate where one ends and the other begins. In our current economy the various ways an organization can co-operate with competitors, suppliers and customers are a common thing, and these boundaries are becoming increasingly blurred. In the discussion on the effects of ICT it is therefore not so simple to distinguish clearly between the effects on the organization itself and the effects on the level of its environment. Nevertheless, in this section we will focus primarily on ICT effects at the level of interorganizational relationships and of the organizational environment.

Interorganizational relationships: from chain to network and beyond

First, we see that within a value system (of suppliers, customers, competitors, and so on) there is increasing pressure on the traditional, serial relationships within the value chain. In a value chain like the one discussed in Chapter 3, mutual relationships meant that an organization received something from a supplier, modified it and then sold it to its customers. According to much literature concerning interorganizational relations, this concept has become somewhat obsolete – many prefer to talk of a value *network*, in which the interactions between the parties involved are pre-programmed to a far lesser extent. A well-known example of this is the process that led to the Boeing 767, where a number of stages in the traditional design process (especially the construction of various costly prototypes) could be skipped, because the demands by the various parties involved could be included in the design at an earlier stage – and visualized thanks to the sophisticated CAD application (Tapscott, 1996).

In addition, we increasingly see organizations trying to solidify relationships with parties in the value system that have become somewhat 'volatile' ('the competition is only one click away') by 'forcing' their customers, for example, to link up to their own electronic order-processing system, or to connect their own business processes to those belonging to their customers.

Furthermore, the role of all kinds of intermediary functions within the value system is changing (see the impact–value framework). Travel agencies, for example, run the risk of becoming obsolete as a result of the fact that customers can purchase their tickets directly from the airline companies via the Internet, as well as book a hotel online. On the other hand, there is a need for new intermediary functions: the amount of available information is huge, and so is its diversity. Intermediaries can provide a degree of order, and indicate which parties are reliable in terms of the content of their information and with regard to the closing of transactions (see Sarkar, Butler and Steinfield, 1995). With regard to the sharing of information, it is interesting to note that there is a great deal of interorganizational co-operation taking place in the area of R&D. The increasing complexity and dynamics in the environment of many organizations means there is also a growing need to benefit from each other's knowledge.

BOX 7.4

Interorganizational co-operation: professionals in occupational health and safety

Van den Hooff *et al.* (2003) report a study concerning interorganizational knowledge-sharing through ICT. On the Internet, two 'communities' for professionals in the area of occupational health and safety were studied.

These professionals have a considerable need to share knowledge with people outside their own organization as the actual professional expertise they need is scarce within their own organization – but can be found with others in the same profession, from different organizations. In order for these people from different organizations and different locations to be able to share their knowledge, ICT was an important facilitator. It was found that identification with the community was high, as well as mutual trust – and both were found to be positively related to the extent to which professionals used the Internet community for both storage and retrieval of information, and for the exchange of information. Identification and trust, in turn, were found to be related to the actual sharing of knowledge within the community.

Members of these communities came from different organizations, from healthcare to education and from technology to the service industry, and they valued the opportunity to share knowledge with like-minded people with related expertise.

This matches a development outlined by Monge and Fulk (1999) – a development towards network organizations that can be placed somewhere between the traditional methods of co-ordination (market and hierarchy). In Table 7.1 these three methods of co-ordination are juxtaposed. The core characteristic of the network organization is that it is not based on the common interests of the various actors – both individuals and organizations (the network organization almost by definition is of an interorganizational nature). While in the market it is the contractual agreements that characterize the mutual relationships, in a hierarchy the key aspects are labour relations and authority (employer–employee, manager–employee). In the network organization, on the other hand, the main factors are common interest and the extent to which actors can mutually benefit – from each other's knowledge, services, products, network and so forth. Network organizations are built on a foundation of ICT, which provides a fast, accurate and cost-effective exchange of information between actors within the network.

TABLE 7.1

Network organizations between market and hierarchy (based on Powell, 1990)

Type of co-ordination	Market	Network	Hierarchy
Normative basis	Contracts Property rights	Complementary Strengths	Labour Relations
Co-ordination	Prices	Relationships	Routines
Conflict handling	'Haggling' Law suits	Reciprocity Reputation	Authority Supervision
Flexibility	High	Medium	Low
Commitment	Low	Medium-high	Medium-high
Mood, climate	Precision Suspicion	Open, mutual Benefits	Formal Bureaucratic
Preferential relations	Independent	Mutually	Dependent
For actors		Dependent	

Building on the idea of the network organization, some authors speak of a 'virtual organization', for which various definitions have been suggested:

- 'A virtual organization is a collection of geographically dispersed, functionally and/or culturally diverse entities that are connected through electronic forms of communication, using dynamic lateral relationships for co-ordination' (DeSanctis and Monge, 1999: 694);
- 'A geographically dispersed organization whose members are connected through a common long-term interest or goal, and who coordinate their work and communicate via ICT' (Ahuja and Carley, 1998: 3); and
- 'A virtual organization is made up of private or public organizations that use ICT to transform business processes within and between organizations in order to enable new forms of joint ventures, alliances or outsourcing' (Dutton, 1999: 474).

These definitions closely resemble the definition of a network organization, although they emphasize more strongly the importance of ICT. What exactly constitutes a 'virtual organization' remains somewhat unclear, it can vary from an ad hoc collection of diverse, geographically and functionally separated individuals that work together on a specific project (heavily supported by ICT) to an organization with a lot of teleworkers and regional offices (also with a great deal of ICT support).

Context: the 'information economy'

Today's organizations operate within a knowledge or information economy, one that has a number of specific features that have to do with the extent to which ICT is being used within this economy. Shapiro and Varian (1999) describe which specific economic consequences that are related to the fact that ICT has made the distribution of information so easy:

- It is expensive to produce information, but (thanks to ICT) easy to reproduce it. In other words, the production of information is characterized by high fixed costs and low marginal costs (the costs involved in making additional copies are virtually negligible). Information products do not deteriorate when they are being used or copied.
- Consequently, the price of information products should not be based upon the costs per unit (which are close to zero), but on the value that the product has to the consumer (value-based pricing). That value also has a specific feature: the value of information, but especially that of ICT, increases as more units are being sold – the above-mentioned phenomenon of *critical mass, network externalities* and so forth.
- *Versioning* facilitates value-based pricing: different versions and variations in packaging of an information product for various target groups at different prices.
- Increased competition will cause the price of information products and services to drop towards marginal costs – in other words, zero. As a result, it is no longer the product itself that will earn the money, but rather the advertising costs and other 'traffic-dependent' revenues. See, for example, the free Internet providers, who hoped to earn back the free access and information they offered their customers through advertising, kick-back fees from telecom operators and by selling user data they collected.

The information and ICT intensity of the current economy leads, then, to a number of specific phenomena. But, Shapiro and Varian warn us, this does not mean that we can simply discard all sorts of traditional economic laws. And this is exactly what a number of the 'gurus' of the 'new economy' were claiming. In particular Kelly (1997) has profiled himself in this manner, by presenting no fewer than 12 'new rules for the new economy', ranging from: 'all of value is free' to 'don't solve problems, go after opportunities'. In the popular press these ideas were translated into the suggestion that in the new economy companies should not make a profit, and that the bigger the losses, the better. A large number of 'dot coms' followed this suggestion meticulously, suddenly finding themselves cast onto the digital scrapyard during the shake-out of 2000-2001.

Economists like Massachusetts Institute of Technology's Paul Krugman (1997; 1998) have rejected this type of rhetoric from the outset. While recognizing that the traditional supply/demand curve does not apply to the information sector (the idea of diminishing marginal costs, and increasing value when more is being sold), he points out that the idea of increasing returns was known among economists as early as the late nineteenth century. In short, Krugman agrees with Shapiro and Varian and many others: it is true that the economy is changing, but that does not mean that all sorts of economic laws are turned upside down. The rather drastic 'correction' of the stock market value of many ICT companies that began at the end of 2001, proves their point. Gordon (2000) has similar arguments, in a thorough analysis that makes clear that this 'new economy' was hardly as miraculous as it seemed, and could not be compared to previous technology-related economic changes.

In spite of this, the information- and ICT-intensive economy does have a few interesting characteristics, which we have discussed above. Even if traditional economic wisdom has not become obsolete, we can conclude that the intensive use of ICT has also had an impact at this 'macro' level.

Organizations between hierarchy and network

Looking at the information presented above we can conclude that, thanks to ICT, the traditional hierarchical bureaucracy has increasingly come under pressure, and we can see organizations that are developing into network (or virtual) organizations. Generally speaking, we see less hierarchy and more market forces, less vertical control and more horizontal co-ordination, and a large diversity of mutual relationships – both within and between organizations, as well as in the economy as a whole. Information and communication technology is an important factor in this development, although it certainly is not the only significant factor. In a great number of areas we can see developments taking place in the environment of organizations that demand more flexible forms of organizing – generally speaking, the environment is becoming more flexible and dynamic (see, for example, Daft, 1995). As we have emphasized before, and as the model by Fulk and DeSanctis indicates, this is by no means a simple case of cause and effect, but ICT is an important factor that, interacting with the four 'key dimensions' (and the autonomous developments that are taking place with regard to each of these dimensions), causes this development towards more network-oriented organizations.

7.6 A CASE STUDY OF ICT EFFECTS: INTERACTION BETWEEN ORGANIZATION AND TECHNOLOGY

Chapter 1 contained a model representing the relationship between organization and ICT as an interaction between demands (made by the organization regarding the technology) and opportunities (that the technology offers to carry out certain activities within the organization differently, and hopefully better). The model by Fulk and DeSanctis (1999), which is used to map the effects of ICT on organizational structures, also assumes this interaction between technological and organizational influences. In this paragraph we will briefly discuss ways in which this interaction plays a role in describing the effects of ICT on organizations.

In Chapter 6, where we discussed structuralistic approaches to media choice usage, we have also discussed this interaction. There we have addressed the process of *re-invention* or *adaptation*, which, as we concluded, in the case of ICT is mainly expressed in a changing perception of the richness of media. In other words, one effect of the use of ICT on the technology itself is a change in the perception regarding the suitability of the application for certain tasks.

Van den Hooff (2000; in press) gives a practical example of this kind of interaction. Based on a longitudinal study into the use of e-mail in one organization (measured in 1993, 1995, 1997 and 2000), insight is provided in the development of an 'organizational innovation process'. This particular innovation process is defined as a learning process in the use of e-mail, defined as: the process whereby users, on the basis of their experience with an ICT application, learn to utilize this technology in ways that may initially not have been expected or intended, but that better meet their needs – and also learn to use this technology more effectively.

This learning process is measured on the basis of the following criteria:

- the *extent* to which the medium is being used;
- a *wider range* of communication tasks for which the medium is being used;
- the use of e-mail in *more externally* oriented communication patterns; and
- an increase in both the first- and second-level effects of the use of e-mail.

This is seen as an innovation process, due to the occurrence of organizational innovation, in terms of a broadening (both in tasks and patterns) of the use of e-mail, and in terms of the effect it has on the organization (more efficient processes and changing communication structures).

Based on the development of this process between 1993 and 2000, four phases emerge:

1 Implementation: the introduction of the ICT application (in this case e-mail) in the organization.
2 Innovation: innovation takes place with regard to all the criteria mentioned.
3 Consolidation: the process stops, there is no further innovation.
4 Reanimation: the process re-emerges, innovation takes place at minimally the same level as in the innovation phase.

According to van den Hooff, the occurrence of the reanimation phase can be explained by technological innovation. The fact that the e-mail system was being renewed between 1997 and 2000 for the first time since its introduction, meant that the system not only offered more functionalities (such as an integrated electronic agenda), but a more user-friendly and modern interface as well. In terms of Chapter 1, a technology was being presented that offered more opportunities, providing the users with a chance to bring the technology more in line with their demands. Technological innovation thus turns out to have an important influence on the development of organizational innovation. Of course, this finding once again confirms that the effects of ICT on an organization are not only part of a complex of effects of various other influences; they also strongly depend on the way individuals and organizations use this technology.

7.7 CONCLUSION

This chapter emphasized that determining the effects of the use of ICT on organizations is a complicated matter, as these effects are part of a complicated interplay between organizational context, individual users and technologies. Effects are strongly determined by the context in which the technology is used. The case that introduces this chapter is a prime example of how important that context can be. Still, we can conclude that ICT is found to have both positive and negative effects on organizations – for the individual employees within an organization as well as for the organization as a whole and its relationship with its environment.

At the individual level the use of ICT leads to a more efficient and effective execution of tasks and to 'empowerment' of the individual employee, whereas it can also lead to a fall in productivity, feelings of uncertainty, dissatisfaction and information overload. The effects at group level, as discussed in Chapter 6 can be related to changing importance of group standards, community formation and so forth.

At the organizational level ICT leads to higher productivity, acceleration and improvement of processes and more flexible structures, but there is evidence to suggest the opposite as well: lower productivity and more control within the organization. Taking an overall view, however, we can conclude that ICT facilitates the development towards the network (or virtual) organization and towards a network economy.

Information and communication technology plays an important role in all these developments, but it is certainly not the only significant factor. In addition to the technological dimension, which certainly plays a role, when we explain the occurrence or absence of certain ICT effects in organizations, we come across the various factors presented in Chapter 1: the extent to and way in which the adoption and implementation are given shape strongly determine the use of ICT. Furthermore, the actual use of ICT in turn helps determine whether or not certain effects are likely to take place. We see these effects in all areas of our model. First we see the *organizational* effects in the sense of changing organizational structures and processes, and effects for the user in the sense of falling or growing productivity, efficiency, job satisfaction, and so on.

At the *economic* level the most important effects are, of course, the productivity effects (controversial though these may be), but also the remaining individual benefits in terms of efficiency, effectiveness and innovation can be interpreted in economic terms. Economically speaking the relationship between the organization and its environment is also significant, as are the associated changes in the economic environment that have been outlined at the end of this chapter. Finally, the *technological* effects are primarily related to changes in the applicability of the technology as a result of the interaction between user, technology and organization that is the central theme of this book: technology is not an objective given, it is something that is actively shaped when it is being used – consequently, it changes in the course of that process.

Describing the effects of ICT, then, is not simply a matter of identifying cause and effect. Information and communication technology is an important factor that interacts with a diversity of other organizational and environmental factors to cause effects to occur in the various areas that have been identified. In this respect it is of central significance that the effects of ICT on individuals and organizations are not only part of a complex of effects of various other influences, but also depend heavily on the way technology is being used by these individuals and organizations. In other words, the extent to and the way in which the effects of ICT manifest themselves in organizations strongly depends on the way previous phases in the process are given shape – on the adoption, implementation and use of the technology.

PART III

8 E-commerce and e-business

CASE STUDY

Plato Online

Plato The Hague is an example of a store that tries to integrate IT and Internet technology in its business strategy. Plato is the name of a number of stores managed by a group of schoolfriends. Although they share the name, the responsibility lies with the individual entrepreneur. A deep and specialized product range and staff with a high level of expertise concerning pop, rock and other music genres characterize Plato stores. They are operating in a niche market. In addition to the store, Plato The Hague also operates its own website. Since May 1997, CDs have been sold over the Internet. Furthermore, the company provides websites for third parties that also sell CDs online. Primarily, the CDs that are sold online are the same ones that can be bought in the store, at the same price. The motivation behind this approach is that price differentiation will affect store sales. In Plato The Hague's strategy the store is leading. Initially the website was very successful. In fact it was so successful that it was top of the list in search engines like Alta Vista, even above, for example, CDNow, which, unlike Plato, paid for its listing. According to Plato's owner/manager, Alta Vista suggested that Plato advertise as well, which the company declined. After that, Plato's name lost its number one listing, and as a result, online sales dropped drastically.

The Internet-based transactions do not yet generate sufficient revenue to earn back all the investments. The investments are earned back above all because the entire back office process (the store automation) is based on Internet technology and dynamic databases. In the heyday period (30,000 to 40,000 visitors per day), before Alta Vista started causing problems, the company worked with IT specialists and contract editors. After the traffic generated through Alta Vista disappeared (currently there are 3,000 visitors a day) the company had to downsize and move towards store automation. At the moment the entire IT department consists of one expert who has an affinity for the industry and who specialize in Linux. Content is generated automatically from various databases. The focus has shifted towards sales and after-sales, where customer relation management (CRM) is a key term. However, in practice the company encounters the limits of technology with CRM.

If the Internet activities were to be made profitable, the website would have to generate a weekly turnover of €11,400. However, there is a tendency for turnover to drop rather than increase. The explanation for this has to do with

CONTINUED

general market trends, among other things the rise of MP3-files. The investments are earned back (relatively quickly) through the store automation: store and cash register automation is linked to the website's back office system. In addition, there are other synergy-related advantages: online orders are processed at times when the store needs less attention: early in the morning or in the course of the afternoon.

In the future, synergy in the Plato case will also take on other forms. At the moment the company is working on an information transfer system from the Internet to the store: using a barcode scanner it will be possible to retrieve information from a dynamic database. Also, people will be able to access music fragments. These types of services have to take some of the pressure off 'the cash register'.

8.1 INTRODUCTION

The case discussed above illustrates that the decision to adopt an innovation, in this case enabling transactions over the Internet (e-commerce), has considerable consequences and that reality is more obstinate than expected. The way e-commerce is eventually given shape, basically resulting in the implementation of Internet technology to support primary and secondary business processes (e-business), is more a gradual process than an abrupt change. Looking for ways to use e-commerce and facilitate customer behaviour is not a simple matter. It takes time to find the right business model for the product one sells, the market in which one wishes to operate and the possibilities the organization has to offer. It is hard to force users to embrace e-commerce, in this instance to buy CDs online. In addition, the case shows that the implementation of e-commerce and e-business is not without consequences for the internal organization: not only did the number of employees fluctuate, the actual job they were hired to do changed as well, with store employees involved in processing the transactions. Furthermore, the operational processes have changed.

E-commerce and e-business are not just about the adoption or implementation of a technological innovation. These concepts have much more to do with looking for new ways to manage and conduct transactions that are enabled by Internet technology. In short, they are about 'new' business models and new, Internet-enabled ways of doing business. We must immediately add a note of caution with regard to the adjective 'new' in new business models. In the next section of this chapter we address the concept of 'business model' and related concepts. In section 8.3 we discuss the decision whether or not to adopt: what is needed to translate a business model into an actual business case. In section 8.4 we examine the way e-commerce and e-business are embedded in the organization, and in section 8.5 we focus on its use. Our insights put a number of popular opinions surrounding e-commerce and e-business into perspective. We discuss these popular myths in section 8.6.

8.2 BUSINESS MODELS

Information and communication technology and Internet technology offer a wide range of possibilities to conduct transactions and organize business processes. Although many terms are used to describe activities surrounding the Internet and ICT within organizations and between organizations and their environment, the resulting terminology is not always equally unequivocal. For that reason we will begin this section by addressing a number of concepts, starting with a broad discussion of e-venturing, gradually narrowing down the concepts, focusing on business models.

Hindle and Dulmains (2000) see e-venturing as the application of all possibilities inherent in the Internet and ICT aimed at the acquisition of any possible benefits for an organization. This rather vague concept includes all activities by all kinds of organizations: governments, not-for-profit and for-profit organizations, and it assumes that the uses of the Internet and ICT are unlimited. The importance of e-venturing as a concept concerns the fact that it shows that the benefits of the Internet and ICT are available not only to companies, but to other organizations as well, and furthermore that the use of the Internet and ICT is important in improving processes in general and that it can produce cost savings.

The restriction of e-venturing to e-business is based on the profit motive of companies. As a result, e-business is defined as, the application of e-venturing principles to activities of organizations whose mission is to realize profits through economic transactions. Turban et al. (1999: 4), define e-commerce as 'the process of buying and selling or exchanging products, services, and information via computer networks including the Internet'. In our vision this can either be through the initiation of a transaction, for example by scheduling an appointment via the Internet, or the actual transaction itself. It can be the actual transaction (sale or purchase) as well as the business processes that precede (information provision, communication, market research) and follow (payment, distribution/delivery, after-sales) the transaction.

In this respect we do not draw a distinction between companies that are only present on the Internet – the all virtuals or dot coms – and companies that, in addition to their presence on the Internet, also have a physical outlet or use a call centre or sales personnel. The latter category is often referred to as click and mortar or clicks and bricks. In our view, such a distinction is hardly relevant. With the exception of companies that can set up a completely digital value chain, dot coms will in time be seen increasingly as part of the regular economy, subject to normal economic laws, taking into account the increasing importance of networks and network formation and the associated network externalities. Traditional companies will increasingly integrate the Internet into their normal business activities as a communication and sales channel. In fact, ICT and Internet technology will be the basis on which to shape internal and external business processes. As far as existing companies are concerned, they often still have to take the step from:

- being present on the Internet (website with company information);
- towards using the Internet as a place to communicate directly with customers;
- through the use of the Internet (or web technology) as a platform to carry out business processes; and
- towards the eventual integration of business processes and the Internet: e-business, the end result that is often referred to as the network economy.

Traditional companies integrate their Internet activities into their existing business models. On the other hand, all virtuals often have not yet determined what business model to use. However, the concept of business model is fairly elusive, due to its popular as well as inaccurate nature. Venture capitalists especially, as well as the popular and business media, are extremely fond of using the term 'concept of business model'. Often the concept of business model is used to refer to strategy, business plan, technology, a product or service, or a mix of these elements.

A detailed definition is provided by Slywotzky (1996: 4), who describes a business model (or design, as he calls it) as: 'The totality of how a company selects its customers, defines and differentiates its offerings (or responses), defines the tasks it will perform itself and those it will outsource, configures its resources, goes to the markets, creates utility for customers and captures profits.'

Many authors (Timmers, 1998, 1999; Cohan, 1999; Rappa, 2000; Weill and Vitale, 2001) have contemplated the question of how to define a business model. For now, we will use the one offered by Weill and Vitale (2001: 25): 'A description of the roles and relationships among a firm's consumers, customers, allies and suppliers that identifies the major flows of product, information and money, and the major benefits to participants.'

In our view the element of added value is of central importance. A business model indicates which party provides which products or services, with added value for the end-user, and which parties are involved in the transaction via the Internet or other wireless or mobile data networks and are thus in a position to create value. In the end, it is a question of the price at which products or services are offered, taking into account the existing cost structure. The following components play a role (see, for example, Faber *et al.*, 2003a):

- Service or product offering: a description of the value proposition (added value of an offering) and the market segment at which the offering is targeted. This has to do with the kind of products or services (tangible, intangible, material and immaterial, homogenous or heterogeneous, level of specificity) and the location in the transaction process (information gathering, order process, fulfilment, transaction and after-sales).
- Business architecture: a description of the organization and organizational units, the value network required to create, realize and distribute the service offering.
- Application and technological architecture: a description of the technical functionality required to realize the service offering.
- Financial arrangements: a description of the way an organization or group of organizations that collaborate in a value network intends to generate revenues from a particular service offering and of the way risks, investments and revenues are divided among the different actors in a value network.

The challenging aspect of analysing business models is that it requires managers to connect and balance various business model components (application and technological architecture, service offering, organizational arrangements and financial arrangements) in the face of technical, market-related and legal developments, the ultimate aim being to create sufficient economic and customer value. We take a closer look at the various elements of business models in section 8.3.

Business models: an overview

In various taxonomies a large number of business models are mentioned (Timmers, 1998, 1999; Rayport, 1999; Mahadevan, 2000; Turban *et al.*, 2000; Afuah and Tucci, 2001; Deitel, Deitel and Steinbuhler, 2001; Raessens, 2001; Rayport and Kaworksi, 2001; and see Bouwman and Van Ham, 2003). The basis for these classifications varies. Some classifications are based on developments in the area of technology, others on marketing concepts or product types. In some classifications elements like value creation or strategy play a role. Classifications tend to be based on new opportunities offered by the Internet. Rappa alone (www.ecommerce.ncsu.edu/topics/models/models.htm) lists over 40 different types of models. It is impossible to analyse all 40 models in depth. Some classifications pop up in a number of places, sometimes in slightly modified or more detailed versions. Basically the business models discussed in these taxonomies are alternative readings of Weill and Vitale's (2001) eight basic models:

- content provider: offers content (information, digital products and services) that may or may not use intermediaries (CNN, *New York Times*, broadcasting companies);
- direct to customer: offers products and services directly to the customer (Nike, Dell, Bol.com, Tower records);
- full service provider: offers a wide range of services in a specific domain (finance, healthcare, Internet) both directly and through third parties (Achmea, Wellowell, WebMD/Healtheon);
- intermediary: brings supply and demand together by bundling information, such as electronic malls (iMall), portals (earthweb.com: IT industry portal); web directories (Yahoo, startpagina.nl), auctions (eBay) and electronic markets (Chemdex, e-transport.ro, Sotheby);
- joint infrastructure provider: brings a number of competitors together by offering a joint IT infrastructure (AMSIX, Covisint);
- value net integrator: co-ordinates activities surrounding a value web, by collecting, bundling and distributing information (Cisco);
- virtual community: creates and facilitates an online community (Talk City, The Gate, WeBNet); and
- whole-of-enterprise/government model: offers one-stop access to a wide range of services from an organization with many different business units (Office Depot/Viking Direct or e-governments).

According to Weill and Vitale, these eight basic models cover the entire range of possible e-business models. As they see it, other business models are merely variations on these basic models. We do not rule out the possibility that they may be right.

There are a number of misunderstandings surrounding business models. Often, business models are confused with marketing models, revenue models or business modelling.

Business models and marketing models

On the Internet it is often hard to distinguish between business models and marketing models. Computer Associates hands out free copies of its McAfee virus scanner, on the assumption that people will automatically come back to the McAfee website when they have a problem and pay to download the repair kit. Buy.com uses a different, though comparable approach. To draw people, this e-tailer sells certain products below cost price. This means they operate at a loss, but because people also buy products with a positive profit margin, they end up making money anyway. For a long time, 'free handouts' were often erroneously associated with the Internet. Music (Napster, MP3.com, KazaA), Internet access (MetConnect in New York, UK4Free in the UK, Freeler in the Netherlands) and newspapers (*Washington Post, Independent*) were, and often still are, free of charge. Although by offering their products and services free companies generate no direct revenues, they do often realize their marketing objectives: attracting potential customers, hoping that they will in fact become paying customers. The creation of customer loyalty is of central importance. Cohan (1999) formulates this even more strongly, as he argues that the 'free handout' strategy is aimed at creating a lock-in relationship, whereby the customer becomes dependent on the provider.

If the idea is to attract people and eventually sell them other things, we are talking about a marketing model. If the intention is to attract people to generate eyeball minutes (for instance in the case of Internet access), which are then sold to advertisers, or to generate kick-back fees from the telecommunications provider, what we have is a business model. This is a business model, incidentally, about which much has been written in media economy literature (Picard, 1989) under the heading 'attention economy' (Shapiro and Varian, 1999) where some people make the mistake of thinking this is a kind of new economy (Kelly, 1997).

Business models and revenue models

Many descriptions of business models create the impression that formulating a business model is a relatively easy affair. All one has to do is describe a number of elements. We feel that this approach is very simplistic, based on the assumption that money is being made when revenues are higher than the costs. Incidentally, such a simple business model is hard to find in reality. In practice one has to combine various revenue models in relation to the complex cost structure of an enterprise. Revenue models are closely linked to business models, but it would be a mistake to confuse one with the other. A revenue model is a quantitative, financial interpretation of a business model. This interpretation is based on assumptions regarding the financial revenue and expenditure flows.

The thinking on models for revenue acquisition is less articulated than on business models. Often, the distinction between the two becomes blurred. Concerning revenue models, Mahadevan (2000) draws a distinction between subscriptions, shopping mall operations, advertisements, computer services, service provision, time usage and sponsoring or free services. This list illustrates the confusion: as a rule, computer services and service provision are offered at a (hefty) hourly rate, and the actual revenue model is simply based on the number of billable hours. In their list of revenue models, Grimshaw, Breu and Myers (2000) draw no distinction between revenue models, value propositions and business models. It is easy to understand the confusion, since in some cases business models and revenue models completely overlap and some business models contain several revenue models. In the media industry (which includes the Internet) that is the case when magazines are sold to subscribers or when advertising space, 'eyeballs', is sold to advertisers.

A revenue model is the financial interpretation of a business model. There are various ways to generate income. We can distinguish between the following revenue models:

- advertisements and associated models (affiliate, banners, click-through);
- transactions (the sale of products, services or information);

- float models, whereby the financial flow is temporarily being used to fund activities (Amazon.com, banks); these include models that focus on commission fees and generating transactions;
- subscriptions;
- licensing models; and
- utility models (the so-called pay-per-use models).

Revenue models are often used in combination. Amazon.com, for instance, makes money from both transactions and float. Revenue models are important because they help clarify where the money is supposed to come from, and as such they are an integral part of a business model.

8.3 ADOPTION: THE TRANSLATION OF BUSINESS MODELS IN PRACTICE

Business models are often abstractions of business practice. A business model describes what should be arranged on an ontological level. It is a generic framework that can be reused. Although in theory it is easy to identify and describe a business model, it is only at the level of a business case that it will prove its worth. A business case is a description and justification of all the practical decisions regarding the way a business model is implemented: which specific product or service is offered, which channels are used to target which specific market segment and what organizational units or partners are or will be involved, how the supporting processes and workflows are organized, what processes have to be in place, what investments are being made by whom, who will take what risks, and so on. In other words, business models are given shape in individual business cases. We describe a business case as the specific application of a (set of) business model(s) for an individual company in a specific situation. A particular business model can be very useful for a certain company, economic sector, industry or geographical market, and be utterly useless elsewhere. This is where the decision by the entrepreneur whether or not to adopt comes into play and he or she has to show the right entrepreneurial instinct.

The challenging aspect of designing and implementing business models is that it requires managers to connect and balance different business model domains (service, technology, organization and the financial domain) in the face of technical, market-related and legal developments, the ultimate aim being to create sufficient economic and customer value (see Figure 8.1).

The central issue in the *service domain* is 'value'. Value is seen as the perceived benefits and total costs (or sacrifice) of (obtaining) a product or service for customers in target markets (Petrovic and Kittl, 2002; Chen and Dubinsky, 2003). The service offering must be perceived as better, and deliver the desired satisfaction more effectively and efficiently, than the one offered by competitors. The key factor is customer or user experience (Bouwman, Staal and Steinfield, 2001; Aron and Sampler, 2003). In many cases customer value as perceived by the end-user has little to do with the customer value that is envisaged in the initial business models, and greatly depends on the user's personal or consumption-related context (Chen and Dubinsky, 2003) and the suitability of the product to be traded over the (wireless) Internet. Intangibles (software, music, information, advice, mobile payment services) are more easily traded and delivered via electronic networks than tangible products. But there are other factors that determine whether a product is suitable for e-com-

FIGURE 8.1

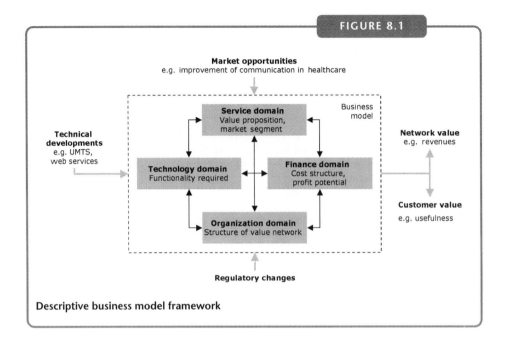

Descriptive business model framework

merce. Homogeneous products with a fairly constant quality are easier to trade electronically than products that are heterogeneous both in terms of form and quality. The specificity of a product – for instance whether it has to be consumed in a certain place (specificity of place) or has a limited lifespan (specificity of time) – indicates whether or not a product is suitable for e-commerce (Bouwman, den Hertog and Holland, 2000). It is to be expected that these qualities have an influence on the service definition in a business model.

BOX 8.1

Customer value of a mobile payment service

Moxmo is a mobile wallet service that allows consumers to make secure and direct payments to anyone who has a mobile or accepts Moxmo as a method of payment. Since mobile payment itself is not a product, Moxmo is collaborating closely with service providers to develop new innovative service concepts that may incorporate mobile payment. This is seen as an important prerequisite for the further growth of mobile payment, and thus of Moxmo in particular. The value proposition of Moxmo towards consumers is that it offers convenient (any time any place) and secure electronic payment. Moxmo currently focuses on the micro-payment product-market segment. It focuses in particular on person-to-person payments, Internet payments, topping-up of prepaid accounts and ticketing. At a later stage Moxmo aims to extend these services to include payment for parking, international transfers, debit card payments, customer cards and, ultimately, for payments in retail stores (this case desciption is based on Faber and Bouwman, 2003).

An important dimension concerns the target market, that is, the actors involved in e-commerce. In addition to companies and consumers, governments also are active in the e-commerce domain both as supplier and as a customer. Table 8.1 provides an overview of the various e-commerce markets. The most common distinction is between B2B – business to business – and B2C – business to consumer.

TABLE 8.1

The various e-commerce markets

Market	Example
G2G	Electronic request for information from the land registry by municipal service against payment
G2B	License applications (against fees)
G2C	Passport applications
B2G	Government buying office furniture (e-procurement)
B2B	Ordering a product electronically, for instance Dell or a marketplace like VerticalNet
B2C	Online bookstore or other type of retail outlet: Barnes and Noble, Bol.com
C2G	Online questionnaires form statistical offices, tax forms
C2B	Customers make or ask an offer for individual or clustered demand: LetsBuyIt, Priceline, Travelbids
C2C	Auction for private persons

Note: G =Government; B=Business; C=Consumer

Business cases can be used to support all or merely a few of the steps in the sales process. In principle, the steps can be conducted electronically. Usually, the following five steps are distinguished:

1 Information gathering: information is gathered electronically regarding the organization in question or more specifically regarding a product offering, an individual product or its price.

2 Ordering/purchasing (order process): this step contains an actual transaction component and is the one that is most commonly associated with e-commerce. It involves the direct electronic ordering (for example by filling in a Hypertext Markup Language [HTML] form) or the indirect electronic ordering/purchasing, for instance by purchasing a product on the basis of information that is provided electronically (in the form of an e-mail address, a telephone or fax number or physical address).

3 Fulfilment: certain products can increasingly be delivered electronically, for instance information products, music and games. Electronic order tracking and tracing can also play a role.

4 Payment: closing the (online) transaction. There are various online payment methods: electronic banking, Trusted Third Parties (TTPs) or credit cards.

5 After-sales service: customers can increasingly be supported electronically, for instance by electronic helpdesks or other forms of client support systems.

The degree to which these steps are conducted electronically varies enormously. For some products, the entire process can be handled electronically (for instance applying for and receiving a report), whereas in the case of other products, payment may be the only electronic step in the process, or customers may gather information online and then purchase the product offline (for example by visiting the store). Business cases, the concrete manifestation of a business model, will usually specify which of the five steps will take place electronically.

The central issue in the *technology domain* is 'functionality'. *Functionality* can be defined as 'the things a system or application can do' for its end-users. Examples of functionality enabled by 2.5G (GPRS) and 3G (UMTS) mobile services are always on capabilities and higher data rates, which are assumed to carry video and sound clips. Future outlooks are directed towards the personal area and wearable networks, with the so-called I-centric services, which automatically adapt to individual requirements (Popescu-Zeletin *et al.*, 2003). Another core concept of the technology domain is 'technical architecture'. A technical architecture describes the fundamental organization of a technical system, which is needed by the firms in the value network to deliver the service offering exhibited in the service domain. Important components of a *technical architecture* are applications, devices, access networks, service platforms and backbone infrastructure. Important characteristics of the technical architecture are centralized versus distributed, open versus closed and interoperable versus non-interoperable.

In general, *organizational arrangements* revolve around the resources and capabilities that have to be made available. In their analysis of business models, Hedman and Kalling (2003) conclude that the bottom line is that economic value is determined by a firm's ability to trade and absorb ICT resources, to align (and embed) them with other resources, to diffuse them in activities and manage the activities in a way that creates a proposition at uniquely low costs or with unique qualities in relation to the industry in which the company is operating. Increasingly, organizations have to work together to deliver customer value in so-called 'value networks' Selz, 1999; Tapscott, Ticoll and Lowy, 2000; Kothandaraman and Wilson, 2001). Depending upon which actor(s) contribute key assets in the creation of value and the operating risks involved, a different configuration of actors is likely to result, some taking structural, integrative roles in the alliance and others taking supporting, facilitating roles (Hawkins, 2003).

Governance is an important element of organizational arrangements. A value network is governed when parameters requiring service and process qualification are set. It is possible to distinguish three forms of value network governance (Kaplinksy and Morris, 2001). First, the basic rules for participating in the value network have to be set. Secondly, it is necessary to audit performance and check compliance with the set rules. Thirdly, value network participants may be supported in meeting the rules. Finally, the question of who is the 'governor' or the 'centre of gravity' in the network and the legitimacy of exerting governance is important.

BOX 8.2

Botfighter: organizational arrangement and governance

Botfighter is the world's first location-based mobile game that uses mobile positioning information from an operator's network and is played using a standard GSM phone with Short Message System (SMS) capabilities. On a website, the player designs a robot, which will be used to carry out a mission. The mission, which is obtained through the phone or website, involves another player, either a friend or one that is randomly assigned. Information concerning the location of the opponent is provided through the robot's radar system (the mobile handset). On the website users can upgrade their robots, buy weapons, view high scores and get information on their current mission. They can also form clans, which gang up on one another. Thus, the website is used for community building and to create an exciting game atmosphere, while the action of the game is carried out on the mobile phone. Botfighter's service network includes both companies and end-users, who provide content via the game's website. The service was conceived by It's Alive!, which maintains the game and organizes the website and the geographical information. The game, along with other Telia content, is hosted on a platform by Mobilaris. Ericsson provides the positioning equipment.

The governance mechanisms employed in the Botfighter case can be described as follows. The relationship between Telia and It's Alive! was initially determined through a contract that provided Telia exclusive rights to offer the game in Sweden. The contract has since expired and new terms and features were included. The relationship between Telia Mobile and Ericsson was formalized in a joint venture called Team Positioning, which develops services based on GSM-based positioning. The participation of end-users in creating content is controlled through website registration, which requires registrants to be Telia customers. (This case desciption is based on Maitland *et al.*, 2003.)

With regard to *financial arrangements* there are three main issues: investment decisions, revenue models and revenue-sharing arrangements (see Chapter 4). Generally speaking the cost side is reasonably well charted. As far as the revenue side is concerned, which from our point of view includes realizing cost reductions but also long-term advantages that stem from intangibles, literature is less uniform (Boulton *et al.*, 2001; Low and Cohen Kalafut, 2002).

An important question is how investments are arranged within complex value networks. Important (internal) stakeholders in complex value systems are next to the core or structural actors, actors that invest, although these might be the same actors. Investment decisions weigh the interests of the actors involved and take the mutual benefits of multiple organizations into account. Organizations that are connected through intended relationships and interdependencies consider risk-sharing, solving common problems and acquiring access to complementary knowledge to be major motivators for collective investments. To facilitate interorganizational investments, organizations go through a collective decision-making process. Compared to internal processes, these joint processes have the following implications (Demkes, 1999):

- They require a lengthy decision-making process.
- They demand multiple rounds of negotiations.
- There are conflicting interests to be sorted out (not always resulting in a win–win situation for all parties concerned).
- There are large costs and possible subsequent disputes.

BOX 8.3

Financial arrangements TMC4U

TMC4U is a co-operation between Siemens and the Dutch motorist association ANWB (like the US AAA) , which provides traffic information on main roads using the Traffic Management Channel (TMC). Siemens is responsible for the technical systems needed for the coding of traffic information into TMC codes. ANWB takes care of the editing of traffic data. At this moment TMC4U is not a profitable initiative for both the ANWB and Siemens. The TMC signal is offered for free. The costs of TMC4U are divided on a 50–50 per cent basis between Siemens and the ANWB. Main sources of revenue are VDO-Dayton, which is a subsidiary of Siemens, and members of the ANWB. VDO-Dayton sponsors TMC4U with a small amount per sold car navigation system with TMC module. Hence, at this moment the sale of hardware sponsors the service. VDO-Dayton sponsors TMC4U because it is of added value to potential buyers of car naviga-tion systems. The ANWB uses a part of its membership contributions to finance TMC4U. The government has committed itself to fund a public TMC service and has put out a public tender. If TMC4U succeeds in winning this tender it receives government funding. TMC4U strives to extend its services to subroads. Besides a public TMC service it wants to set up a commercial variant, which makes use of coded access. (This case desciption is based on Faber *et al.*, 2003b.)

Interorganizational investments require explicit articulation and collective agreement on the terms of investment and timing (Miller and Lessard, 2000). The share of each participant and the corresponding partnership ratio must be defined. It will be deter-mined what each member will contribute in terms of financial and technical expertise. The success of these arrangements hinges on whether or not the role of each member within the terms of institutional framework is clearly defined (ibid.).

Creating customer value is not an easy task due to the difficulty of extracting user requirements and *conflicting design requirements*. Design choices in the service domain may affect those of the technology domain and vice versa. For instance, what might make sense from the point of view of technology (for example, deployment of high-precision positioning technique) may make no sense at all from a user perspective (for example, privacy concerns). Hence, service providers need to balance technical and user requirements. Creating value for business actors (network value) is a rather complex task due to the *conflicting strategic interests of partner organizations*. Actors often originate from different industries (for example network operators, financial institutions, and retailers), each with their own strategic interests (for example, gen-erate traffic, extend services to customers, generate transactions). Design choices in the organization and finance domain may to a greater or lesser extent serve the strategic interests of the actors involved. For instance, operator and content providers may disagree on how to brand an information service and who needs to pay whom. Knowledge on how effectively to balance requirements and strategic interests is largely missing in business model literature (Hedman and Kalling, 2003; Seddon and Lewis, 2003). To develop an insight into how organizations can design 'balanced' business models, researchers need to go beyond identifying simple success prescrip-tions and try to understand the critical design issues in business models and their interdependencies.

Business models and the value-web

When we consider business models surrounding the Internet, we can look at them from two perspectives. The first involves the way value is commonly added within the industry in which the company operates, for instance the financial or pharmaceutical sector, while the second looks at the way value is added within the Internet value chain. Suppose we want to describe a business model for an electronic insurance agent. On the one hand; the agent can be placed in the value chain of insurance companies; on the other hand, it can be seen as a company providing electronic services. In this chapter we will focus primarily on the latter of the two perspectives.

Usually a creative use of new possibilities offered by the Internet, and increasingly by wireless and mobile technologies, leads to the most successful business cases. These cases in particular find themselves at the crossroads of the traditional value chain and new communication technologies. The Internet makes companies take a fresh look at their traditional roles (Earle and Keen, 2000) or produces forms of reintermediation or bypassing (Wigand, Picot and Reichwald, 1997: Sarkar Butterand Steinfield, 1998). Concrete business cases assume not only a thorough knowledge of the Internet, but also, above all, knowledge of and experience in a specific sector. As discussed in Chapter 7, it can no longer be assumed that value chains are linear (Porter, 1980). Increasingly, what is referred to as a value-web is a temporary network of independent companies characterized by a lack of hierarchy and vertical integration, and which is based on transparent, flexible and dynamic relationships (Tapscott, Ticoll and Lavry 2000; Wigand, 2000). Other terms that are used in this context are complex value systems, c-commerce or cyber markets. The interaction model between various actors, suppliers and clients is no longer one to one or one to many, but one to any. In this model, partners share the risk, and applications are aimed at co-operation and a real time exchange of information. Increasingly, we assume that value creation takes place via a web or within a network (Earle and Keen, 2000).

The decision on how to integrate business models in a specific case and how they should be embedded in the organization is a strategic management decision which implies the adoption of business models and (wireless) Internet technology in concrete cases. To summarize, in our view there are a number of basic models, as we discussed above. We talk about a business case when a business model is embedded in everyday practice through concrete decisions. On the one hand, these decisions depend on the possibilities and resources within the organization or the value-web in which the organization operates, including the IT infrastructure, applications and so on; on the other hand, it is determined in the business case what customer value one wants to offer to whom and in which phase of the transaction process, and what the products and/or services will be.

The choices that are made determine what processes play a central role within the organization and what channels (Internet, mobile, physical) one will use to reach the customer and offer customer value. The business case also makes it clear how one intends to earn money, by selecting certain revenue models. The decisions concerning all these elements are closely connected.

IMPLEMENTATION: EMBEDDING E-COMMERCE AND E-BUSINESS IN THE ORGANIZATION

The case presented at the beginning of this chapter illustrates how an existing company can use Internet technology both in the transaction process and in organizing its back office. Existing companies are often organized on the basis of an existing business case. Company management tries to combine the existing business case with the possibilities offered by the Internet. The virtual presence is used to strengthen the existing business case. Such companies are often referred to as click-and-mortar companies (Steinfield, 2003; see also http://place.telin.nl).

If we focus on the business models of existing companies, a complex set of issues emerges that requires examination (see also Viscio and Pasternack, 1996). This has to do with adapting the existing organization, infrastructure and business cases to the possibilities of the Internet. Relevant issues in this respect are the role of technology, the use of the multi-channel approach, the importance of customer relation management, organizational consequences, outsourcing questions and learning effects. In addition, by making clever use of the Internet and ICT, companies are able to realize cost reductions, improve efficiency and quality, and share knowledge. Research into all of these elements has to provide an insight into the way e-business can be realized. It is expected that these click-and-mortar companies that come from the traditional sector will in time outperform the dot coms. Click-and-mortar companies use so-called synergy strategies, combining the best of two worlds, the physical and the virtual (Steinfield *et al.*, 2001a). This means that in the various phases of the transaction process they alternate between physical and virtual channels. It would appear that these applications are most suitable for companies that already have a physical presence.

Much can be said about synergy effects, especially in terms of which elements are compared to one another. Is the website a reflection of the physical store, or is the physical store designed to match the virtual website? Venkatesh (1999) distinguishes six types of Internet strategies:

1 Pre-Internet: here, companies make a deliberate decision not to become active on the Internet, for instance because they do not have the resources or because they expect the Internet to offer little by way of added value. One can think of the neighborhood barbershop whose customers do not use the Internet much.

2 Mirror: here, virtual and physical presence are designed to be as much alike as possible. However, although the look and feel are the same, the underlying business processes have not been fully integrated and are not yet completely transparent.

3 Parallel: here, the decision is made to develop the physical and virtual channels parallel to and independent of each other (see Figure 8.2, the presentation of parallel transaction processes). Both channels offer different products or approach a different target group. The two channels do not refer to each other, for instance because the company wants to keep its online customers from finding out that it is in fact a small firm wanting to operate on a global scale.

4 Synergy: in a synergy strategy companies look for ways the physical and virtual channels can complement and reinforce each other (see Steinfield, Bouwman and Adelaar, 2001). The physical outlet, for instance, may help reinforce trust, as it makes the company visible. In genuine synergy strategies both channels comple-

ment and reinforce each other. See, for instance, Figure 8.2 where it is illustrated how different channels can be used in the transaction processes, for instance using the physical channel in order to get an idea of the look and feel of product, while it is ordered online after online price comparison.

5 Virtual: here, companies choose to have a virtual presence only, relinquishing any physical presence.

6 Anti-mirror: here, the physical presence is adjusted to match the virtual presence. The presence on the web makes companies redesign their business processes, for instance, to establish a better match with their Internet-activities.

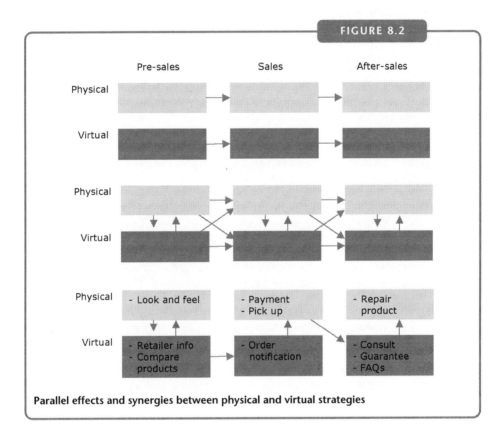

FIGURE 8.2

Parallel effects and synergies between physical and virtual strategies

On the basis of research, we have established that a seventh strategy has to be added to the six described above. In this seventh strategy there is complete transparency between the physical and virtual channels. It makes no difference to the customer whether he or she approaches a company via the Internet, a call centre or a sales representative. On the basis of a well-designed database (the sales representative or customer service agent of) the company immediately knows the customer's identity, what their likes and dislikes are, and so on. Processes are fully integrated and transparent.

BOX 8.4

Cisco, leader in e-business

Cisco is one of the world's leaders in e-commerce. By 1999 year end, online ordering exceeded 90 per cent of sales, resulting in more than $10 billion expected online sales in 2000. Cisco is a supplier of networking software and hardware, providing roughly 80 per cent of the routers and switches that keep the Internet humming and power the local area networks within most large corporations. Hence, Cisco is also known as 'the plumber of the Internet.' Cisco started selling online in July 1996. However, Cisco's first step into e-commerce was customer support.

Cisco has a relatively long history in electronic customer service. As early as 1985 the company set up e-mail support from company engineers to customers (Ernst and Young, 1997). Since 1989, Cisco's customers can download software via the Internet, and since 1990 customers can access Cisco's bug report database (Seybold, 1998). The company's earliest self-help support solution, primitive by today's standards and established in 1992, provided technical tips via an electronic bulletin board (Cisco Systems Inc., 1998). From 1993, attention shifted towards the web. In 1993 a call-tracking system was put in place to monitor each technical support call and its route to completion. This system was designed to be used both for a telephone-based call centre and for a virtual call centre via the web (Seybold, 1998). In 1994 the goal was to improve the self-help bulletin board application, and provide ubiquitous access by using the web. In July 1994, the website Cisco Connection Online (CCO) had 5,000 registered users and provided bulletin board information, answers to frequently asked technical questions and access to technical documentation. By January 1995, customers could open a technical support case or check the status of a support case on CCO. Later that year, the interactive 'Open Forum' was launched along with commerce agents for order and pricing status. In the 'Open Forum' users can pose networking questions, after which both Cisco's technical support staff and other Cisco customers and resellers start working on the answers. Often several helpful suggestions and workarounds are proposed (Seybold, 1998). By July, 1996 the 'Internetworking Product Center' was available, allowing users to configure, price, route and submit orders directly to Cisco (Ernst and Young, 1997). The decisions made and applications introduced in this period still form the heart of Cisco's Customer Support success. This success is illustrated by the fact that customer satisfaction rose from 3.4 to 4.05 (on a five-point scale) between July 1994 and August 1995, and then slowly up to 4.25 by July, 1998 (Cisco System Inc., 1998). Between July, 1994 and March, 1998 the number of logins per month has steadily grown from 5,000 to over 900,000 (Ernst and Young, 1997). In short, popular applications were introduced relatively early, and the use of those applications by customers, resellers and partners has steadily grown over a longer period.

Behind the questions 'what' and 'when' lie the more interesting questions 'why' and 'how'. During the 1990s Cisco experienced annual growth rates of approximately 70 per cent. In 1993 and 1994 it became difficult to find enough skilled engineers to service networks that were increasingly large and complex. With a vision of more growth to come, that was a very serious problem.

Fortunately, there were some signs that the Internet could become a useful customer support tool, especially after 1992, when browsers made the Internet accessible in a ubiquitous and user-friendly way.

Based on these early signs, Cisco's first step away from servicing via traditional call centres was automation of customer support, using information from their 1993 (virtual) call centre tracking system. In these automation efforts they cleverly used the 80–20 rule: 'After you understand the flow of events, focus your resources on streamlining the process where 80 per cent of the activity occurs ... use staff only to handle the exceptions' (Cisco System Inc., 1998). Cisco's 1993 (virtual) call centre tracking system was instrumental in providing insight into 'the flow of events'.

Thus the idea of a web-based customer service centre was born. Between July, 1994 and July, 1996 major customer support services were introduced on the site (see above). As a result, by the end of 1997 customers could obtain self-service answers to roughly 80 per cent of routine support questions, and roughly 60 per cent of technical support questions (Ernst and Young, 1997). As a consequence, the questions that did reach the call centre were much more difficult than they had been in the past (Ernst and Young, 1997; Seybold, 1998). The nature of support provided by the call centre had changed considerably, and had become complementary to that of the web. To achieve these high levels of voluntary adoption of service automation, Cisco did two things. First, on the marketing research side the company 'constantly surveyed customers and asked them what they needed. They said, "I can't find out the status of the order I placed", "Your price lists are out of date and useless", "No one can figure out how to configure your products", "Your ordering process is horrendous." So [Cisco] addressed each of these issues one by one,' according to Mark Tonnesen, Cisco's director of customer advocacy in (Seybold, 1998). Secondly, on the organizational side the company dedicated teams to specific tasks aimed at developing a high-level service website and attracting users. 'Cisco specifically created a telemarketing group tasked with contacting potential customers, generating awareness of and interest in the Internet services, and registering them as users' (Ernst and Young, 1997). '[On top of a dedication to using self-help technical support] a team representing both business and technical sides of the company conducted wide-ranging discussions about the company's goals, business needs and technical capabilities' (Cisco System Inc., 1998).

Finally, the changing role of customers in relation to Cisco should not go unmentioned. Cisco has managed to exploit the fact that its customers have experiences that exceed those of Cisco. This first became apparent with their large multinational customers that were deploying global networks in very complex environments. They would often encounter new combinations of hardware and software that nobody at Cisco had ever seen before. A customer would search Cisco's database to see if similar situations had been encountered in the past, and see how they had been resolved. Then, if he could not find an answer to his particular question, he of she would post the question in the Open Forum. Cisco's technical support staff would begin to work on finding the answer, but, interestingly, so would other Cisco customers! Whoever came up with the answer first, posted it (Ernst and Young, 1997; Cisco, 1998; Seybold,

1998). In 1997, an average of 4,500 technical questions were answered each week in Cisco's Open Forum. And each week they are polished and added to the company's technical knowledge base (Ernst and Young, 1997; Cisco Systems Inc, 1998; Seybold, 1998). So Cisco uses the expertise of customers to let them help each other, to improve its problem resolution database, and to learn about the ways its products are used. (This case description was presented earlier as a paper for 2nd McMaster World Congress on the Management of Electronic Commerce, Hamilton Canada, 17–19 January 2001 by Luuk Simons.)

Finding and exploiting synergies between physical and virtual channels is by no means an easy task (see the Cisco case in Box 8.4). Managers list a number of important challenges facing companies that wish to benefit from e-commerce and e-business (Steinfield, Bouwman and Adelaar, 2001). There are four critical challenges: avoiding conflicts between the channels, the need for extensive IT investments, non-realistic expectations on the part of customers, and logistical restrictions (Steinfield, Bouwman and Adelaar, 2001).

Avoiding conflicts between channels

Despite the best intentions on the part of management it may be difficult to avoid conflict between channels and a certain level of cannibalization with regard to the sales of physical channels. As virtual channels become easier to use and customers become familiar with online transactions, a (partial) shift towards the virtual channel is unavoidable. Furthermore, we see that even those companies that try to redirect revenues that are generated online towards physical outlets are increasingly feeling the pressure to use online revenues to pay for the development and maintenance of virtual channels. Companies that practise channel specialization (meaning that services are assigned to the most suitable channel), the way many financial institutions do, illustrate the fact that this is also a moving target. The evolution of online facilities means that a growing number of services can be provided at lower costs. The underlying message is that in the future it will be hard to avoid any kind of cannibalization of the physical channel. The challenge facing management is to recognize conflicts at an early stage and to design reward mechanisms that encourage interchannel co-operation.

The need for extensive IT investments

To benefit from the advantages offered by synergy it is necessary to promote interchannel co-operation by 'virtualizing' physical outlets. To enable customers to see the physical stock online refined database systems and networks have to be developed. Web services make it possible to connect legacy systems, systems that have been designed specifically for a company, to the web.

Non-realistic expectations on the part of customers

An important challenge facing companies is to manage customer expectations. It is logical for customers to expect that any contact they may have with one of the channels of a company be transmitted to other channels. Customers expect channels to be integrated seamlessly. However, that level of integration is hard to achieve, mostly because channels are embedded in specific organizational units, and that they are very costly. Companies have to be careful in communicating the extent to which integration has been achieved. As an alternative they can develop business processes aimed at preventing crucial transaction errors. When one American company that provided its customers with information on its stock at one point realized that there would always be a possibility that a customer in one of its stores purchased the last item of a certain product before it could be processed in the information presented to its online customers, it decided to postpone confirmation of online orders until the goods had been set aside by its store personnel. The actual confirmation was given by the store itself.

Logistical restrictions

Local distribution may not always be able to keep track if the virtual channel really becomes a success. The logistical problems involved in delivering at home and a lack of local supplies and storage room are among the reasons mentioned. Free Record Shop, a Dutch retailer that sells CDs, DVDs and other entertainment products, for instance, decided to centralize its distribution of CDs and DVDs and reduced the product range because from a logistical point of view that produces a better result. Companies have to find a balance between local order processing and the lower costs involved in central distribution. Here, we see opportunities for the developers of e-commerce applications to build logistical solutions that allow companies to realize the optimum combination. Companies like the American firm Sameday.com have emerged to build those kinds of solutions, whereby stock supplies are managed locally as well as centrally, based on what is known about consumer behaviour and user requirements.

Companies that have turned their synergetic e-commerce approach into a success use reward systems to encourage co-operation and avoid conflicts between the e-commerce and physical channels. Co-operation was the outcome of an explicit effort to ensure that existing outlets would not be penalized for the success of e-commerce, by offering compensations and rewards. In the case of the Rabobank, a major Dutch bank, a system was developed whereby local branches where the customers were registered benefited from revenues generated by online transactions. In other cases, for instance Free Record Shop, customers were able to collect the goods at physical stores, in which case the stores recorded the sale. The pattern is clear: if there is a reward system for revenues generated through local outlets, the e-commerce channel has to be developed in such a way as to boost rather than reduce local sales.

Implementing e-commerce and e-business activities is not without consequences. First, staff will have to be convinced of the use and benefits of e-commerce and e-business, and resistance to change will have to be overcome. In Chapter 5 we addressed these issues in great detail and in this chapter we have seen how some companies try to stimulate co-operation between channels and commitment among employees or franchisees. In addition to gaining support for e-commerce activities, the integration of activities within the organization also plays a role.

The implementation of e-commerce and e-business will often require expertise and experience that existing organizations in many cases do not possess: web designers, webmasters, online marketers and e-commerce or project managers. The decision to acquire this kind of expertise or to outsource certain activities is a strategic decision that has considerable implications. In practice, many organizations start out by outsourcing and then build up the necessary expertise themselves, gradually taking over activities that were initially carried out by others. On the other hand, there are also examples of marketing or ICT departments that introduce e-business solutions and decide to outsource activities when they find it difficult to expand their activities. This leads to the follow-up discussion as to how best to embed these kinds of activities within the organization: distributed, as a separate unit in the organization or as a separate enterprise. The answer to this depends on the type of organization, the environment in which it operates, and so on.

8.5   E-COMMERCE AND E-BUSINESS: ADOPTION AND USE

After the initial success stories from various dot coms it became clear in the course of the year 2000 that all kinds of high expectations with regard to the so-called new economy, successful business models and business cases had to be tempered. This development has since continued at increasing speed. At present, people tend to overreact and talk of dot bombs, dot gones and dot cons. We feel that the current negative attitude surrounding the possibilities of e-commerce and e-business is unrealistic. Many people base their opinion on negative stock market developments and the bankruptcy of various dot coms, rather than on an accurate analysis of actual developments. Developments outside the over-hyped Internet world deserve our attention, in particular developments surrounding the use of Internet technology by more traditional companies. Traditional companies increasingly realize that Internet technology can support all kinds of business processes (e-business) and, in combination with other channels, can also play a role in the pre-sales, sales and after-sales processes. The use of Internet technology by existing companies is also referred to as the second wave of e-business. We find ourselves in the middle of a transitional phase. The use of Internet technologies in business processes is an innovation and a learning process. It is a process that takes time and money.

As yet, we are only at the beginning of that process, as becomes clear from a study into the synergy strategies of click-and-mortar companies in the Dutch city of Rotterdam (Bouwman, Fielt and Smit, 2001). In this study, a representative sample from the databases of the Chamber of Commerce was examined. Some 1950 companies were approached, 570 of which did not respond and 925 of which were not relevant because they did not have a website. Of the companies that did have a website, 62 per cent used it exclusively to provide information. The remaining companies either enabled or initiated online transactions, for instance by offering customers the opportunity to obtain a quotation or to schedule an appointment with a sales representative. A similar study conducted by Steinfield (2003) in the US showed that 33 per cent of the companies investigated in that study facilitated online transactions. Data of Statistics Netherlands (CBS, 2001) show that seven per cent of all companies have e-commerce facilities, meaning that they process orders online, enable customers to pay online or offer customers online support. In the study conducted by Bouwman, Fielt and Smit this was the case for 12 per cent of all valid respondents.

In light of these figures, it may be clear that e-commerce and e-business have not yet been universally adopted. However, an increasing number of people are aware of what the new electronic media can do. On the other hand, the trends with regard to B2C e-commerce are mixed. The market for electronic shopping is still limited, data from different countries show a volume of around two per cent of the total retail shopping being Internet transactions, but the volume of shopping is gradually increasing.

Research into consumer behaviour with regard to the demand side is still limited. We hardly know anything about user motives and patterns. One of the most extensive studies was conducted by Dahlén (1999), who tested eight hypotheses. The first hypothesis is that shopping behaviour is stable: people who are currently buying things online will continue to do so in the future, in contrast to non-shoppers. Internet shoppers are not average customers. Dahlén's study shows that there are three groups of Internet shoppers: regular shoppers (17 per cent), people who have made one attempt, but who have given up after that (11 per cent), and a large group of people who have never bought (or attempted to buy) anything online (72 per cent). Whereas the first group will continue to shop online, the third group will hardly be prepared to do so in the future and about a third of the second group will at some point buy things online. The first hypothesis is accepted.

The second hypothesis has to do with orientation towards shopping in relation to buying online. The existing orientation towards shopping – economic rational shopping behaviour, aimed at personal service provision, ethically responsible shopping behaviour or shopping as a form of relaxation – will influence online shopping behaviour. Rational and apathetic shoppers especially are active online. Their Internet shopping behaviour correlates with specific product categories.

The third hypothesis is partly confirmed. It concerns the profile of Internet shoppers. Shopping on the Internet correlates with socio-economic status (high), occupation (professionals), age (young) and sex (male). When occupational groups are concerned there are no significant variations.

The fourth hypothesis refers to the assumed risks. The perception of the risks associated with online and offline shopping will affect people's willingness to buy online. If the perceived risks are big, people will be more reluctant to buy online, but if they have prior experience with online shopping the perceived risks will be lower and their willingness to buy online will increase. This hypothesis is accepted.

The fifth hypothesis has to do with the relationship between the perceived problems involved in getting to a physical store and online shopping. When people expect major problems with regard to physical shopping this will have a positive impact on Internet shopping. This hypothesis is confirmed as well. The sixth hypothesis involves the relationship between an awareness of where one can shop online and willingness to shop online. This hypothesis is also confirmed. The seventh hypothesis has to do with the relationship between Internet shopping and the degree to which people are innovation oriented. This hypothesis is rejected. The eighth hypothesis is that people will shop online more easily when they are experienced Internet users. This hypothesis is confirmed.

The image emerging from Dahlén's study is that experienced Internet users will shop online more easily, and that people who have had positive experiences are prepared to continue using the Internet for e-commerce activities. The second category, those who at one point tried to use the Internet to buy something, will in time do so again and continue to do so if the experience is a positive one.

Research conducted by Liao and Cheung (2001) partly confirms these results. They found that online shopping depends on the perception of security, education, price, prior experience, experience with the Internet, the perception of the quality of the companies selling products on the Internet and an assessment of the network capacity. With the exception of the last variable, these variables correlate positively with willingness to shop online. Partly based on the TAM approach we discussed earlier, Eastin (2002) finds that prior use of telephony for the same activity, perceived risk, self-efficacy, Internet use and perceived financial benefits play a role in the adoption of online shopping, banking, investing and electronic payment of Internet services. Koufaris (2002) found that shopping enjoyment and perceived usefulness have an effect on the willingness of online consumers to make unplanned purchases via the Internet. Individual beliefs and attitudes towards e-commerce services, such as perceived usefulness, attitudes toward the Internet and perceived risks are determinants of the adoption decision. However, little attention has been paid to the role of the context in which users decide whether or not to use a specific e-commerce service, more specifically the choice of channel (medium), or to the characteristics of the information products, services or goods being offered. Furthermore, issues such as personalization and trust play an important role in relation to the choice in favour of a specific channel.

Based on data concerning the supply of e-commerce activities and what little user-oriented research has been conducted, we have to conclude that e-commerce and e-business are becoming more and more integrated in a traditional way of doing transactions. The unrealistic expectation that e-commerce and e-business would become the dominant force has to be modified. The main trend is that the Internet and ICT technology enable e-commerce and e-business to become part of the normal way of doing business.

ON THE EFFECTS OF E-COMMERCE AND E-BUSINESS: SOME MYTHS RECONSIDERED

There are a number of misconceptions surrounding e-commerce and e-business. First, there is the idea of a worldwide market where any company could sell its products on a global market via the Internet. Furthermore, all kinds of intermediaries that are active in value chains are expected to become obsolete. The Internet would wipe out information inequality: after all, everybody has access to all the available information. Information asymmetry, which supposedly prevents economic markets from functioning perfectly, would be a thing of the past. We will now briefly discuss these assumptions.

Death of distance

The hypothesis that in e-commerce distance no longer plays a role and that any company can sell products or services on a global market thanks to the Internet, is one of the many unfounded assumptions regarding the possibilities of the Internet. It is often assumed that e-commerce means that customers no longer come from the local community and that it allows companies to turn people from all over the world into loyal customers as well (Adelaar, Bouwman and Steinfield, 2004). Bouwman, Fielt and Smit (2001) have presented companies that are active in e-commerce with a number of statements regarding the relationship between local orientation and loyalty, and maintaining customers.

These click-and-mortar firms are of the opinion that their customers are not from the immediate vicinity (a 10 kilometre radius) (77 per cent). Click-and-mortar e-commerce companies have loyal customers (68 per cent); they find it easy to get follow-up orders (62 per cent); there is a certain balance between customers from within the region (33 per cent) and from outside the region (30 per cent); there are more requests for information from outside the region (59 per cent). They are not sure if they are good at maintaining local customers (33 per cent give a neutral answer), but the score is also neutral when it comes to maintaining distant customers.

The study further shows that Dutch companies and consumers are considered the desired target group. The focus on the local market is less than on the international market. The study indicates that in practice the actual market is also a national market, but that the local and regional markets are at least equally important.

Dis- and re-intermediation

The benefits offered by e-commerce and e-business are not restricted to the producers of goods and services. Intermediaries can also use the Internet, e-commerce and e-business to improve their internal business processes as well as those business processes related to suppliers and customers. In practice we see that, because markets are not functioning perfectly, intermediaries (continue to) play an important role in bringing together supply and demand.

Above we have also seen that the linear nature of value chains is gradually disappearing and that it is easier for companies to enter into temporary coalitions to provide certain products and services. On the other hand, we witness the emergence of all kinds of marketplaces. Marketplaces are an elaboration of the intermediary business model. Business-to-business marketplaces are places where supply and demand are brought together. The marketplaces can be defined either in a broad sense (an entire sector) or in a narrow sense (supply surrounding a single company). The services offered vary from simple product presentations up to and including real-time information, from systems for dynamic pricing to payment services and fulfillment. The B2B concept comes close to supply chain management, value chain optimization and e-procurement (purchasing via the Internet or EDI). Some of the Internet's promises– transparent markets, skipping links in the chain – are fulfilled by marketplaces, which may explain their swift emergence in the last few years. It is evident, however, that only a few marketplaces will be able to survive in each sector. Real-time information is like oxygen for marketplaces. Transparent markets where information is readily available lead to lower prices and that is interesting for buyers. For other parties in the value-web it is also interesting to have access to relevant information enabling them to save costs and allowing them to better match the links in the value chain.

The importance of having the right information in the right place can lead to enormous advantages in various places in the chain. The promises vary from increased customer satisfaction to better specifications for product development. The benefits (or the added value) of marketplaces as far as consumers are concerned are the following (McKinsey and Co., 2001):

- Marketplaces increase the potential markets for everyone involved.
- Marketplaces lead to lower prices for buyers. Research shows that bulk goods on average are 7 per cent to 10 per cent cheaper, and that more specialist products can be up to 25 per cent cheaper.
- Marketplaces lead to a reduction in the operational costs for buyers, because the time-consuming procurement process becomes more efficient.
- Marketplaces serve as a benchmark for best practices.

In the end, processes within user organizations will improve (both internally – better information between the links within the company – and externally – better information between the various parties in the value-web).

8.7 CONCLUSION

E-business has emerged as one of the most prominent and promising areas for the application of ICT. E-business is about much more than 'just' technology, however. This concept is related to new ways of doing business, of interacting with consumers, competitors, internal and external contacts – about new business models, in other words. Business models describe the added value of the service offering, the organizational and technical integration and the financial flows, and describe the roles and relationships among different parties involved. It is precisely in these relationships that e-business brings about fundamental changes.

The central issue is how 'value' can be generated within these relationships, and that is not an easy task, as we described. In this respect, it is remarkable that literature and research are still very much focused on the strategic opportunities for companies, that have to collaborate in complex value systems. This more or less illustrates the push character of e-commerce and e-business.

Although for a long time there was something of a hype regarding the alleged possibilities of the Internet, a hype that was primarily the result of attention to dot coms and all virtuals, we have illustrated in this chapter that e-commerce and e-business offer all kinds of new opportunities, especially for existing companies. A distinction is often made between 'all virtual' companies and 'click-and-mortar' enterprises, which combine their presence on the Internet with physical outlets. As more and more companies integrate the Internet in their activities, this distinction becomes less relevant. It does point towards an interesting challenge, though: managing different, possibly conflicting, channels (physical and electronic) of delivery. These delivery channels are increasingly going to be a mix of (wireless and mobile) Internet channels and traditional physical channels. Other challenges facing e-business today are the need for extensive investments, non-realistic expectations on the part of customers, and a number of logistical restrictions.

Still, e-business seems to be taking off, and after the 'dot com bust', this is considered to be the 'second wave of e-business'. We are only at the beginning, as we pointed out. Adoption and use are increasing, but e-business is far from being universally adopted. There is also a lack of well-researched insight in consumer considerations and behaviour. Also, there are a number of myths surrounding e-business that seem to hinder its further development – creating unrealistic expectations with both suppliers and consumers. The assumption that mobile and Internet channels will replace existing channels has proved to be wrong, for instance. The new opportunities of these channels will be integrated in existing business processes and behaviour of customers. Also, distance (physical location of parties involved in a transaction) will remain a relevant variable, and the fact that consumers and suppliers can interact more directly may make some intermediaries obsolete – but it will create the need for new ones. Still, our conclusion is that e-business is here to stay.

9 E-government

CASE STUDY

Electronic government in Canada and Finland

Together with Canada, Finland is among the forerunners when it comes to e-government. E-government projects have been embedded in a clear infrastructure. Important drivers in this area are the Ministry of the Interior and Finance and the Advisory Committee on Information Management in Public Administration. The Advisory Committee has set over 40 IT standards. Agencies that are involved are encouraged to formulate explicit objectives as well as strategies to achieve these goals. Of the 161 services for which the government is responsible, 151 are offered electronically. In the area of e-procurement the Finnish government is leading. Furthermore, there are a number of government projects that contribute to electronic provision of services, examples of which are the Electronic Citizen Card and the citizen portal:

> The Citizen Card is a service card containing a Public Key Infrastructure-based certificate. The card allows its holder to be identified electronically on the Internet and to make use of various public and private sector services, for instance Internet banking. The Population Register Centre and Finnish telecom operators are working together in a program directed at creating a service for electronic identification of persons on mobile terminals, whereby the Electronic Citizen Card will be matched with the module cards of the subscribers' mobile phones.

The Finnish government has three central government portal projects, of which the citizen portal is one. The others are directed at business and government employees. The citizen portal (www.suomi.fi.suomi) was launched in 2002, and is linked to most of the key services. The quality and degree of sophistication of services varies because the services have been agency led. One of the services is the automatic updating of the voting registry system, which is linked to the population register. No intervention on the part of citizens is required. Another much used service is the collection of data by Statistics Finland via the Internet. Compulsory schools are required to fill in questionnaires via the Internet, a system that was set up after consultation with schools and takes into account their needs and Internet access. The Internal Revenue Service asks taxpayers to check information that is included in a tax proposal, to make amendments and/or corrections and to submit these to the Inland Revenue Service. (Multiple sources, including Accenture, 2003; OECD, 2003)

INTRODUCTION

After the chapter on e-business we now move to the subject of e-government. This concept has been defined both in broad and in narrow terms. In the broadest sense of the word, e-government refers to the use government makes of ICT – of which the Internet is a part – in its public tasks and the underlying (internal) work processes, (external) provision of services and interaction with stakeholders, for instance citizens. The public tasks and work process can be divided as follows:

- public information provision;
- public provision of services;
- policy-making and decision-making, including citizen participation; and
- internal management of government.

In this chapter we describe how ICT can be used in these processes, and what problems may arise in the adoption, implementation, use and effects of ICT in government organizations. What are the differences and similarities compared to ICT in the business community? We begin by mapping out the tasks government has to perform. Next, we take a look at the environment in which it has to operate and what demands are made by that environment. We conclude this chapter with an inventory of the strategic possibilities of ICT with regard to government activities.

In the following section (9.2) we investigate to what extent government has actually adopted these possibilities. What are the factors that play a role in the adoption and implementation of ICT by government agencies in general and by civil servants in particular? In section 9.3 we look at the actual use of ICT in government, and in section 9.4 we examine the effects that have been or have yet to be realized. Are the strategic possibilities being fully exploited and the policy objectives realized?

9.2 DIFFERENCES AND SIMILARITIES WHEN COMPARED TO E-BUSINESS

When it comes to the application of ICT, a government organization resembles a company in several respects. The problems involved in the adoption, implementation and use of ICT that we described earlier apply to both types of organization. Also, they both use ICT to increase the efficiency, effectiveness and innovation of their activities. Nevertheless, in this chapter we will emphasize that the difference between commercial businesses and government organizations in terms of their objectives has an impact on the implementation and use of ICT.

One important difference is, of course, the fact that business serves a private interest (making a profit) that is led by market regulation, as opposed to the public interest government agencies serve and which is led by political regulation. In this chapter we shall see that this difference has consequences for the concrete application of ICT. Government agencies have to take the public interest and citizens' rights into consideration. This is translated into a regulation that is much broader than that which applies to the private sector. Although the latter is also considerable in scope when we look at existing market regulation, social legislation, environmental protection and consumer protection, when it comes to the application of ICT, government agencies are faced more directly, and to a larger extent, with legislation and regulation. In many cases the application of ICT is even a direct translation or implementation of legislation.

In this chapter we shall see that the political and legal preconditions cause many complications with regard to the application of ICT by government. In addition, this application is often standardized and has to be the same with all similar types of government institutions, which means that innovation and change are more difficult to realize.

Another difference is that a government is at the same time referee and player in the area of government, policy and provision of services. The political branch of government issues laws that have to be implemented by its own agencies. As a result, it is harder to monitor government and to hold it to account with regard to its performance. Although it is true that businesses are also bound by legislation and regulation, these rules are imposed externally. Government applies legislation and regulation to itself as well as implementing the rules, which is why institutions such as parliaments, regulatory authorities, auditors, ombudsmen, and so on, exist. Governments are monitored indirectly by these institutions, usually on the basis of citizens' complaints.

A third difference has to do with the composition of government. This is not a single organization but a complex of organizations that are difficult to manage centrally. In addition, certain layers of government, such as municipalities and regions, enjoy a certain level of autonomy. In the past, this autonomy has led to so-called 'island automation' with regard to the application of ICT. Each part of government had and still has its own administrative organization, including the associated information systems, standards, programs and applications. A central ICT management was, and in many countries continues to be, impossible. In the first half of the 1990s the adoption of the so-called *BIOS-nota 2* (Tweede Kamer 1990–91) in the Netherlands meant a political decision was made to streamline government ICT and integrate government services through an increased standardization of ICT applications. However, this is easier said than done. After all, such a decision has far-reaching consequences for the way government is organized. It may, therefore, take considerable time before the ideal of a smoothly running, integrated and transparent government with the appearance of one single organization will be achieved, if indeed it ever will.

A final difference is that businesses deal only with consumers, whereas governments deal with customers that are at the same time consumers, clients with certain rights as well as voters, which has an impact on the ICT applications used by government. Government is supposed to involve its customers as citizens in policy issues, among other things the development of public services. As clients of those services, of which government is the sole supplier, citizens have certain rights as well. A consequence of that state of affairs is that government has to spend a lot of energy on policy-making and citizens' participation, and also uses ICT to do so. Businesses do not face anything like that level of involvement from consumers.

 GOVERNMENT IN NETWORKS OF INFORMATION, COMMUNICATION AND TRANSACTION

In the last 10 to 20 years, important shifts have occurred in the internal relationships of government and in the relationships between government and its environment. Both types of relationships are beginning to take on a *network structure*. This fast-changing and growing organizational form is made possible by the use of ICT networks. Traditionally, government has what is called a *departmental structure*, based on a territorial principle (country, region, municipality) and is organized vertically (top-down authorities which are organized independent of the environment). This departmental structure was reinforced by the principle of government autonomy and by classic bureaucratic forms of government and management.

The development of a network structure allows for a simultaneous scaling up and scaling down (van Dijk, 1997). Government increasingly has to deal with international bodies and flow of goods, services, money and people (scaling up), while at the same time having to serve demanding customers that require tailor-made, fast and local services (scaling down). In the second half of the twentieth century, the tasks facing government have increased both in number and in complexity (partly as a result of its own regulation). Information and communication technology was considered a tool with which that complexity might be reduced. Without modern technology, government would simply not be able to carry out its tasks. It would get bogged down in an infinite paper bureaucracy.

The growth of the above-mentioned network structure means that to an extent government departments become more independent, allowing them to enter into a more direct relationship with their environment, with citizens or businesses. At the same time the various parts of government remain connected and can thus be managed centrally. A combination of centralization and decentralization is the organizational principle of networks (Castells, 1996; 2001; van Dijk, 2001). In networks a shift takes place from vertical towards horizontal *co-ordination* (see Chapter 7). At the same time, the vertical supervision changes its form and content. Supervisors are replaced by information systems used by people at the top and bottom of an organization. At the top, government bureaucracy is replaced by an 'infocracy' (Zuurmond, 1994), and at the bottom government institutions and civil servants are given more room to improve communications with their environment.

Government is itself part of a complex network structure, the main actors of which are the components of political and public government. These actors in turn consist of several networks at every level (national, provincial, local). Political and public government are at the centre of the network. As a result of the decentralization or 'relocation' of politics in Europe, and as a result of the virtualization (independence from place and time) and decentralization that is made possible by ICT, the role of citizens, businesses, social organizations and supervisory bodies is strengthened. They are given a bigger role in an ICT application strategy called *the socialization of politics and government* (Depla, 1995; van Dijk, 1997). Some people have a different vision and feel government will play a more modest role (Frissen, 1996; Commissee ICT an Overheid, 2001). In their view, government should no longer govern, but instead act solely as a facilitator of networks that are increasingly self-regulating. Others, on the other hand, argue in favour of a stronger role for government, using ICT to steer, support and provide services within the complex of networks. This is called the strategy of *reinforcing institutional politics and public government* (Depla, 1995; van Dijk, 1997).

STRATEGIC POSSIBILITIES OF ICT FOR GOVERNMENT

When we follow the *impact–value* grid for the application of ICT in organizations (Chapter 3), we can list the following strategic possibilities of e-government. The applications listed here will be described in greater detail further on.

Efficiency

Information and communication technology can contribute to an *acceleration of organizational processes* involving government. This applies both to the internal and external provision of information and to the provision of services, policy-making, decision-making and internal management. In policy documents regarding electronic government, ministries and municipalities are keen to point out that information and services are available on a 24 hours a day, seven days a week basis. They also mention the possibility of declaring one's taxes faster, as well as the increased speed with which government departments can exchange information. These kinds of electronic applications can lead to cost reductions, cheaper services and management, once the investments have been written off.

BOX 9.1

E-procurement in Italy

E-procurement – all activities involved in obtaining items from suppliers via electronic networks – is one of the domains where government bodies, like businesses, are extremely active. There are numerous examples of e-procurement within government organizations. Many a government plan of action explicitly mentions e-procurement, often to increase internal efficiency and effectiveness, but also to act as a launch pad for customers and thus stimulate e-commerce activities in a broader sense. Australia, Canada, Finland, Germany, Norway, the UK and the USA are among the vanguard in this respect.

Recently, the Italian government has developed a new e-procurement system. On the one hand, a revision and centralization of policy and procedures was involved, while on the other hand the budgetary autonomy of government agencies had to be respected. Laws were changed, as was the existing procurement approach, ICT applications were developed and processes redesigned. Three procurement channels were introduced, that is online catalogues, e-auctions and an e-marketplace. The new e-procurement website was implemented, based on the three platforms, enabling a fully transnational and e-enabled capacity allowing for online bids and purchases. The result is a 30 per cent reduction in the overall costs involved in the entire goods and services procurement process. (Culbertson, 2002)

The second range of possibilities does not refer so much to a market expansion as to a *wider reach of government services and tasks*. Via the Internet and government telephone exchanges, low-threshold access to government information and services can be provided. In addition, government databases can be linked over large distances. In principle, this can lead to a reduction in costs.

Another important strategic possibility is the *removal of links* in service and information provision, and in policymaking and implementation. There can be one point where people can access all services, and in addition 'open counters' can be used. This type of one-stop shopping counter is referred to as 'open' because information and data that used to be available only in a number of back offices have now been brought together in a front office via a network. The result of removing links is that the relationships within government, and between government on the one hand and citizens and businesses on the other become more direct, possibly closer and more efficient.

BOX 9.2

E-government, Mexican style

The Mexican government has set up a portal (www.gob.mx) where information and services are ordered thematically in a system that includes over 1,500 information and transaction services of 100 institutions. The theme 'work', for instance, includes a job centre that brings supply and demand together. In addition, information is offered regarding labour law and taxation, information on public housing and soft financing for low-income workers. Other themes are, for instance, youth and drugs. The thematic channels are co-ordinated by thematic leaders who co-ordinate the work of several dozens of agencies. (OECD, 2003)

Effectiveness

The most important feature of ICT in organizations has to do with the *improvement of organizational processes*. By replacing traditional ways of providing services and information (in writing, by telephone or face to face) with an electronic approach, the electronic government hopes it can improve the quality of its services, based on the speed, accuracy, selectiveness and automatic registration of digital services and information. There is also an opportunity to improve policy-making and decision-making processes through interactive policy-making, with active participation on the part of citizens. Thirdly, fraud prevention and detection can be made more effective by linking the databases of various government agencies. Finally, there is a possibility to streamline all basic government data concerning private persons, businesses, real estate, buildings and addresses. This would mean a huge improvement with regard to government database management and the associated supervision, management and implementation processes.

Streamlining basic data is an important condition for *management and supervision at a distance* through ICT. When the various components of government are connected in a network structure, there is a need for an integration of departments and for transparent structures. Integration means that the various independent departments co-operate according to joint tasks and guidelines. Information and communication technology can help improve supervision in this respect through a constant monitoring of measures, indicators and targets. As a result, transparency will increase as well, first of all for the civil servants involved and also for citizens. To achieve all this government databases have to be connected on a large scale; the result will be *smart government*.

An example of smart government is a proactive provision of services. Citizens can be informed that they are entitled to subsidies or the Inland Revenue Service can fill in tax forms and all citizens have to do is indicate whether the information is correct. In Finland, the latter of these services is already in place (www.vero.fi).

It will take considerable time before government structures will have attained this level of transparency and are seen as a smoothly running and efficient machine. This depends not only on effective structures, guidelines, indicators and open technical standards and interfaces, but on ICT knowledge as well. In a broader sense this refers to the importance of *knowledge management*. Knowledge management can contribute to the mobilization and bundling of the existing knowledge of civil servants, citizens and businesses, with the aim of using that knowledge as effectively as possible. Although within government there is a great deal of knowledge concerning citizens and material provisions, that knowledge is extremely scattered.

Innovation

What appeals most to the imagination are actual innovations in government provision of services and management. The use of the term e-government suggests several innovations of that kind.

First, it refers to *new high-quality services*, such as the above-mentioned examples of proactive government. Generally speaking, the most important innovation is the transformation of all kinds of supply-oriented services into demand-oriented services that are designed with the individual citizen's point of view in mind. Such a transformation represents a veritable revolution in the way civil servants think, act and are organized. Thus far, civil servants tended to operate on the basis of the values, wishes and approach of government organization. A demand-oriented approach implies an overall redesigning of the government services. Clusters are formed, for instance, of services that are closely related as far as citizens are concerned, but that at present are offered by separate departments. Subsequently, the services involved are integrated into virtual front offices to provide fast and tailor-made services. Examples of this are the English government's website offering services based on people's various lifecycle phases (www.ukonline.gov.uk) or the US government's website aimed at students (www. students.gov). Setting up these kinds of counters does imply, incidentally, that there is a direct link to the back offices that provide and process the information involved. The basic data of citizens and businesses have to be collected only once and can then be made available to all relevant government agencies, as is currently already the case in Belgium. Citizens and businesses are thus spared the hassle of having to provide information time and again. This kind of well-organized database containing the basic information of citizens and businesses offers government the same possibilities that are available to businesses, who use direct marketing and CRM to collect and store information they can then use in relation management and customer contacts. Examples of this are the states of California (www.ca.gov/state/portal/myca_homepage.jsp) and Michigan (www.michigan.gov), which both offer people the opportunity to customize their websites, and in the process manage to collect information on the people visiting the sites. Innovations with regard to internal management are also within reach, as is shown by the state of Arkansas's auction site (www.arstatesurplus.com/index.hteml), where surplus government materials can be purchased.

Canada, on the other hand, uses a multi-channel strategy. Although the Canadian government's focus was initially on offering electronic services online, that focus has shifted towards a client-centred service delivery across the range of service delivery channels, that is the Internet, in person and telephone. This demands a high degree of co-ordination and integration across the whole of government. To make an integral multi-channel approach possible guarantees that services are client-oriented, responsive, cost-effective, accessible, trusted and secure, work has to be done in the areas of service transformation and channel integration, shared and secure infrastructure, policy and standardization.

THE ADOPTION OF ICT BY GOVERNMENT

Motives for adoption

Of the three main motives for the adoption of ICT in organizations mentioned in Chapter 4 of this book (demands from an organization's environment, availability of technology and the behaviour of others), demands from within the organization and the availability of the technology appear to be the most important. The main share of government ICT investments is dedicated to internal management processes. Of the strategic benefits mentioned earlier, efficiency is given top priority, followed by effectiveness and innovation. Information and communication technology is used above all to support and streamline the enormous flows of standardized data within (semi-)government. It is therefore more important that ICT meet the government organization's requirements than that it meet the requirement of the organization's environment. The environment and the behaviour of others are less influential because government has a monopoly in most of the tasks and services it performs. When investment decisions are made, virtually no attention is paid to the outside world (clients) or market developments. There is above all *input management* (budget management): the only thing government has to do is demonstrate that it did not exceed its annual ICT budgets. In the business sector budgets are assigned on the basis of the expected yield and contribution to added value, which cannot always be translated into concrete cost–benefit analyses. The tension between government budgeting and ICT investments is illustrated in Table 9.1

TABLE 9.1

Traditional budgeting and budgeting for ICT investments (adapted from OECD, 2003: 34)	
Focus of traditional government budgeting	Characteristics of high value ICT investments
Single year (or biennial) expenditures	Multi-year investment
Programme-by-programme performance	Enterprise or cross-boundary performance
Financial costs benefits	Financial and non-financial benefits
Level of effort within existing workflows	Changes in workflow
Ongoing operations	Start-up costs
Control	Innovation

Increasingly, all kinds of alternative financing and budgeting rules are being developed and implemented. Since 1998, for instance, the UK uses a Capital Modernization Fund, set up to support capital investment to improve public services, such as e-government projects or projects to reduce delay in the criminal justice system, while improving the quality of service to court users. Other countries that work with central funding criteria or with encouragement and/or co-ordination measures aimed at stimulating joint investments of government services are Canada, Italy, the USA and Mexico (OECD, 2003: 38).

The behaviour of others is only important to the extent that they encourage civil servants to keep up with the application of ICT in the business sector. Modern government implies that the strategic possibilities outlined above be used at least to a certain extent. When the business sector as a whole shifts towards demand-led and customer-oriented provision of services, direct marketing and CRM, government feels it cannot lag behind. However, the budget remains the main determining factor.

Parties involved in the adoption

An important difference between the business sector and government is that, in addition to strategic management, line management and ICT staff, various political bodies are involved in the adoption decision as well. In many cases the adoption of ICT by government is a political matter as much as it is a management-related affair. Often, the approval of all kinds of representative bodies and/or committees, councils or boards is required, which means that it can take a long time before an application is implemented. This is often also the case with regard to internal management applications, especially when these applications have a direct impact on government revenues or expenditure, or when contact with citizens is involved. It takes many years before people agree on the design of the basic administrations, social legislation and cost-calculation models of large government projects. In many cases the legislation and regulation directly influences the design of information systems. In a worst case scenario, a change in legislation has to be implemented in the calculation rules of the supporting software, which often leads to impossible and dramatic revisions in software and programs that take considerable time. One could say that a law, including its many detailed stipulations, would have to be approved and in place, before the relevant systems and applications could be adopted, developed, built and implemented. As this would often take too long, a start is often made with the technological development before the legal details have been worked out. As a result, there is a chance that politicians and civil servants implementing the policies are restricted by the limitations of a specific technical system (van Dijk, 1997: 143–5), giving technicians an inordinately big influence on the actual legislation. It is to be expected that these kinds of dependencies will be reduced in times to come due to the development of transparent architectures, middleware and an increase in the use of XML based web services (isb.oio.dk) (see Box 9.3).

BOX 9.3

SAGA: Standards and Architecture for e-Government Applications

SAGA (www.bund.de/saga) is leading with regard to the implementation of e-government in Germany. This standard has to contribute to a transparent exchange of information between citizens, businesses and government and as such it has to enable electronic services. Data models are defined to make integrated e-government application possible. Above all, SAGA is a document that is continuously being developed and that describes standards and architectures, including the goals, basic agreements, responsibilities and application areas for SAGA, the architectural building blocks, which is to say the components that are necessary for a functioning e-government data-management system, platform for payments, and so on, as well as interfaces.

Thus far, we have talked about collective adoption decisions. The next phase, involving the various adoption decisions of civil servants, by and large is similar to the general situation outlined in Chapters 4, 5, and 6, with one important difference. Civil servants are under constant pressure from citizens with certain rights that are fully independent of a certain service. This goes one step further from serving customers with various options in the private sector. Many civil servants have a specific professional attitude when it comes to helping people using collective services. One of the problems of many standardized ICT applications is that they do not allow a great deal in terms of the civil servants' personal autonomy and room for manoeuvre. The civil servants have to follow the prescribed procedure as presented to them on their computer screen and lose the ability to look for compromise in certain cases where they believe it might be beneficial. In cases where the new application is imposed from above, and, to make matters worse, is lacking in user-friendliness, as was the case with the Amsterdam Social Service Department (see Chapter 5), one may expect a great deal of resistance with regard to the adoption of the application in question.

Government innovativeness

Many government bodies see ICT supported innovation as a low priority. However, there are exceptions. In Finland, a smart card was introduced to replace existing identity cards. In addition to the traditional identification-related possibilities, this card offers possibilities for electronic identification and digital signatures, as a tool for encrypting sensitive documents, and as an enabler for information exchange among citizens and public authorities, as well as for secure transactions. Although the card is innovative in itself, the slow adoption of the card can be ascribed to the lack of private–public collaboration in developing user solutions and interactive services.

Adopted applications

We present a list of ICT applications that in the last 10 to 15 years have been adopted by governments (Table 9.2). Their description serves as an introduction to the next sections concerning the implementation, use and effects of ICT in government bodies. In line with what was described earlier, we will divide the applications into the

TABLE 9.2

Applications of ICT by government

	Information provision	Provision of services	Policy-making and decision-making	Management
Externally	Legislation and regulation on the Internet Information sites by government bodies Product catalogues and form services Internet in public places Parliamentary and council information systems	Electronic citizens' services (passports, licences, etc.) Citizens' service card/digital signature and *public key infrastructure* Virtual counters and service centres Proactive services Integration front office and back office services	Electronic polls Research and referendums Internet discussions Electronic votes Decision support systems (GDSS)	E-mail (address) for all civil servants Links and exchange of data with services and businesses outside government Government intranet Team support (CSCW) Linking and exchanging information between government sectors
Internally	Management information systems			

following categories: information provision, provision of services, policy-making and decision-making, and management. The applications have been arranged on the basis of the extent to which they are either externally or internally oriented.

Information provision

Government uses the Internet on an increasingly large scale to provide access to *legislation and regulation* and parliamentary minutes. In the 1990s electronic publications of this kind were often still in the hands of commercial publishers, but in the second half of the 1990s many governments developed websites. Since then the number of *government websites* containing information, search functions and possibilities to communicate, has grown considerably. The main value of the government's information provision is its accessibility. Attempts are made to increase this accessibility through high-quality search and reference functions.

In addition, ICT is used to improve the internal provision of information of government. For governments, parliaments and municipalities this involves *parliamentary systems and council systems*, which can also be made available to the public. Intranets also serve a largely internal purpose of providing information. Finally, most large government agencies have so-called *management information systems*. They are used for the internal management of people and resources.

Provision of services

Transforming government services into electronic services is much more than simply changing information on paper into electronic information. There has to be a user demand for these services, and they have to be individualized ('tailor-made') and integrated ('one-stop shopping'). Evidently this means that the organization of government changes drastically. It is easy to offer relatively straightforward standardized and administrative services provided by the register (passports, marriages, births and so on) and some licences electronically, but other services require considerable effort, organization and changes in processes.

In the development of electronic services a number of phases can be distinguished. The simplest form is the electronic provision of information, as discussed above. The second phase refers to the provision of services by predominantly innovative government bodies. According to Accenture (2003), countries like Mexico, Portugal, Brazil and South Africa currently find themselves in this phase. Often a central vision and basic infrastructural provisions with regard to security and certification have yet to be developed. Especially those sectors where benefits are easiest to achieve are leading and an example to others. In the third phase, in which – again according to Accenture (2003) – countries like the Netherlands, Spain, Japan and Malaysia find themselves at the moment, governments have usually set up a portal and are trying to offer as many services as possible, which requires the collaboration of several institutions. The first transaction services are made available. The focus is very much on the user of the services. In the fourth phase the portals are organized thematically and services are clustered. It is clearly defined who is responsible for the services, especially since co-operation between institutions at various levels becomes increasingly important. Policy is no longer formulated in terms of availability, but in terms of functionalities that are relevant to citizens. Countries like Singapore, the USA, Australia, Hong Kong, the UK, Ireland, Belgium and Finland are currently in this phase. The final phase focuses on the multi-channel integration, and government is just one of the players involved in offering a cluster of services. There is a redefining of processes and organizational change within and between government institutions. Canada is said to be in this phase right now. In the final and ultimate phase government operates proactively. In terms of principle, however, this certainly takes things a step further, as in this phase the initiative lies not with citizens but with government. After linking databases, a government agency may decide, for example, that a citizen is eligible for a tax refund or that a company may apply for subsidies, and then alert the parties in question. This application has already been set up in Finland (http://www.euro.fi). The addressee can then respond online or via regular mail. This application requires that the users' privacy and right to self-determination be respected. Another but similar form of provision of services is making sure citizens and businesses are not asked to provide information that is already available elsewhere in government organizations. Belgium is one of the countries that have such a database ('Kruispuntbank Ondernemingen'). In these databases all businesses have a unique identification number. Based on that unique number government agencies know what information is already available with regard to a specific company. Government agencies that need information from a company are required to check the database before approaching the company. The goal is to make sure that companies are not asked to provide information unnecessarily.

Policy-making and decision-making

The use of ICT for policymaking and decision-making consists of political applications that do not serve the same purpose in the business sector. Although the applications may be similar, their function is determined by government on the basis of the legal rights of citizens. The overriding political objective of government when it comes to the use of the applications we will discuss below is to improve the relationship between politics and public government on the one hand, and citizens and their organizations on the other (Hacker and van Dijk, 2000; van Dijk, 2001).

BOX 9.4

Live+: Switzerland Internet transmission of parliamentary debates

Live+, an audiovisual Internet relay system, was launched in 1999 and transmits live the debates of the National Council and the Council of States of the Swiss Parliament, as well as providing information to put the debates into context. Users use multiple windows to follow the debate, to access information with regard to issues at stake or the speaker involved. The main objective of Live+ is to achieve greater transparency for citizens, media and the stakeholders involved in the work of Parliament. (www.parliament.ch)

Government institutions, political parties and media with increasing frequency conduct electronic polls among the population, similar to the way businesses carry out market research. In these polls facts are presented and people are asked to give their opinions. The results can play a role in the policymaking process.

Electronic *citizens research* has a more specific objective, in that it is mostly about measuring the quality of government services, often municipalities, as perceived by the population. This kind of research can also be conducted in the form of 'quality panels' evaluating government services on a continuous basis.

Citizens consultation is an opinion poll among the population (at municipal level) resembling a referendum. In 1993, the Dutch municipality of Hoogvliet used the local two-way cable to ask a panel of 293 of its citizens concerning matters ranging from neighbourhood safety to dog poop in the streets (Paans, 1993).

The second half of the 1990s saw the emergence of *Internet discussions* as a semi-official way to involve citizens and social organizations in policy-making at an early stage (van Dijk, 1999). We call these tools semi-official because the government agencies in question are not obliged to follow up on the results, although generally speaking they have in fact done so.

Some countries experiment with *electronic voting*. There are a number of problems with this type of voting, such as its general accessibility, establishing the identity and legitimacy of the voters, making sure the ballot is secret and the possibility of voters being influenced when the electronic polling booth is but one click removed from all sorts of election propaganda. In 2004, the Dutch experimented with online voting by ex-patriates for the European elections. Many countries are still looking for ways to safeguard the security and preconditions that are required (Bouras, Katris and Triantafillou, 2003). Although to an extent the barriers for innovative use of online participation are of a technical nature, there is a definite resistance on the part of politicians and policy-makers to develop new forms of partnership with citizens.

A more direct form of democracy appears to be possible through new information and communication technologies, although there are still some question marks (see McLean, 1989; van Dijk, 1997). These question marks have to do with the assumptions regarding the form of democracy – participatory versus direct – and the involvement of citizens. The latter concerns both the access to the required technologies and the cognitive possibilities. Traditional stakeholders know how to exert their political influence anyway, and to them these new technologies are merely an additional way of getting their voice heard (Bentivenga, 2002). However, it is inevitable that the increasingly frequent direct electronic polls, consultations, discussions and ballots will start to have an impact on a political system based on representation. Viewed in that light ICT changes the way government is organized in a fundamental way. Based on recent studies it remains to be seen whether this development is a positive or a negative one (Rice, 2002).

Management

As argued above, the most important applications of ICT in government, at least in terms of the investment they require, are the ones that are used to improve internal management. In this respect the connection and exchange of databases within and between government sectors, and between certain government agencies and companies, is of crucial importance. The basis for this is laid in projects aimed at acquiring unequivocal basic data. In these projects attempts are made to organize government data management, by setting up authentic registrations designed to serve as a unique data source. This includes not only the basic information regarding individuals, but companies, real estate, buildings, addresses and basic geographical maps as well. These data can be used, for instance, for tax purposes, crime-fighting and social and medical services. The idea is that the data have to be collected only once, after which government agencies can be obliged to use them.

To improve the efficiency of the administrative organization of government it is necessary to *connect databases* within government and between government and businesses or social institutions. It is also required for the realization of a 'one-stop counter', for proactive services, to ease the administrative burden on businesses and to realize a transparent government where individual citizens are given access to their own information and have the opportunity to correct any errors. An important condition is that privacy legislation be in place and that so-called *privacy-enhancing technologies* be used, if necessary in collaboration with *Trusted Third Party* services, whereby information is encrypted and the encryption keys are entrusted to independent third parties, who can only provide those keys to others under the strictest of conditions, for instance when Justice Departments need them to fight crime.

Adoption of electronic government services by citizens

Developments on the supply side of government services, especially with regard to systems development, the use of web services and architectures, receive a lot of attention. It is therefore remarkable that hardly any attention is paid to the adoption of services, citizens' consultations and so on, by citizens. General diffusion research presents a picture of middle-class users with Internet access and knowledge, with an above average education and a higher income (Jaeger and Thompson, 2004). This resembles the adoption of e-commerce when it was introduced on the consumer market. It may be expected that e-government services will also be adopted more broadly in the longer term. One of the few more theory-oriented studies was conducted by Wang (2002). Using the extended TAM model, Wang has looked at the adoption of the electronic tax-filing system, as an example of an e-government system in Taiwan.

IMPLEMENTATION AND USE OF ICT BY GOVERNMENT

The history of ICT implementation by government

Before describing the actual use of ICT, we feel that some remarks concerning the context are in order. Since the 1980s, four phases can be distinguished when it comes to the implementation of ICT by government.

In the first phase, which took place in the 1980s, the emphasis was almost exclusively on the use of ICT for *internal management*. Large-scale standardized information systems were designed to automate the colossal government administrations. These administrations were tackled separately, which led to the aforementioned 'island automation'. The implementation problems associated with these systems were, and continue to be, twofold. The first type of problem has to do with the fact that the systems do not function faultlessly and that they are often user-unfriendly. The reason for this state of affairs is that the information systems in question were often used as tools to implement legislation that is complex, detailed and often contains internal contradictions. The second type of problem is related to the formal and informal resistance from government agencies and individual civil servants when automation appeared to lead to a redefinition or erosion of the competences of certain civil servants. Proposals were being deliberately frustrated and people were clinging stubbornly to their own competences and system standards (Brussaard, 1992: 142).

In the second phase all kinds of possibilities relating to internal and external *communication* were added to the ICT applications (from IT to ICT). This took place from 1990 onwards, although as a large-scale development it only really took off around 1995–97. With regard to the internal communications, this involved systems that supported knowledge-sharing and co-operation, such as intranets or CSCW and GDSS. As far as external communications were concerned, websites were developed that contained all kinds of information and interactive possibilities for citizens. One of the typical problems in this phase was that civil servants continued to prefer a face-to-face approach. As far as external communications were concerned most websites were little more than a collection of online documents and brochures to which some search facilities were added. Interaction, which mostly involved e-mail, was and still is limited. When citizens asked questions or provided feedback, this hardly affected the internal organization and communication processes of government. It is still largely a one-way affair. One of the causes of this situation is that many civil servants – especially at a local level – have insufficient skills to work with interactive electronic communication.

In the third phase, which started around 1998, government took things one step further by offering electronic services and transaction facilities and by using ICT to encourage citizen participation in policy-making and decision-making. This led to a large number of new implementation problems. To begin with, front offices had to be set up, both virtually and physically, with new electronic services. To do so, the right people had to be found. All kinds of job descriptions had to be modified, and people had to be (re-)trained. This in turn led to a lack of motivation and in a number of cases resistance. Finally, the front offices had to be connected to existing or new systems (that had yet to be built) in the back offices, which was probably the hardest task of all.

Regarding the use of ICT for citizen participation in the decision-making process in political and public government, numerous obstacles have to be overcome. Citizens and politicians are often uncertain about their roles and attitudes. Electronic polls and discussions are fast and immediate. The existing political system – which is based on representation – is, however, slow and cumbersome. It is based on a constant weighing of priorities and on discussions between various components. After all, representational democracy and the management of complex issues require time. The first experiences with citizen participation and ICT showed that they clash quickly with the existing political and administrative culture (van Dijk, 1999). In the eyes of citizens, politicians and civil servants are too slow to respond and they seem reluctant to act on the results of electronic 'consultation'. Often, civil servants have to answer politically charged questions, which is really the politicians' job, but the politicians often lack the time, inclination of (ICT) expertise.

In the fourth phase, which began in the early years of the new millennium, attempts are made to transform the entire government organization by connecting all applications, both internal and external. This means that all back offices and front offices that are related to certain government tasks are connected and integrated. This requires a *business process redesign* and a redefining of the government organization, for instance through shared service centres. The implementation problems that occur in this phase are numerous, as it involves a transformation that touches at the heart of the government organization. Entire departments will be merged and reorganized. Jobs, tasks, competences and authorities will have to be re-examined and redefined. It is hardly surprising that this leads to a great deal of conflict. Certain services, departments, committees and categories of civil servants protest when they expect to be worse off under the new situation. It will, therefore, take considerable time before this transformation will show any visible results.

Generally speaking, government has the best interest of citizens in mind when it implements all kinds of e-government services, citizen consultations, and so on. Many government agencies have explicit guidelines about taking into account the user requirements of citizens in general, and those of specific groups – for instance the disabled – in particular, when designing websites and electronic government services.

Use of government services

Remarkably, as far as the supply of services by government, the use of electronic government services, electronic citizen consultations, and so on are concerned, hardly any research has been conducted at all. One gets the impression that the market for e-government services is still under development. Development of advanced government services is still in the early stages or has been adopted to such an extent (for instance filling in tax forms or finding government-related information online) that research is not necessary. In the area of eEurope, research is conducted into some 20 services in the areas of, for instance, income taxes, job search, social security benefits, personal documents, reports to police, and so on, but also services that are specifically aimed at businesses, such as customs declarations, submission of data to statistic offices and public procurement. Sweden offers 87 per cent of these services electronically, followed by Ireland (85 per cent), Denmark (82 per cent) and Finland (76 per cent). Closing the ranks are Belgium (47 per cent) and Luxembourg (32 per cent) (eEurope, 2003:15). It is remarkable that a study conducted among webmasters involved in offering these kinds of services shows that 75 per cent of them do not know how many people use the services or how many transactions are realized online http://europa.eu.int/information_society/eeurope./2005/doc/highlights/whats_new/capgenini4.pdf. The motivation citizens have to use these services has to do with time efficiency (84 per cent), flexibility (66 per cent), faster service/reply (39 per cent), more and better information (37 per cent), more in control (31 per cent), money (30 per cent) and better help (19 per cent). This research also shows that the user-friendliness of e-government services leaves a lot to be desired.

Research conducted in Finland (OECD, 2003: 107) shows that citizens are, above all, aware of services that are offered at a local level, but that they are hardly aware of the electronic services of other public institutions. In Canada, on the other hand, the federal websites and services are visited most (70 per cent), whereas local services show a much lower score (55 per cent) (Erin, 2003). Generally speaking, user data are hard to find, never mind the motivation citizens have for using electronic government services, nor is more fundamental scientific research available. User data are often related to general Internet-use and access-related issues. More specific data on the use of e-government services are available to a limited extent only.

Although the media pay a great deal of attention to the use of ICT for *policy-making and decision-making* purposes, quantitatively speaking this is something that is still in its early stages. The first government-initiated (semi-)official Internet discussions that took place in the late 1990s attracted a limited number of participants (Bongers *et al.*, 1998; van Dijk, 1999). These discussions dealt with new guidelines on which government wanted to gauge the opinions of citizens at an early stage. In the Netherlands, it appeared that citizens with higher education are more interested in these discussions than lower educated citizens and that men were more interested than women (Dialogic, 2001)

There is, however, an increase with regard to electronic polls and citizen research conducted by government research bodies and large municipalities. In all sorts of areas electronic panels and monitors are set up. In Italy, the municipality of Modena frequently uses this tool to consult its citizens. Through Mo-Net all kinds of interest groups are given the opportunity to participate in policy issues (OECD, 2003: 57). More and more experiments are carried out with electronic ballots. In Brazil electronic voting machines are used. The 390,000 or so voting machines make it possible to process around 14 million votes within a few hours (Accenture, 2003: 49). The exact scope of the use of group systems (GDSS) by civil servants and politicians is unknown.

Despite the shift of applications towards information provision, provision of services and policy-making, the use of ICT for *internal management* is still more significant, both in terms of investment and of political and administrative importance. Remarkably enough, we hardly have any insight into the use of the new possibilities ICT has to offer within government. Research in this area appears to be lagging.

9.7 CONCLUSION

In the previous section we have argued that thus far, the results of the application of ICT by government can mainly be found in the first two columns of the *impact–value* framework – in other words, efficiency and effectiveness rather than innovation. There are more first-level than second-level effects. Chances are that processes will become more efficient and effective rather than lead to improved government relationships. In the 1980s and 1990s, cost reductions with regard to the increasingly complex and costly government administration were a primary motive for ICT investments.

In spite of this, innovation in the area of relationships (both internal and external) is crucial for the position of government in the political-administrative network system. In the execution of their tasks national and local authorities are faced increasingly with competition from businesses, organized citizens and their social organizations, and international bodies. Many government services have been liberalized and privatized over the past 15 years. In principle, this could happen to all government tasks. Proposals have been made to privatize the prison service, to outsource the social security system and to have research consultancies prepare policy documents. If government wants to continue to carry out these tasks or work together or compete with departments that have already been liberalized or privatized, relation management is crucially important. A service-oriented attitude and a smooth-running government will prove decisive.

Clearly, the greatest progress has been made in the area of *information provision*. A lot of government-related information is available online. Poor interactivity and a low level of user-friendliness are major problems in relation to government websites providing information and services (La Porte, 1999). Overall, there is too much one-way traffic. When we talk about *online government services*, information has to flow both ways. Citizens want to be helped quickly and expertly. They expect the use of ICT to increase the speed and quality of the services. Government faces the challenge of living up to those expectations, as citizens will increasingly start to compare government services to those offered by commercial companies.

Within Europe and the OECD countries quality monitors and user panels are increasingly being used to evaluate the quality of services. They have to shed light on the accessibility, interactivity and topicality of services and related information. In each of these areas the quality of e-government services needs to be improved considerably. Generally speaking, electronic services imply that they are faster, more direct and more effective (customization) than traditional services. Improved accessibility of government services, however, does not automatically mean that the civil servants are more *approachable* and prepared to negotiate. The opposite is often the case. The electronic front office and e-mailbox are often used as a kind of buffer. The civil servant working in the front office may appear friendly and the website may look magnificent, the question whether or not a citizen will get the licence, or social security benefit, he or she applied for is answered by a computer system or someone in the back office. Times were when one could directly address civil servants who had certain authority and discuss the details of, say, a building permit. Nowadays, all one sees is a response form on a website or a civil servant who may have a computer that is connected to the network, but who lacks the authority to make any decisions.

The promised increase in citizen participation in the areas of policy-making and decision-making has hardly or not at all been realized (van Dijk, 2001). To begin with, participation is limited to the make-up of the Internet population that uses these applications. It is quite difficult to persuade a sufficiently large group of people to take part to ensure the required level of representation. With regard to Internet discussions, the situation is even more one-sided. To a large extent, the people taking part in these are politically interested, highly educated young men, which means people with a lower education, women and immigrants are underrepresented (van Dijk, 1999: 208).

Another problem is the poor level of interaction in Internet-discussions (Rojo and Ragsdale, 1997; Bongers *et al.*, 1998; Van Dijk, 1999). Usually all people can do is respond once to an opening document or to statements other people have made previously. Opinions are often divided and tend not to come together in the course of the discussion. In face-to-face discussions the discussion lines are longer and there is a certain group pressure to arrive at a consensus and draw conclusions. As a result, politicians and civil servants are unlikely to adopt the results of Internet discussions. This is the main problem facing these kinds of applications. They have hardly led to changes in the political decision-making process, which is disappointing for the people taking part, who no longer see the need to do so and, as a result, the gap between government and citizens becomes wider rather than smaller. Nevertheless, governments do try to use these applications to mobilize an untapped potential of expertise and creativity among the population, and to extend participation beyond the 'usual suspects' that are traditionally interested. We can expect the applications to become more important in terms of their political and administrative importance in times to come.

Despite the emphasis on the use of ICT for *internal management*, government agencies are lagging behind some parts of the business sector in this respect, especially with regard to the services and industrial sectors. Added to the aforementioned problems of organizational transformation, this means that the extremely ambitious objective – streamlining the internal government administration and making the internal management more flexible, accessible and transparent – will be hard to realize in the short or medium term. The intention is to make government operate as 'a single entity and to realize a valid link between front office and back office'. It is only through such a far-reaching integration that concrete objectives like the 'one-stop counter', the one-time only collection of data, the linking of databases and the offering of proactive services can be realized.

10 Some concluding remarks and research agenda

In the previous chapters we have presented our model for the analysis of the process of adoption, implementation, use and effects of information and communication technologies in organizations, and applied it to the application of said technologies in both the private and the public sector. In this final chapter we evaluate to what degree we think the model is helpful in analysing these processes and to what extent a number of our central premises remain valid, and present a research agenda that emerges from our analyses.

10.1 OPPORTUNITIES AND DEMANDS IN RETROSPECT

Our central premise is that the value of ICT for organizations takes shape in an interaction between organization, users and technology. We have presented various models concerning such an interaction: for instance a model balancing opportunities and demands in Chapter 1, a model concerning technology push and technology pull (in the development of technology) in Chapter 2, a model concerning technology push and market pull (in the diffusion of technology) in Chapter 4, the strategic alignment model in Chapter 5 and the structurationalist model of media use in Chapter 6. Although all these models are based on different assumptions, starting points and objectives, and focus on specific domains, they do have something in common: they try to find a balance between, on the one hand, the opportunities technologies offer, and the demands and requirements that organizations and users have. In this book we have presented a number of studies that support this central premise.

As far as *adoption* is concerned, the final decision to adopt (or reject) an ICT application is made after carefully assessing technology and organization, taking into account the demands made of organizational processes and structures with regard to the means of communication and the possibilities ICT offers in terms of facilitating, changing and improving these processes and structures. In the adoption phase, the interaction between organization and technology plays an important role. Information and communication technology providers have to be aware of organizational demands and the demands of potential users and they need to match these demands with technology and vice versa.

In terms of *implementation*, we have used the strategic alignment model for illustrative purposes. This model, although it is not very recent, focuses on the relationship between the organizational domain on the one hand, and the ICT domain on the other. To some degree, implementation is about balancing these two domains, about mutually adapting business and ICT strategies (functional integration). The balance between push and pull is relevant in the implementation phase as well, as users to some degree should be involved in the implementation process (to integrate their needs and create a kind of 'market pull'), whereas, on the other hand, organizations have certain objectives they want to realize with the implementation process and need a certain amount of 'push' to realize these objectives (strategic fit).

In terms of *use* and *effects*, the structurationalist approaches towards ICT in organizations have been very valuable. The view that the use and consequent effects are shaped in a continuous interaction between users, technologies and organizational environments has shed additional light on the role of ICT in organizations. Since none of these characteristics are fixed, and they all evolve over time, this perspective proves very helpful in understanding and explaining the dynamic nature of the use and effects of ICT in organizations.

In practice, of course, we see that this 'balancing act' is taking place as well. Both for *e-business* and for *e-government*, the application of ICT within processes is guided by the need to support existing processes on the one hand, and by perceptions of technological possibilities (and consequent innovations) on the other. There is, however, a clear difference between the two domains. We have seen that in *e-government*, the application of ICT focuses primarily on improving efficiency and effectiveness in existing processes, and not on radically altering information, communication and transaction processes between government and citizens. Hence, in e-government we see more first-level than second-level effects. We have argued that innovation in the area of relationships (both internal and external) is crucial for the position of government in the political–administrative network system. In other words, governments may want to shift their perspective from one that focuses primarily on the demands their existing processes put on information and communication technologies, towards one that puts greater emphasis on the innovative opportunities these technologies offer – and thus, for instance, increase participation in the area of policy-making and decision-making.

We have concluded that for *e-business* the picture is somewhat different. We have noted that literature and research focus on the strategic opportunities that new enabling technologies offer companies. To reap these strategic and – more often than not – intangible benefits, companies have to collaborate in complex value systems. This more or less illustrates the push-character of e-commerce and e-business, and the primary focus on technological opportunities as offered, for example, by mobile and wireless developments. Especially in the heydays of the e-commerce hype, there was a tendency to focus on technological possibilities, without any realistic analysis of what the new emerging technology could do for organizations and how the new opportunities could be integrated into existing activities and thus allow an organization to realize synergies. This has subsided by now, and the 'second wave of e-business' seems to be based on more realistic expectations, and on a quest to find a careful balance between organizational demands and technological opportunities.

10.2 PHASES AND FACTORS IN RETROSPECT

Our model, which integrates a number of perspectives on the adoption, implementation, use and effects of ICT in organizations, has proven to be analytically useful, and has helped us analyse the various relevant aspects in detail.

Adoption was defined as an organizational decision process, the outcome of which is a decision whether or not to implement a certain ICT application and to provide the application to the organization's members. The course and outcome of this process are affected by a number of factors, represented by the various perspectives. Although in terms of *relative advantage* (expectations concerning improvements in relation to the expected efforts required to realize those improvements), a number of *economic criteria* in terms of costs, benefits – both tangible and intangible – and risks are of central importance, there are a number of *technological* features of the ICT application that play a role as well. The organizational decision-making process concerning such factors is an issue in itself, one which is strongly influenced by *economic, technological* and, above all, *organizational* considerations.

Implementation was defined as the stage in the process at which the adopted ICT applications are introduced within the organization, with the aim of removing reservations and stimulating use of the application. First, an important distinction was made between the *technical* implementation of an ICT application, on the one hand, and the organizational implementation on the other. Technical implementation primarily refers to system design, whereas *organizational* implementation, has to do with changing attitudes within an organization. In both types of implementation processes a central question is to what degree *users* should be involved. In a *technical* implementation users are consulted primarily to formulate user requirements, either at an early stage of the design or on a recurring basis, and the systems and applications are built according to user specifications. *Organizational* implementation focuses on employee behaviour, user training, expectations with regard to changes, hierarchies and organizational change occurring as a result of ICT systems and applications. Thus, to a degree the user is central to both kinds of implementation, but apart from that a technical implementation is guided primarily by *technological* variables, whereas an organizational implementation is guided primarily by *organizational* variables. We have noted that, in general, organizations tend to pay relatively little attention to the economic and psychological aspects of implementation. The primary focus is on how a technology can be applied, taking into account organizational and technological aspects.

We have concluded that the *use* of ICT is not simply the result of the introduction of a new application in an organization. There are *technological* variables such as medium characteristics (for instance perceived usefulness, perceived ease of use and richness), *organizational* variables such as tasks, co-workers, group norms, culture and structure, *user* variables such as innovativeness, social influence, experience with technology and task, and individual preferences. All these variables somehow influence the degree and way in which members of an organization use a certain ICT application. Although economic criteria are hardly discussed in theories concerning the use of ICT, they are of course relevant as well, for instance in terms of costs for management and maintenance. In our discussion of media choice theories, the relevance of our theoretical framework has become clear: the degree and way in which technology is actually being used to a large extent is determined by technological, organizational and user-related factors.

In terms of *effects*, we emphasized that the effects of ICT are part of a complicated interplay between organizational context, individual users and technologies. The effects are strongly determined by the context in which the technology is used. For the individual *user*, the use of ICT leads to a more efficient and effective execution of tasks and to 'empowerment' of the individual employee, whereas on the other hand it can lead to a fall in productivity, feelings of uncertainty, dissatisfaction and information overload. For the *organization*, ICT is expected to lead to higher productivity, acceleration and improvement of processes and more flexible structures; on the other hand, there is evidence to suggest the opposite as well: lower productivity and more control within the organization. At the *economic* level the most important effects are of course the strategic and productivity-related (controversial though these may be) effects, but also the remaining individual benefits in terms of efficiency, effectiveness and innovation, as well as the relationship between the organization and its environment.

Finally, the *technological* effects are related primarily to changes in the applicability of the technology as a result of the interaction between user, technology and organization, which is the central theme of this book: technology is not an objective given, it is something that is actively shaped when it is being used – and it consequently changes in the course of that process. Our discussion on effects also re-emphasizes the importance of our process perspective: the extent to and way in which the effects of ICT manifest themselves in organizations strongly depends on the way previous phases in the process have been given shape – on the adoption, implementation and use of the technology.

In our descriptions of *e-business* and *e-government,* our framework has proven valuable. We have seen how the adoption and use of e-business, for instance, have been influenced by economic, technological and organizational variables. We have also seen what the effects of e-government can be in terms of participating organizations and individual users – and what organizational measures are necessary to take e-government to the next level, to name another example.

10.3 FUTURE DEVELOPMENTS AND RESEARCH AGENDA

In this section, we suggest future areas for research concerning ICT and organizations. We first sketch a number of developments in relevant areas that guide such a research agenda, and then address several methodological issues that we consider relevant for future research. Based on these discussions, we present our research agenda.

Relevant developments

In Chapter 1, we distinguished four different perspectives on ICT and organization: technological, organizational, economic and user-related. Within the area of each of these perspectives, recent developments (some of which were discussed in the preceding chapters) have helped us define relevant areas of future research.

In the area of *technology,* we have discussed how technology tends to develop towards more intuitive, image-oriented (that is, richer) applications. Issues of usability, user-friendliness and ergonomic design are important here and need to be researched further. Designing applications with the user's point of view in mind is becoming increasingly important. Especially in the domain of mobile and wireless applications I- and we-centric concepts, taking into account a high degree of personalization as well as group orientation, context awareness and concepts of self-management are driving the development of new technologies. Developments at middleware level make information and communication services more and more agile and adaptive, while taking into account privacy and security settings. At the service level we have also signalled an increasing integration of information, communication and transaction services, as well as an integration of external and internal applications. Convergence and integration are key elements here. Also, we see an increase in transaction-oriented applications, not only between services and users, and business and customers, but also between independent devices that will negotiate services between themselves in network grid computing, proactively supporting users, both in an organizational and in a private setting. Hence, the role of ICT in organizational communication will develop further, and become richer, more flexible, adaptive and agile. More external and more integrated applications become available and are being used. Information and communication technology applications will continue to be of increasing strategic importance, both for internal processes and for processes between organizations and their environment. These developments will make ICT an integral and important part of the information and communication landscape available to organizations. We are long past the stage where ICT facilitated communication was seen as a primarily technological peculiarity. For information and communication technology, it is no longer the technology but the communication and information processes that are the point of departure. Information and communication technology is accepted and fully integrated in communication and information processes and it is available to organizations and their members. Competitive advantage and strategic success increasingly depend upon experience with, and incorporation of, information and communication technology in everyday practices. Such experiences will also lead to a further adaptation of technologies, tailoring technology to user expectations. We will see that users are increasingly going to be limited in their use of innovative ICT due to strict organizational requirements with regard to security (firewalls) and privacy. As far as adoption is concerned, in Chapter 4 we discussed how providers play an active role in the ICT adoption process. The crucial role of providers in the development of applications is an issue that also needs to be looked at in greater detail. The increasing dependency of the providers of applications could lead to a new form of technology determinism, due to path dependency. If a choice in favour of, for instance, a certain ERP-system is made, this may lead to a situation where an organization becomes dependent on the provider or is locked in. Path dependency may hinder the implementation of other, perhaps more attractive systems.

We have to keep in mind, however, that adoption and implementation rate varies between organizations, and although information and communication technology as a commodity increasingly is a given, there are still numerous organizations that struggle with the basic decisions about adopting and implementing technology, trying to find out in which way technology can help achieve their objectives. While companies are still struggling with the automation of basic processes, others are dealing with their business and technical architectures, and the most advanced organizations may have reached the point where they can incorporate learning practices in communities.

In the *organizational* area, we have discussed how the boundaries between organization and environment, and thus between internal and external communication, are increasingly becoming blurred, partly due to the pervasiveness of ICT, developments towards total business integration and the mobile and wireless availability of many applications. Henceforth, the distinction between primarily internal (for example, intranet) or primarily external (for example, websites) applications of ICT becomes increasingly irrelevant, in line with what was discussed in the previous section. A relevant question here concerns the integration of ICT in interorganizational processes. Also, looking at the interorganizational use of ICT, it will be interesting to see how interorganizational processes of co-ordination and collaboration are supported by ICT applications. And what are the effects of that use on such interorganizational processes and networks, and also on control over and accessibility of databases, servers, and so on? Building on this, we see the emergence of new organizational forms (such as network or virtual organizations), where ICT applications can play a crucial role. This in turn raises new questions – for instance, with regard to adoption, can we still distinguish two 'units of adoption' in these network organizations, where there is hardly any hierarchy? And what kinds of implementation strategies are appropriate for such organizational forms? What kind of co-ordination issues will emerge? Also, organizations are becoming increasingly knowledge-intensive, in the sense that an organization's knowledge has become a crucial resource for its performance. The role of ICT (both in terms of its contributions *and* its limitations) in processes concerning knowledge management is thus an important area of research. What role, for instance, does ICT play in facilitating knowledge-sharing within communities, teams or groups in organizations? Concerning the organizational use of ICT, more and more organizations are now in the stage where they are experienced with the use of ICT based media – which means that ICT is used on an ever increasing scale, leading to a critical mass for many applications. Thus, issues of collective action concerning the interorganizational use of ICT, as described in Chapter 4, form a relevant avenue of research: is the prerequisite of a critical mass of users or applications still necessary, in light of the pervasiveness of information and communication technology? Information and communication technology is increasingly being integrated with other media for organizational communication, and as a result, ICT should perhaps not be studied as an isolated phenomenon, but increasingly in the broader context of organizational information and communication processes. The same may be true with regard to e-business, as e-business becomes just business. It is expected that ICT will increasingly be seen as another resource organizations have at their disposal, albeit a very fundamental one. Imagine what will happen to an organization if there is a temporary energy cut or they cannot access the Internet

In terms of *economy*, the developments sketched above lead to an increasing economic dependence on ICT. As the use of information and communication technology within organizations is increasing, influencing more and more processes and individuals inside and outside organizations, and as this use becomes increasingly strategic, the economic performance of organizations is increasingly affected. And as the use of applications increases, it makes economic sense to adopt applications for which a critical mass of users exists. E-commerce is gradually becoming a broadly accepted and applied way of doing business. More and more consumers are conducting their banking affairs through the Internet. An increasing number of business processes is being conducted almost entirely electronically – on the whole, the economy is increasingly dependent on such technologies. The risks of such a dependency are, therefore, an important area of research. Security issues are of prime importance when more and more business is conducted in this way, and research concerning computer crime, viruses and spam will be increasingly important. Also, with the growing importance of ICT, there will remain increasing attention not only for risks but also for a balance between cost and strategic, intangible and short-term tangible, economic benefits. The relationship between the costs and (in)tangible benefits of ICT is still an unresolved issue, and fundamental research is necessary to establish exactly what its economic contribution is. We will see the development of economic tools that monitor developments, and governance of information and communication technology based on performance parameters will become more central in relation to a more strategic approach. At the organizational level as well as the macro level, the question is whether the productivity paradox is still an issue. A continued search for sound productivity measures (and their relationship with the use of ICT) is called for, even more so as input and output relations in networks of collaborating organizations become increasingly complex. Also, research can provide tools to help managers control the implementation, management and maintenance costs of ICT applications, and determine quantifiable and non-quantifiable benefits.

Finally, as far as the *user* is concerned, the most crucial development is that users are becoming increasingly *experienced* with and *skilled* in the use of ICT, stimulated by the increasing ease of use and the commodification of information and communication technology. Together with the technological developments discussed above, this will lead to an increase in the perceived 'richness' of ICT, and the increasing use of ICT applications for a broad range of tasks – from simple and routine tasks to complex ones. As ICT will no longer be regarded as a special phenomenon, but as part of the palette that is available for organizational communication, it becomes a question of what to apply under what conditions. What is the optimal degree of user involvement in an implementation process? What is the role of rationality in an individual's decision whether or not to use a certain application? To what degree does substitution take place, and with what effects? And looking beyond ICT as 'just a medium', in terms of advanced technologies, there are interesting questions concerning the way perceptions and cognitions take shape in virtual environments. We also see a number of serious threats as far as the user is concerned, however. The increasing use of ICT leads to an increased feeling of information overload. Intranets, the Internet, multiple e-mail accounts, conferencing systems, web cam video-conferencing opportunities, participation in a number of different groupware systems, each with its own routines and lack of logic, and other new emerging mobile applications, with push and pull routines, will all contribute to an avalanche of information coming towards the user, and users who are not skilled in sifting through this information and selecting what is relevant, will become overloaded, have trouble remembering all their passwords, pin codes and so on, even when parameters are defined in self-management systems and personalization is in place. Handling all the different devices will divert users from their key tasks and activities, affecting personal and organizational productivity. This feeling is further augmented by the fact that for many people, their e-mail inbox is now dominated by 'spam' or mails containing dangerous viruses. Also, there is the issue of abuse – in the sense that employees surf pornography websites or send private e-mails, confidential information gets 'leaked' and other uses of ICT that are contrary to an organization's goals. And, related to that, there is the issue of 'electronic surveillance', the increasing monitoring of employees' activities. Also, people are increasingly expected to be on call and available, because information and communication technology kills time and distance. All these developments create negative sentiments towards ICT, which may be detrimental to its use – and to its potentially positive contributions. Such negative issues certainly warrant research in order to provide a realistic insight into the threats to the potentially positive contribution of ICT to task execution and communication within and between organizations.

Methodological issues: multiplicity

Throughout this book we have used a multi-theoretical and multi-level framework (in terms of Monge and Contractor, 2003). In the preceding chapters, theories from the areas of organization science, media use, social psychology, economics and technology (to name but a few) have been used to describe and explain the process of adoption, implementation, use and effects of ICT in organizations. Also, we have described this process at different levels of analysis – individual, group, organization and environment.

Where Monge and Contractor (2003: 46) argue that 'utilizing multiple theories should improve our explanations of network evolution as well as significantly increasing the amount of variance accounted for by these theoretical mechanisms', we feel the same can be said for the process of adoption, implementation, use and effects of ICT in organizations. Rice (1999: 40) presents a similar argument, stating that:

> We feel that it is important to consider multiple paradigms when studying a complex social phenomenon such as the implementation of information systems in organizations, as each paradigm emphasizes and highlights different, though often overlapping, aspects of the phenomenon. Furthermore, each paradigm emphasizes different sources of data and different analytical approaches.

Our framework does just that, integrating theories and research from various disciplines to explain the process under study as clearly as possible. For future research, we feel it is important to maintain such a multi-theoretical approach. The developments sketched in the previous section underline this: we see important developments in various areas in which different theories and paradigms are prevalent, and to incorporate these developments in our further studies of ICT in organizations, a multi-theoretical approach is crucial. Alternative theories make differential predictions about the role of ICT in organizations, and for a complete analysis of this subject integration is necessary.

A similar conclusion can be drawn for the multi-level character of our framework. We have discussed how different levels of analysis are of varying importance when we consider the various stages in the process of diffusion of an ICT application. In Chapter 1, we concentrated on the individual, organizational and environment level, but Chapter 6 has made it clear that the group level warrants some explicit attention as well. In Chapter 7 we discussed how difficult it can sometimes be, on the one hand, to distinguish such levels of analysis (what is an individual effect, what is an organizational effect?) and to integrate them as well (how to aggregate individual measures to organizational or societal levels). Nevertheless, the discussion throughout this book has emphasized the importance of such distinctions and integrations, and they should be an integral part of future research. Future research should not only apply a multi-theoretical framework in order to provide optimal explanations, it should also incorporate (*and* distinguish) the different levels of analysis. Monge and Contractor's (2003: 46) observation with regard to network data is valid for the subject of this book as well: 'data are either transformed to a single level of analysis ... that necessarily loses some of the richness in the data, or are analysed separately at different levels of analysis thus precluding direct comparisons of theoretical influences at different levels'. Thus, in future research, data should be collected at different levels of analysis, and multilevel analysis techniques should be applied to avoid such analytical problems.

And, of course, we also argue for multiple methods and multiple sources of data (cf. Rice, 1999). Different theoretical approaches and levels of analysis call for different methodological approaches. Determining the relationship between the use of ICT and organizational performance, for instance, may require a detailed statistical analyses of large datasets from agencies such as the Organization for Economic Co-operation and Development (OECD) or the US Department of Commerce, combined with large-scale surveys or log-data from system use. Analysing the influence of group norms on the use of ICT, on the other hand, implies laboratory experiments in which such processes can be studied in detail. A study of the role of individuals' resistance to the implementation of ICT can very well take the form of a number of case studies, in which qualitative methods such as participative observation, interviews and narrative analyses, as well as a more quantitative approach using questionnaires, are applied to explore this issue.

Finally, in line with our process perspective, we argue in favour of multiple measurements – in other words, longitudinal research. As Rice (1999) and van den Hooff (in press) show, collecting data at different points in time enables researchers to maintain a sharper distinction between causes and effects than can be achieved in cross-sectional studies. Such longitudinal studies provide insight into the way different stages in the process of diffusion follow and influence each other, the way perceptions of task and medium characteristics are influenced by an increase in experience, the way different kinds (and levels) of ICT effects influence each other, and so on.

In short, when considering our research agenda, keep in mind that we argue for multiplicity: multiple theories, multiple levels of analysis, multiple methods and data sources, and multiple measurements. Such multiplicity, we feel, provides rich insight into the dynamic process of adoption, implementation, use and effects of ICT in organizations.

TABLE 10.1

Research agenda

	Adoption	Implementation	Use	Effects
Technology	– role of ICT-providers in development of applications – path dependency and technical choices – relative advantage: from estimate to experience	– usability and user-friendliness, I– and we-centric services – basic ergonomic design, in addition to co-creation of applications	– reinvention and adaptation – development in the extent to which applications are used	– convergence and detachment of technology – redesign of applications and interfaces
Organization	– integrating ICT in interorganizational processes – validity of 'two units of adoption' in new organizational forms	– implementation strategies in new organizational forms – adaptability and flexibility of systems – implementation of business architectures, taking into account strategic consideration both as practical opportunities and consequences	– interorganizational use of ICT – co-ordination and cooperation in organizational networks – ICT in knowledge management – communities, groups and distributed teams	– effects on value chains/ value webs/ interorganizational networks – longitudinal studies to determine effects on all levels
Economy	– further analysis of cost/ benefit models, taking into account risks and intangible benefits – increasing critical mass with increasing adoption (collective action)	– estimating and controlling implementation processes from a cost perspective – making hidden costs explicit	– costs of ICT maintenance and management – costs of upgrading	– economic risks due to computer crime, viruses and spam – productivity measures at micro, meso and macro level
User	– role of rationality in decision–making process	– optimal degree of user involvement – resistance to change	– perception and cognition in interactive/virtual environments – reinvention and adaptation – computer literacy, computer fear – relationship to and substitution of other media	– aversion to ICT due to information overload, spam and viruses – performance indicators on micro level

Research agenda

This all leads to the research agenda presented in Table 10.1. In this table, we have organized possible areas of research along the process stages of adoption, implementation, use and effects on the one hand, and along the technological, organizational, economic and user perspectives on the other. Based on the developments we sketched earlier, we give some examples of possible research subjects within each cell of the table. This is a limited list of examples, of course, and we invite the reader to come up with his or her own research subjects for each of these processes and perspectives.

10.4 CONCLUDING REMARKS

On the basis of everything we have said above, we feel that our framework helps provide insight into the process of adoption, implementation, use and effects of ICT in organizations. A word of warning, though: the framework should not be taken too literally, in the sense that we realize that this not a neat linear process but one in which incremental steps are taken, different stages occur at the same time, stages mutually influence each other, are skipped altogether, and so on. Also, the model can be criticized for at least appearing to be quite deterministic, with unidirectional arrows from the different factors to the different stages in the process. Again, we should emphasize that a model is by definition a simplification of reality, and that we are fully aware of the fact that in reality, influences are rarely linear and unidirectional. As we have emphasized throughout the book, it is the *interaction* and mutual influence between users, organizations and technology that shape the process of adoption, implementation, use and effects of ICT in organizations. For analytical purposes, however, we are convinced that our framework has value, and that it offers a potentially valuable basis for further research in the area of information and communication technology in organizations.

Glossary of concepts

Accessibility, affective	User-friendliness of a technology, ease of use, day-to-day behaviour
Accessibility, physical	Availability and reliability of technology
Adaptive structuration theory	Theory that integrates decision-making school, like media richness, and institutional school, oriented on social structures, in a social technology perspective. Structuration is the process by which social structures are produced and reproduced in social life
Adaptation	See Reinvention
Adhocracy	Organizational form in which project teams of experts formed on ad hoc basis
Adoption	The phase of exploration, research, deliberation and decision-making to introduce a new system into the organization
Advantage, relative	The degree to which an innovation is considered 'better' than the idea, practice or object it is supposed to replace
Architecture, application	Blueprint of how applications in the information and communication domain are working together
Architecture, business	Embedding of business strategy based on blueprint of organizational structure, process and function that serves as a starting point for the application, information and communication architecture as well as the technical architecture
Architecture, information and communication (platform)	Blueprint of technical resources necessary to support information and communication applications, such as computer, network and peripherals, operating systems, database management systems, user interface networks, system services, middleware and so on
Architecture, technical	Blueprint of technical resources necessary on an infrastructure and middleware level to support information and communication applications
Asynchronous communication	Communication where there is a time interval between a message and a reaction to that message, does not require simultaneous presence of communication partners
Balanced score card	A tool, approach for measuring the performance of an organization, developed by Kaplan and Norton

Bandwagon effect	Copying of a popular view or vision, free riding on success of a certain development or successful movement. 'Me too' behaviour
Benefits (intangible)	Immaterial revenues and values that are hard to quantify
Benefits (tangible)	Material, quantifiable revenues
Bounded reality/rationality	Decision-makers do not have all the information to take the 'best' decision. Bounded rationality is a response on rational decision-making theory
Bureaucracy (machine)	An organizational form characterized by large size of organization with an extensive staff and technological structure, and a dominating management
Bureaucracy (professional)	See organization, professional
Business IT alignment	Theoretical framework that advocates that strategy of business and IT have to be functionally integrated and strategy and operation need a strategic fit
Business model	Description of roles and relationships among a firm's consumers, customers, allies and suppliers that identifies the major flow of product, information and money, and the major benefits to participants
Business process redesign	Almost continuous re-engineering of business process due to new opportunities enabled by information and communication technology
Cascading method	System engineering method that follows a linear path
Channel (communication)	Carriers of the diffusion process, more general carriers of information
Channel expansion	Subjective approach of media choice concept in which earlier experiences with channel, with message topic and other criteria play a role
Client-server software	Software that can be installed both on a computer and on a network server and that can only execute tasks when used in combination
Client, thick	A client that contains the major part of the software on the local computer
Client, thin	A client that contains the minor part of the software on the local computer
Collective action	Members of a social system having high costs to realize a collective good without being certain that others will invest as well
Communality	Availability of a generally accessible collection of information
Compatibility	The degree to which an innovation is consistent with existing values, previous experiences and the needs of potential users
Compatibility, technical	The degree to which a technology is consistent with the infrastructure, hardware and software, middleware and applications
Conformation	Degree to which people will adopt prevailing group values

Connectivity	Possibility on the part of parties to communicate directly with one another
Control, vertical	Degree to which hierarchical, top-down control is exerted on tasks and processes in organization
Convergence	The integration of information technology, (tele) communication and media technologies and/or industry sectors
Co-ordination, horizontal	Changes in the level of and way in which lateral relationships between organizational departments and entire organizations emerge
Co-ordination, forms of	Forms of economic co-ordination like markets, hierarchy and network
Cybermediairy	A concept used to describe intermediaries in the domain of Internet, e-commerce, telecommunication
Datamining	The collection of, analysis of and access to data from data warehouses, based on specifications and specific research questions, and mostly directed to personalized marketing
Datawarehousing	A collection of data collected in primarily logistic, production, transaction and marketing processes. These data are being used for further analysis to support organizational goals
Determinism, technology	Vision of technology in which it is assumed that people will be convinced of the benefits of technology only on basis of the capabilities of technology itself
Dis-intermediation	Bypassing intermediaries in value chains
Diffusion process	Process in which innovation is communicated through certain channels over time among members of a social system
Digitization	Translation of information in digital values, 0 and 1, making transferring, switching, manipulating and checking data more effective and efficient
Division	Organizational form developed from a machine bureaucracy: the organization has been split up into different divisions that each make their own products
Dystopian	Stressing the negative sides of (information and communication) technology for organizations. Pessimistic view on technology
Ease of use, perceived	Degree to which a person believes that using a particular system would be free of effort
Early adopters	Units of adoption that play the role of opinion leaders within the community of which they are a member, and who adopt innovation at a relatively early stage, but are less venturesome than innovators
Early majority	Those units of adoption that adopt an innovation before the 'average' person or organization does so
E-business	Support of business process based on the use of Internet and information and communication technology

Economies of scale	The more products are being produced the more the production costs decrease and the lower prices of products become, resulting in a mass market
Economies of scope	Diversifying products for specific markets based on market analysis
E-commerce	Process of buying and selling or exchanging products, services and information via computer networks, including the Internet
E-government	Support of processes in the domain of government based on the use of internet and information and communication technology
Effect, first-level	Consequences of ICT use for individual tasks – anticipated, technical effects, such as planned efficiency gains or productivity gains that justify an investment in new technology
Effect, second-level	Consequences of ICT use for the social structure in the organization: changing and new communication patterns, new roles within social networks, new patterns of dependence between actors
Effectiveness	Realization of objectives
Efficiency	Achieving maximum result with minimum resources
Equivocality	Absence of clear definition of a situation
Implementation	The phase of internal strategy formation, project definitions and activities in which the adopted ICT applications are introduced within the organization, with the aim of removing resistance and stimulating the optimum use of the application
Information economics	Method for analysing investment in ICT taking into account financial, but also business and risks criteria
Information overload	Cognitive overload as a consequence of the availability of an increasing amount of information
Initiation phase of adoption	All activities concerning the gathering of information, outlining and planning that lead to the decision to adopt
Innovation	Idea, practice or object that is perceived as new, by an individual or another unit of adoption
Innovation decision, authoritative	Innovation decision in an organizational innovation process is *authorative*, if the choice is made at the top level of the organization, and the individual decision depends on the organization decision
Innovation decision, collective	Innovation decision in an organizational innovation process is *collective*, if the choice is supported by the members of the social system
Innovation decision, contingent	Innovation decision in an organizational innovation process is *contingent*, if the choice of an individual member of an organization depends very much on the decision made by the organization

Innovativeness	The degree to which an individual or other unit of adoption is relatively earlier in adopting new ideas than the other members of a system
Innovators	Units of adoption that actively look for information regarding new ideas and who adopt these innovations at a very early stage
Intermediation	Brokerage between two parties in a value-chain
Interoperability	The degree in which different information and communication systems are able to work together
Knowledge economy	Economy in western, industrialized countries in which knowledge-intensive organizations are the predominant organizational form
Knowledge, explicit	Knowledge that can be articulated in words, documents, figures and information systems, and thus is relatively easy to transfer to others.
Knowledge-intensive organization	Organizations in which knowledge is a crucial production factor and production workers are directly involved in the production process
Knowledge management	Process of creating or capturing, storing updating and maintaining (tacit and explicit) knowledge within an organization
Knowledge, tacit	Knowledge that exists inside people's heads, is directly related to their actions and is not easily articulated or transferred
Laggards	Conservative units of adoption with few external contacts and a primarily suspicious attitude towards new ideas, who will not adopt an innovation until a very late stage (or not at all)
Late majority	Units of adoption that are somewhat sceptical and wait until the 'average' person or organization has adopted the innovation before deciding to do so themselves
Legacy system	Existing ICT systems that most often are are outdated and hinder the implementation of new systems, due to the fact that they are deeply rooted in the organization and interlinked with existing structure and processes
Levels of analysis	Different levels at which the process of adoption, implementation, use and effects takes place and is to be studied: individual, group, organizational and environment.
Marketing (technology) pull	Process of acceptance and use of technology that is based on the understanding of users' needs and preferences
Media choice	Choice for a specific channel for a communication task, dependent on tasks and organizational and social context
Media, cold, hot	Classification of media according to McLuhan
Media richness	Degree to which media are suitable for equivocal information tasks. 'Rich' media score high on instant feedback, capacity to convey multiple cues, use of natural language and personal focus

M-commerce	E-commerce via mobile or wireless telecommunication and data networks
Microprocessor	That part of a computer that executes logical transformations, such as computations
Middleware	Middleware is software that arranges the communication between a client and a database.
Miniaturization	Combination of increased processing capacity combined with more efficient use of energy that leads to smaller devices
Model, technology acceptance	Model that starts from the theory of reasoned action to explain use of information and communication services and applications based on users attitude to technology/services and intentions to use
Multi-channel strategy	Strategy in which synergy between channels in a marketing approach is sought
Network externalities	Increase of the value of a network due to additional nodes added to a network
Observability	The extent to which the use and effects of an innovation are visible to other members of the social system
(Real) option theory	Investment theory based on analysis of future (technical) options, based on concepts from the options stock markets, benefits are analysed on basis of options in future projects
Organization	Abstract system of formal positions, held by individuals, with explicit objectives, tasks, processes and assets
Organization, culture	Long-standing, shared values, that express the way members of the organization behave
Organization, professional	Organizational form characterized by largely separated operational cores with highly educated professionals
Organization, structure	Abstract configuration of internal relationships as expressed in the division of labour and tasks
Organization, virtual	Collection of geographically dispersed, functionally and/or culturally diverse entities that are connected through electronic forms of communication, using lateral relationships for coordination.
Perceived ease of use	See Ease of use, perceived
Perceived usefulness	See Usefulness, perceived
Portal	An access website that offers multiple services for instance via the Internet
Process, learning	The process whereby users, on the basis of their experience with an ICT application, learn to utilize this technology in ways that may initially not have been expected or intended, but that better meet their needs – and learn to use this technology more effectively
Product, heterogeneous	Product with a varying quality and form
Product, homogeneous	Product with a fairly constant quality and form
Product, intangible	Immaterial products, like digital information products and services

Product, tangible	Material products
Productivity paradox	Relation between investments in information and communication technology and the lack of a visible increase in productivity
Protocol	A protocol is a collection of agreements and instructions used by software in nodes of a network in order to make the exchanges of data between these nodes possible
Prototype	First, original model, nowadays a model that is developed in order to test its functionality before it will be introduced to the market
Prototyping	System development method that is cyclical in nature
R&D	Research and development: all combined efforts in the domain of research and product development
Rational decision-making model	Model for decision-making based on the assumption that people behave rationally (homo-economicus)
Real time	Real time implies that data are updated constantly with the consequence that the data reflect the actual situation
Re intermediation	Opposite to dis-intermediation: emerging of new intermediary activities
Reinvention	Affection of the perceived characteristics due to daily use, and as result a change in use entirely different from that originally intended
Relative advantage	See Advantage, relative
Revenue model	Description of how a company will earn income; a quantitative, financial interpretation of a business model, including tangible and intangible benefits, and risks
Return, diminishing	First investments that yield considerable results (positive feedbacks) in the first phase of adoption, whereas later investments yield decreasing results
Return, increasing	Large investments made in the first phase of adoption while the benefits are low but will increase in the long run
Social influence model	Model that assumes that media use is a context-dependent result of subjective perceptions of task and media characteristics
Social information processing	Theory of media choice and use, which challenges social presence and media richness theories by stating that regardless of the medium used, communicators will want to establish meaningful social relationships, and adapt their linguistic and textual behaviours in order to be able to communicate socially relational signals via 'lean' media as well
Social presence	Degree to which users experience the psychological proximity of other individuals via media that differ in non-verbal signals, proximity, orientation and physical appearance
Social system	A set of interrelated units that are engaged in joint problem-solving to accomplish a common goal

Standardization	The degree to which open or closed standards are being used to allow infrastructure, hardware and software, middleware and applications to be interoperable and compatible
Strategy, authority, force	Implementation strategy based on authoritative approach and sanctions
Strategy, competitive potential	Change in strategy driven by the introduction of new information and communication technology, one of the four ways to move through the strategic alignment model
Strategy, empirical–rational	Implementation strategy based on the assumption that members of an organization act rationally and will use an application if convinced of its value
Strategy execution	Change in ICT infrastructures and processes driven by change in operations, one of the four ways to move through the strategic alignment model
Strategy, normative-re-educative	Implementation strategy based on the assumption that members of an organization are geared towards satisfying context-dependent needs, and focusing on influencing norms and perceptions
Structural model of technology	Theory based on principal of duality of technology (result of human action and tool) and interpretive flexibility of technology
Structuration	Process by which social structures are produced and reproduced in social life
Suitability	Fit between the tasks that have to be performed and the possibilities that technologies have to offer
Synchronous communication	Communication where there is a simultaneous presence of partners in the communication process
System development	Method for developing systems, that is, information and communication systems, based on system engineering principles
Technology Acceptance Model	See Model, technology acceptance
Technological determinism	See Determinism, technology
Technology pull	Clear demand for specific technological solutions
Technology push	Autonomous process of developing knowledge and technology resulting in technologies that are useful and will be adopted and used
Technology, social shaping of	Technology seen as an outcome of complex social interactions that define the meaning and use of technology
Technology transformation	Change in strategy driven by technology, one of the four ways to move through the strategic alignment model
Terminals	Devices at the border of a network that present or make entry of data possible
Tracking and tracing	Distant monitoring of products, persons and transportation vehicles
Triability	The extent to which an innovation can be tested and experimented with on a limited scale

Trust	Knowing what can be expected from others
Unstructured messages	Electronic messages that do not have a fixed format, such as e-mail and short message services, contrary to structured messages, such as electronic data interchange exchanges that have a fixed format
Use	Application of ICT in their daily activities by members of an organization
Usefulness, perceived	Degree to which a person believes that using a particular system would enhance his or her performance
Utopian	Positive view of technology, stressing the benefits of (information and communication) technology for organizations
Value, business	Trade-off between preceived benefits and total costs (or sacrifices) for delivering a product or service for customers in target markets
Value, customer	Trade-off between perceived benefits and costs (or sacrifices) of (obtaining) a product or service for customers in target markets
Workflow management	Management of work and process-related activities
Workflow management systems	Soft-and orgware that supports the management of work and process-related activities

References

Accenture (2003) 'Egovernment leadership: engaging the customer', http://accenture.ca.

Adams, D.A., Nelson, R.R. and Todd, P.A. (1992) 'Perceived usefulness, ease of use, and usage of information technology: a replication', *MIS Quarterly,* 16(2): 227–247.

Adelaar, T., Bouwman, H. and Steinfield, C. (2004) 'Enhancing customer value through click and mortar e-commerce: implications for geographical market reach and customer type', *Telematics and Informatics,* 21(2): 167–182.

Aerts, A., Goossenaerts, J., Hammer, D. and Wortmann, J. (2004) 'Architectures in context: on the evolution of business, application software and service platform architectures', *Information and Management,* 41(6): 781–794.

Afuah, A. and Tucci, C. (2001) *Internet Business Models and Strategies.* Boston, MA: McGraw-Hill, Irwin.

Ahuja, M.K. and Carley, K.M. (1998) 'Network structure in virtual organizations', *Journal of Computer-mediated Communication,* 3(4), http://www.asusc.org/jcmc/vol3/issue4/ahuja.html.

Ananova (October 2001) 'Staff sacked by e-mail', retrieved from http://www.ananova.com/business/story/sm_415508.html, February 2004.

Ananova (September 2003) 'Jail for men who divorce wives by text', retrieved from http://www.ananova.com/news/story/sm_816051.html.

Ananova (5 September 2003) 'Workers "need help turning computers on"', retrieved from www.ananova.com.

Anderson, M.C., Banker, R.D. and Ravindran, S. (2003) 'The new productivity paradox', *Communications of the ACM,* 46(3): 91–94.

Andriessen, J.H.T.H. (1989) 'Nieuwe media in organisaties: gebruikt of niet?' (New media in organizations: used or non-used?), in H. Bouwman, and N. Jankowski (eds), *Interactieve Media op Komst* (*The Rise of New Media*). Amsterdam: Otto Cramwinckel Uitgever. pp. 17–28.

Andriessen, J.H.T.H. (1994) 'Conditions for successful adoption and implementation of telematics in user organizations', in J.H.T.H. Andriessen and R.A. Roe (eds), *Telematics and Work.* Hove: Lawrence Erlbaum Associates. pp. 409–439.

Aron, D. and Sampler, J.L. (2003) *Understanding IT: A Manager's Guide.* Harlow: Prentice Hall.

Au, Y.A. and Kauffman, R.J. (2003) 'What do you know? Rational expectations in information technology adoption and investment', *Journal of Management Information Systems,* 20(2): 49–76.

Automatiserings Gids (AG) (2004) *Automatiserings Gids,* 2 April.

Baily, M.N. and Chakrabarti, A. (1988) *Innovation and the Productivity Crisis,* Washington, DC: Brookings Institution.

Bannister, F. and Remenyi, D. (1999) 'Value perception in IT investment decisions', *Electronic Journal of Information Systems Evaluation,* 3(1), http://is.twi.tudelft.nl/ejise.

BBC News (8 January 2004) 'Messaging programs bring instant risk', retrieved March 2004 from http://news.bbc.co.uk/2/hi/technology/3378647.htm.

Bedell, E.F. (1985) *The Computer Solution: Strategies for Success in the Information Age.* Homewood, IL: Dow-Jones Irwin.

Bemelmans, T.M.A. (1991) *Bestuurlijke informatiesystemen en automatisering* (*Management Information Systems and Automation*). Leiden/Antwerpen: Stenfert Kroese.

Bentivenga, S. (2002) 'Politics and new media', in L. Lievrouw and S. Livingstone (eds), *Handbook of New Media*. London: Sage. pp. 50–62.

Berghout, E. and Meertens, F.J.J. (1992) 'Investeringsportfolio voor het beoordelen van voorstellen voor informatiesystemen' (Investment portfolio for the assessment of proposals for IT systems), *Informatie*, 34: 677–689.

Boehm, B. (1988) 'A spiral model for software development and enhancement', *Computer*, 21(5): 61–72

Bongers, F. and Holland, C. (2001) 'Elektronische vergadersystemen als medium voor interactief beleid' (Electronic meeting systems as medium for interactive policy), in H. Bouwman (ed.), *Communicatie in de informatiesamenleving* (*Communication in Information Society*). Utrecht: Lemma. pp. 191–215.

Bongers, F., Bouwman, H., Holland, C. and Kerkhofs, J. (1998) *Interactief beleid in bits and bytes, Een evaluatie van de Internet-debatten over 'Transmurale Gezondheidszorg' en 'Technologie & Criminaliteit'* (*Interactive Policy in Bits and Bytes: Evaluation of Internet Debates on 'eHealth' and 'Technology and Crime'*). Delft: TNO-STB.

Boonstra, J.J. (1992) *Integrale Organisatie-ontwikkeling, vormgeven aan fundamentele veranderingsprocessen in organisaties*. 2^e druk. Utrecht: Lemma.

Botan, C.H., and Vorvoreanu, M. (2000) 'What are you really saying to me? Electronic surveillance in the work place', paper presented at the International Communication Association Conference, Acapulco, Mexico.

Boulton, R., Elliott, T., Libert, B. and Samek, S. (2000) 'A business model for the new economy', *Journal of Business Strategy*, July–August: 29–35.

Bouras, C., Katris, N. and Triantafillou, V. (2003) 'An electronic voting service to support decision-making in local government', *Telematics and Informatics*, 20(3): 255–274.

Bouwman, H. (1998) 'Effectiviteit van Intranet en andere vormen van ICT' (*Effectiveness of Intranets and other ICT-application*), in V. Damoiseaux and A. van Ruler (eds), *Effectiviteit in het communicatiemanagement. Zoektocht naar criteria voor professioneel succes* (*Effectiveness in communication managememt: Search for Criteria for Professional Success*). Houten: Bohn, Stafleu and Van Loghum. pp. 115–128.

Bouwman, H. and Christoffersen, M. (1992) 'Videotex in a broader perspective: from failure to future medium?', in H. Bouwman and M. Christoffersen (eds), *Relaunching Videotex*. Dordrecht: Kluwer Academic. pp. 165–176.

Bouwman, H. and Ham, E. van den (2003) 'Business models and eMetrics, a state of the art', in B. Preissl, H. Bouwman and C. Steinfield (eds), *Elife after the Dot.com Bust*. Berlin: Physica Verlag. pp. 65–82.

Bouwman, H. and Neijens, P. (1991) 'Een meta-analyse van videotex-literatuur: een aanzet tot een acceptatiemodel voor de consumentenmarkt' (A meta-analysis of videotex literature: an impulse towards an adoption model for the consumer market), *Massacommunicatie* (*Mass Communication*), 19(2): 134–149.

Bouwman, H. and Slaa, P. (1992) 'L'adoption du vidéotex par un marché de consommateurs: tentative de prédiction d'une masse critique (Videotex adoption by consumers: a tentative prediction of critical mass)', *Technologies de l'information et société* (*Technologies of Information and Society*), 4(1): 75–95.

Bouwman, H., Fielt, E. and Smit, A. (2001) *Click and Mortar E-commerce in Rotterdam*. Enschede: Telematica Insituut.

Bouwman, H., Hertog, den, P. and Holland, C. (2000) 'Measuring e-commerce', *Trends in Communication*, 2000(6): 13–35.

Bouwman, H., Staal, M. and Steinfield, C. (2001) 'Klantenervaring en Internet concepten', (Consumer experience and Internet concepts), *Management & Informatie* (*Management and Information*), 9(6): 52–60.

Bouwman H., Hes, R., Porte, La T. and Westerveld, J.R. (2000) *ICT in huis. De Magnetron als informatiebron. Trends in Informatie- en communicatietechnologie in de huiselijke omgeving in het jaar 2010*. (ICT at Home: The Magnetron as an Information Source: Trends in ICT in the Home Environment in 2010). Den Haag: SCP.

Brown, J. S. and Duguid, P. (2000) *The Social Life of Information*. Boston, MA: Harvard Business School Press.

Brussaard, B.K. (1992) 'Informatisering en het functioneren van de openbare sector' (Information systems and public functions), in P.H.A. Frissen, A. Koers and I. Snellen (eds), *Orwell of Athene? Democratie en informatiesamenleving* (Democracy and Information Society). Den Haag: NOTA/SDU. pp. 131–150.

Brynjolfsson, E. (1993) 'The productivity paradox of information technology: review and assessment', *Communications of the ACM*, 26(12): 67–77.

Brynjolfsson, E. and Hitt, L.M. (1998) 'Beyond the productivity paradox: computers are the catalyst for bigger changes', *Communications of the ACM*, 41(8): 49–55.

Business Week (2003) 'WiFi means business', *Business Week*, 28 April, retrieved March 2004 from http://www.businessweek.com/magazine/content/03_17/b3830601.htm.

Carlson, J. R. and Zmud, R.W. (1997) 'Channel expansion theory and the experiential nature of media richness perceptions', *Academy of Management Journal*, 42(2): 153–170.

Castells, M. (1996) *The Information Age: Economy, Society and Culture, Vol. I: The Rise of the Network Society*. Cambridge, MA, and Oxford: Blackwell.

Castells, M. (2001) *The Internet Galaxy, Reflections on the Internet, Business and Society*. Oxford: Oxford University Press.

CBS (2001) *De digitale economie 2001* (Digital Economy 2001). Voorburg: CBS, Ministerie van EZ.

Chau, P.Y.K. and Hu, P.J.W. (2002) 'Investigating healthcare professionals' decisions to accept telemedicine technology: an empirical test of competing theories', *Information & Management*, 39(4): 297–311.

Chen, Z. and Dubinsky, A. (2003) 'A conceptual model of perceived customer value in e-commerce: a preliminary investigation', *Psychology and Marketing*, 20(4): 323–347.

Cisco Systems Inc. (1998) *Building a Global Networked Business; Global Networked Business Approach and Architecture Overview*, San Jose, CA: Cisco Systems, http://www.cisco.com/warp/public/779/ibs/solutions/.

Clark, K.B. (1989) 'Project scope and project performance: the effect of parts strategy and supplier involvement on product development', *Management Science*, 35(10): 1247–1263.

CNN (September 2003) 'Firm bans e-mail at work', retrieved from http://cnn.technology.printthis.clickability.com, February 2004.

Cohan, P. (1999) *Net Profit: How to Invest and Compete in the Real World of Internet Business*. San Francisco, CA: Jossey-Bass.

Cohen, M.D., March, J.I.G. and Olsen, J.P. (1972) 'A garbage can model of organizational choice', *Administrative Science Quarterly*, 17(1): 1–25.

Coleman, J.S. (1990) *Foundations of Social Theory*. Cambridge, MA: Harvard University Press.

Commissie ICT en Overheid (Cie. Docters van Leeuwen) (2001) *Burger en overheid in de informatiesamenleving* (Citizen and Government in the Information Society). Den Haag: Ministerie van Binnenlandse Zaken, http://www.minbzk.contents/pages/00007384/eindrapport_comm_ict_overheid_9-01.pdf.

Computerworld (2003) 'Wireless gets down to business', *Computerworld*, 5 May, retrieved March 2004 from http://www.computerworld.com/mobiletopics/mobile/story/0,10801,80864,00.html.

Conner, K.R. and Prahalad, C.K. (1996) 'A resource-based theory of the firm: knowledge versus opportunism', *Organization Science*, 7(5): 477–501.

Contractor, N. and Eisenberg, E. (1990) 'Communication networks and new media in organizations', in J. Fulk and C.W. Steinfield (eds), *Organizations and Communication Technology*. Newbury Park, CA: Sage. pp. 143–172.

Cozijnsen, A.J. and Vrakking, W.J. (1986) *Handboek voor strategisch innoveren. Een internationale balans* (*Handbook for Strategic Innovations: An International Balance*). Deventer: Kluwer.

Crafts, N. (2001) 'The Solow productivity paradox in historical perspective', www.j-bradford-delong.net/articles_of_the_month/pdf/newsolow.pdf

Culbertson, S. (2002). *Transformed Government: Case Studies on the Impact of E-government in Public Administrations*. Cited in OECD E-Government Task Force (2003) 'The case of e-government: excerpts from the OECD report "The E-government Imperative"', *OECD Journal on Budgeting*, 3(1): 61–96.

Daft, R.L. (1995). *Organization Theory and Design*. St. Paul, MN: West Publishing.

Daft, R.L. and Lengel, R.H. (1984) 'Information richness: a new approach to managerial behavior and organizational design', in L.L. Cummings and B.M. Staw (eds), *Research in Organizational Behavior*, vol. 6. Greenwich, CT: JAI Press. pp. 191–233.

Daft, R.L. and R.H. Lengel (1986) 'Organizational information requirements, media richness and structural design', *Management Science*, 32(5): 554–71.

Dahlén, M. (1999) 'Closing in on the web consumer: a study in Internet shopping', in E. Bohlin (ed.), *Beyond Convergence, Communications in the New Millennium*. Amsterdam: Elsevier. pp. 121–137.

Davis, F.D. (1989) 'Perceived usefulness, perceived ease of use, and user acceptance of information technology', *MIS Quarterly*, 13(3): 319–340.

Davis, F.D. and Venkatesh, V. (1996) 'A critical assessment of potential measurement biases in the technology acceptance model: three experiments', *International Journal of Human-Computer Studies*, 45(1): 19–45.

De Vries, E.J. (1998) 'Information at the moment of truth: case study design', *Primavera Working Paper 98–10*. Amsterdam: University of Amsterdam/Primavera.

Deitel, H.M., Deitel, P.J. and Steinbuhler, K. (2001) *E-Business and e-Commerce for Managers*. Upper Saddle River, NJ: Prentice Hall

Demkes, R. (1999). 'COMET; A Comprehensive Methodology for Supporting Telematics Investment Decisions'. PhD. Dissertation, Telematica Instituut, Enschede.

Depla, P. (1995) *Technologie en de vernieuwing van de lokale democratie, Vervolmaking of vermaatschappelijking* (*Technology and Change in Local Democracy*). Den Haag: VUGA.

DeSanctis, G. and Monge, P. (1999) 'Communication processes for virtual organizations', *Organization Science*, 10(6): 693–703.

DeSanctis, G. and Poole, M. (1994) 'Capturing the complexity in advanced technology use: adaptive structuration theory', *Organization Science*, 5(2): 121–147.

Dialogic (2001). *E-government: de vraagkant aan bod: Een inventarisatie van de wensen en verwachtingen van burgers over de elektronische overheid.* (*E-government: the demand side: an inventory of needs and expectations of citizens with regard to the digital government*). Utrecht: Dialogic, htp://www.minbzk.contents/pages/00007384/eindrapport_comm_ict_overheid_bijlage_dialogic_9-01.pdf.

Dimmick, J., Kline, S. and Stafford, L. (2000) 'The gratification niches of personal e-mail and the telephone', *Communication Research*, 27(2): 227–248.

Dos Santos, B.L. (1991) 'Justifying investments in new information technologies', *Journal of Management Information Systems* 7(4): 71–90.

Ducatel, K. (1994) *Employment and Technical Change in Europe: Work Organization, Skills and Training*. Edward Elgar.

Dutton, W.H. (1999) 'The virtual organization; tele-access in business and industry', in G. DeSanctis and J. Fulk (eds), *Shaping Organization Form: Communication, Connection and Community.* Thousand Oaks, CA: Sage. pp. 473–495.

Earle, N. and Keen, P. (2000) *From .com to .profit: Inventing Business Models that Deliver Value and Profit*. San Francisco, CA: Jossey-Bass.

Eason, K. and Harker, S. (1994) 'Developing teleinformatics systems to meet organizational requirements', in J.H.E. Andriessen and R.A. Roe (eds), *Telematics and Work*. Hove: Lawrence Erlbaum Associates. pp. 355–367.

Eastin, M.A. (2002) 'Diffusion of e-commerce: an analysis of the adoption of four e-commerce activities', *Telematics and Informatics*, 19(3): 251–267.

eEurope (2003) 'Web-based survey on electronic public services', http://europa.eu.int/information_society/eeurope/2002/documents/CGEY.report3rd.measurement.pdf.

Ende, J. van den (1998a) 'Techniek in het kantoor' (Office technology), in *Techniek in Nederland in de twintigste eeuw. Deel I, Kantoor en informatietechnologie (Technology in the Netherlands in the Twentieth century. Part 1 Office and Informationtechnology)*. Zutphen, Stichting Historie der Techniek, Walburg Pers. pp. 211–217.

Ende, J. van den (1998b) 'De Computerrevolutie' (Computer revolution), in *Techniek in Nederland in de twintigste eeuw. Deel I, Kantoor en informatietechnologie. (Technology in the Netherlands in the Twentieth century. Part 1 Office and Informationtechnology)*. Zutphen, Stichting Historie der Techniek, Walburg Pers. pp. 341–348.

Erin Research (2003) *Citizens First*. Toronto: Institute of Public Administration of Canada.

Ernst and Young (1998) Creating value through global networked business: Cisco case study, updated from 1997 original, http://www.cisco.com/warp/public/779/ibs/solutions/.

Faber, E. and Bouwman, H. (2003a) 'Designing business models for mobile sevices. Exploring the connections between customer value and value networks. 3rd International Conference on Electronic Business, Business Paradigms: Strategic Transformation and Partnerships', paper presented at the International Conference on Electronic Business, Singapore.

Faber, E., Ballon, P., Bouwman, H., Haaker, T., Rietkerk, O. and Steen, M. (2003b) 'Designing business models for mobile ICT services', paper presented to Workshop on concepts, metrics and visualisation, at the 16th Bled Electronic Commerce Conference eTransformation, Bled, Slovenia.

Faber, E., Haaker, T., Bouwman, H. and Rietkerk, O. (2003) 'Business Models for personalized real-time traffic information in cars: which route to take?', in J. Gordijn and M. Jansen (eds), Proceedings of the First International E-services Workshop, ICEC 2003, Pittsburg. pp. 29–37.

Fishbein, M. and Ajzen, I. (1975) *Belief, Attitude, Intention, and Behavior: An Introduction to Theory and Research*. Reading, MA: Addison-Wesley.

Flichy, P. (1995) *Dynamics of Modern Communication: The Shaping and Impact of New Communication Technologies*. London: Sage.

Fokkinga, L., Glastra, M. and Huizinga, H. (1996) *LAD – Het lineair ontwikkelen van informatiesystemen (Linear Development of Information Systems)*. Schoonhoven: Academic Service.

Frambach, R.T. (1993) 'An integrated model of organizational adoption and diffusion of innovations', *European Journal of Marketing*, 27(5): 22–41.

Frissen, P.H.A. (1996) *De virtuele staat, politiek, bestuur, technologie: een postmodern verhaal (Virtual State: Politics, Administration, Technology: a Post-modern Story)*. Schoonhoven: Academic Service.

Fulk, J. (1993) 'Social construction of communication technology', *Academy of Management Journal*, 36(5): 921–950.

Fulk, J. and DeSanctis, G. (1999) 'Articulation of communication technology and organizational form', in G. DeSanctis and J. Fulk (eds), *Shaping Organizational Form; Communication, Connection and Community*. Thousand Oaks, CA: Sage. pp. 5–32.

Fulk, J., Heino, R., Flanagin, A.J., Monge, P.R., Kim, K. and Lin, W-Y. (2000) 'Intranet functionality as collective action', paper presented at the International Communication Association conference, Acapulco, Mexico.

Fulk, J., Schmitz, J. and Steinfield, C.W. (1990) 'A social influence model of technology use', in J. Fulk and C.W. Steinfield (eds), *Organizations and Communication Technology*. Newbury Park, CA: Sage. pp. 117–142.

Fulk, J., Steinfield, C.W., Schmitz, J. and Power, J.G. (1987) 'A social information processing model of media use in organizations', *Communication Research*, 14(5): 529–552.

Galbraith, J. (1973) *Designing Complex Organizations*. Reading, MA: Addison-Wesley.

Gartner Group (1995) 'Electronic mail', conference presentation, Stamford, CT, Gartner Group.

Gordon, R.J. (2000). 'Does the "new economy" measure up to the great inventions of the past?', *Journal of Economic Perspectives,* 4(14): 49–74.

Grant, R.M. (1996) 'Toward a knowledge-based view of the firm', *Strategic Management Journal,* 17(Winter Special Issue): 109–122.

Grimshaw, D,. Breu, K. and Myers, A. (2000) *Exploiting E-business: A Survey of UK Industry.* Cranfield: Information Systems Research Centre, School of Management, Cranfield University.

Gurchom, M. van, Wit, D. de, and Franken, H. (1996) 'Strategisch inzetten van IT en Telematica toepassingen' (Strategic application of IT and applications of telematics), *Management & Informatie,* 4(4): 48–58.

Gustafsson, J., Herrmann, A. and Huber, F. (2003) 'Conjoint analysis as an instrument of market research practice', in J. Gustafsson, A. Herrmann and F. Huber (eds), *Conjoint Measurement, Methods and Applications.* Berlin: Springer. pp. 5–46.

Hacker, K. and Van Dijk, J. (eds) (2000*) Digital Democracy, Issues of Theory and Practice.* London, Thousand Oaks, CA: Sage.

Hambeukers, D. (2001) 'Business cases AGPS', master thesis, Delft University of Technology, Delft, the Netherlands.

Hammer, M. and Mangurian, G.E. (1987) 'The changing value of communications technology', *Sloan Management Review,* 28(2): 65–71.

Hawkins, R. (2003) 'Looking beyond the .com bubble: exploring the form and function of business models in the electronic marketplace', in B. Preissl, H. Bouwman and C. Steinfield (eds), *E-life after the dot.com Bust.* Berlin: Physica Verlag.

Hawryszkiewycz, I. (1997) *Designing the Networked Enterprise.* Boston, MA: Artech House.

Hedman, J. and Kalling, T. (2003) 'The business model concept: theoretical underpinnings and empirical illustrations', *European Journal of Information Systems,* 12: 49–59.

Heliview (2000) *ICT Monitor 2000.* Breda: Heliview.

Henderson, B. (1984) *The Logic of Business Strategy.* Cambridge: Ballinger.

Henderson, J.C. and Venkatraman, N. (1993) 'Strategic alignment: leveraging information technology for transforming organizations', *IBM Systems Journal,* 32(1): 4–16.

Hindle, K. and Dulmains, P. (2000) 'Beyond e-commerce: an entrepreneurial business modelling method for profitable e-venturing', in S. Klein, B. O'Keefe, J. Gricar and M. Podlogar (eds), *Proceedings of the Electronic Commerce Conference in Bled. The End of the Beginning.* Research. Kranj: Moderna Organizcija. pp. 21–49.

Hinds, P. and Kiesler, S. (1999) 'Communication across boundaries: work, structure and use of communication technologies in a large organization', in G. DeSanctis and J. Fulk (eds), *Shaping Organization Form: Communication, Connection and Community.* Thousand Oak, ca: Sage. pp. 211–246.

Hochstrasser, B. (1994) 'Justifying IT investments', in L. Willcocks (ed.), *Information Management – the Evaluation of Information Systems Investments.* London: Chapman and Hall. pp. 151–169.

Hofstede, G. (1991) *Cultures and Organizations: Software of the Mind.* London: McGraw-Hill.

holtz.org/Library/Social%20Science/Economics/Historical%20Productivity.pdf.

Huysman, M. and De Wit, D. (2000) *Kennisdelen in de praktijk. Vergaren, uitwisselen en ontwikkelen van kennis met ICT (Knowledge Sharing in Practice: Collection, Exchange and Development of Knowledge with ICT).* Den Haag: Van Gorcum.

Huysman, M. and Van Baalen, P. (eds) (2001) 'Communities of Practice', *Trends in Communication,* 4(8): pp. 3–5.

Information Week (3 November 2003) 'Keep far–flung employees close', retrieved March 2004, from http://www.informationweek.com/showArticle.jhtml?articleID=15800300.

Information Week (4 March 2004) 'Microsoft shows off technology you don't know you need yet', retrieved March, 2004, from http://www.informationweek.com/story/showArticle.jhtml?articleID=18201933.

Internet Week (5 March 2004) 'Automakers adopt EBXML for e-business', retrieved March 2004, from
http://www.internetweek.com/breakingNews/showArticle.jhtml?articleID=18311208.

Internet Week (30 October 2003) 'E-mail use eroded by spam and IM', retrieved March 2004, from http://www.internetweek.com/breakingNews/showArticle.jhtml?articleID=15800271.

Irsel, H.G.P. van and Swinkels, G.J.P. (1992) 'Investeren in IT: take IT or leave IT' (Investment in IT: take IT or leave IT), *Informatie* (*Information*), 34(Special Issue: Evaluation of IT investments): 624–636.

Jaeger, P.T. and Thompson, K.M. (2004) 'Social information behavior and the democratic process: information poverty, normative behavior, and electronic government in the United States', *Library and Information Science Research*, 26(1): 94–107.

Jankowski, N. and Van Selm, M. (2001) 'ICT en samenleving, vier terreinen voor onderzoek' (ICT and society: four research domains), in H. Bouwman (ed.), *Communicatie in de informatiesamenleving.* (*Communication in Information Society*). Utrecht: Lemma. pp. 217–250.

Janssen, M. (2003) 'Webservices and component-based developments', TU Delft white paper.

Janssen, M., Wagenaar, R. and Beerens, J. (2003) 'Towards a flexible ICT-architecture for multi-channel service provisioning', Hawaii International Conference on System Sciences (HICSS-36), Hilton Waikoloa Village, Big Island, 6–9 January (proceedings on CD-Rom).

Johnson, B. and Rice, R.E. (1987) *Managing Organizational Innovation: The Evolution from Word Processing to Office Information Systems.* New York: Columbia University Press.

Jong, M.W. de (1993) 'De productiviteitsparadox in de dienstensector' (Productivity paradox in the service sector), *Management & informatie*, 1(4): 25–34.

Kaplan, R.S. and Norton, D.P. (1992) 'The balanced scorecard: measures that drive performance', *Harvard Business Review*, 70(1): 71–79.

Kaplinsky, R. and Morris, M. (2001)' A handbook for value chain research', retrieved on 6 December 2004, from www.ids.ac.uk/ids/global/pdfs/VchNov01.pdf.

Katz, J. and Rice, R.E. (2003) *Social Consequences of Internet Use: Access, Involvement and Interaction.* Cambridge, MA: MIT Press.

Kelly, K. (1997) 'New rules for the new economy', *Wired*, 5(9): 140–144, 186–197, http://www.wired.com/wired/5.09/newrules_pr.html.

Kiesler, S., Siegel, J. and McGuire, T.W. (1984) 'Social psychological aspects of computer-mediated communication', *American Psychologist,* 39(10): 1123–1134.

Kim, S.-H. and Lee, J. (1991) 'A contingency analysis of the relationship between IS implementation and IS success', *Information Processing and Management*, 27(1): 111–128.

Kim, W. (1990) 'Object-oriented databases: definition and research directions', *IEEE Transactions on knowledge and data engineering*, 2(3): 327–341.

Kling, R. (1996) 'Hopes and horrors: technological utopianism and anti-utopianism in narratives of computerization', in R. Kling (ed.), *Computerization and Controversy.* San Diego, CA: Academic Press. pp. 40–48. (1st edn, 1991, edited with C. Dunlop.)

Kothandaraman, P. and Wilson, D. (2001) 'The future of competition: value creating networks', *Industrial Marketing Management*, 30: 379–389.

Koufaris, M. (2002) 'Applying the technology acceptance model and flow theory to online consumer behaviour', *Information Systems Research*, 13(2): 205–223.

Kraut, K.E., Rice, R.E., Cool, C. and Fish, R.S. (1998) 'Varieties of social influence: the role of utility and norms in the success of a new communication medium', *Organization Science,* 9(4): 437–453.

Krcmar, H. (1992) 'Computer aided team. Ein Uberblick' (Computer aided team: an overview), *Information Management*, 7(1), 6–9.

Krim, J. (2003) 'Spam's cost to business escalates', *Washington Post*, 13 March.

Krugman, P. (1997) 'Speed trap. The fuzzy logic of the "new economy"', *Slate*, 19 December, http://slate.msn.com/id/1927.

Krugman, P. (1998) 'Entertainment values. Will capitalism go Hollywood?' *Slate*, 23 January, http://slate.msn.com/id/1929.

La Porte, T.M. (1999) 'National differences in how governments use websites', in T. Sprehe (ed.), *The Internet Connection: Your Guide to Government Resource.* Washington, DC: Thomas Sprehe. pp. 21–28.

Lahti, R.K. (1996) *Group Decision Making in Organizations: Can Models Help?* CSWT Reports, University of North Texas, http://www.workteams.unt.edu/reports/lahti.htm.

Lee, A. (1994) 'Electronic mail as a medium for rich communication: an empirical investigation using hermeneutic interpretation', *MIS Quarterly,* 18(2): 143–157.

Legris, P., Ingham, J. and Collerette, P. (2003) 'Why do people use information technology? A critical review of the technology acceptance model', *Information and Management,* 40(3): 191–204.

Lewin, K. (1954) 'Frontiers in group dynamics', in D. Cartwright (ed.), *Field Theory in Social Science: Selected Theoretical Papers by Kurt Lewin.* Chicago, IL: University of Chicago Press. pp. 188–237.

Liao, Z. and Tow Cheung, M. (2001) 'Internet-based e-shopping and consumer attitudes: an empirical study', *Information and Management,* 38(5): 299–306.

Lieshout, M. van and Mol, A. (1989) 'Integratie van IT in de samenleving: een sociaal experiment?' (Integrating IT in society: a social experiment?), in H. Bouwman and N. Jankowski (eds), *Interactieve media op komst (New Media Emerge).* Amsterdam: Otto Cramwinckel Uitgever. pp. 158–166.

Limburg, D. (2002) *Making Telework a Reality.* Enschede: Twente University Press.

Linton, J.D. (2002) 'Implementation research: state of the art and future directions', *Technovation,* 22(1): 65–79.

Low, J. and Cohen Kalafut, P. (2002) *Invisible Advantage: How Intangibles are Driving Business Performance.* Cambridge, MA: Perseus.

Maes, R. (1999) *Reconsidering Information Management through a Generic Framework.* Amsterdam: PrimaVera Working Paper 99–15.

Mahadevan, B. (2000) 'Business models for Internet-based e-commerce', *California Management Review,* 42(4): 55–69.

Maitland, C., Van de Kar, E., De When Montalvo, U. and Bouwman, H. (2003) 'Mobile information and entertainment services: business models and service networks', in G.M. Giaglis, H, Werthner, V. Tschammer and K.A. Froeschl (eds), *2nd International Conference on Mobile Business.* Osterreichische Computer Gesellschaft. pp. 69–86.

March, J.G. and Simon, H. (1993) *Organizations* (2nd edn). Cambridge, MA: Blackwell. (1st edn, 1958).

Markus, M. L. (1987) 'Toward a "critical mass" theory of interactive media: universal access, interdependence and diffusion', *Communication Research,* 14(5): 491–511.

Markus, M.L. (1990) 'Toward a critical mass theory of interactive media', in J. Fulk and C.W. Steinfield (eds), *Organizations and Communication Technology.* Newbury Park, CA: Sage. pp. 194–218.

Markus, M.L. (1994a) 'Finding a happy medium: explaining the negative effects of electronic communication on social life at work', *ACM Transactions on Information Systems,* 12(2): 119–149.

Markus, M.L. (1994b) 'Electronic mail as the medium of managerial choice', *Organization Science,* 5(4): 502–527.

McAfee, A. (2003) 'When too much IT knowledge is a dangerous thing', *MIT Sloan Management Review,* 44(2): 83–89.

McCreadie, M. and Rice, R. (1999) 'Trends in analyzing access to information. Part I: Cross-disciplinary conceptualizations of access', *Information Processing and Management,* 35(1): 45–76.

McDonagh, J. (2001) 'Not for the faint hearted: social and organizational challenges in IT-enabled change', *Organizational Development Journal,* 19(1): 11–19.

McKinsey and Co. in collaboration with CAPS Research (2001) *Coming in to Focus Using the Lens of Economic Value to Clarify the Impact of B2B E-marketplaces.* CapsMcKinsey 200 Colorcom.pdf.

McLean, I. (1989) *Democracy and New Technology.* Cambridge: Polity Press.

McLoughlin, I. and Clark, J. (1995) 'Technological change and work', in N. Heap, R. Thomas, G. Einon, R. Mason and H. MacKay (eds), *Information Technology and Society.* London: Sage. pp. 149–178.

McLuhan, M. (1964) *Understanding Media: The Extensions of Man.* New York: McGraw-Hill.

Mierlo, S. van (1999) 'Het blijft sukkelen met systeem GSD Amsterdam' (Pervasive problems with benefit system municipality Amsterdam), in *Automatisering Gids,* 31 December.

Miller, R. and Lessard, D. (2000) *The Strategic Management of Large Engineering Projects: Shaping Institutions, Risks and Governance.* Boston, MA: MIT Press.

Miller, S.J., Hickson, D.J. and Wilson, D.C. (1996) 'Decision making in organizations', in S.R. Clegg, C. Hardy and W.R. Nord (eds), *Handbook of Organization Studies.* London: Sage. pp. 293–312.

Mintzberg, H. (1983) *Structure in Fives: Designing Effective Organizations.* Englewood Cliffs, NJ: Prentice Hall.

Mintzberg, H. (1989) *Mintzberg on Management: Inside Our Strange World of Organization.* New York: Free Press.

Mogard, K. (2000) 'Information and communication technology empowerment – and the dual potentialities of ICT', master thesis in European communication. Amsterdam: ISHSS.

Monge, P. and Contractor, N. (2003) *Theories of Communication Networks.* Oxford: Oxford University Press.

Monge, P. and Fulk, J. (1999) 'Communication technology for global network organizations', in G. DeSanctis and J. Fulk (eds). *Shaping Organization Form: Communication, Connection and Community.* Thousand Oaks, CA: Sage. pp. 71–101.

Monge, P.R., Fulk, J., Kalman, M.E., Flanagin, A.J., Parnassa, C. and Rumsey, S. (1998) 'Production of collective action in alliance-based inter-organizational communication and information systems', *Organization Science, 9*(3): 411–433.

Morrison, C.J. and Berndt, E.R. (1990) 'Assessing the productivity of information technology equipment in the US manufacturing industries', National Bureau of Economic Research Working Paper #3582.

Nahapiet, J. and Ghoshal, S. (1998) 'Social capital, intellectual capital, and the organizational advantage', *Academy of Management Review, 40*(2): 242–266.

Newell, S., Scarbrough, H. and Swan, J. (2001) 'From global knowledge management to internal electronic fences: contradictory outcomes of intranet development', *British Journal of Management,* 12(2): 97–111.

Ngwenyama, O. and Lee, A. (1997) 'Communication richness in electronic mail: critical social theory and the contextuality of meaning', *MIS Quarterly,* 21(2): 145–167.

Nonaka, I. and Takeuchi, H. (1995) *The Knowledge-Creating Company.* New York: Oxford University Press.

OECD (2003) 'OECD e-government flagship report. The e-government imperative', *GOV/PUMA (2003)6/ANN. 27th session of the Public Management Committee,* Paris, http://webdomin01.oecd.org//connect/PUM/egovproweb.int/viewhtml/index/$file/the%2 0e-government%20imperative%20%20final.pdf.

Oirsouw, R. van, Spaanderman, J. and De Vries, H. (1993*) Informatie-economie. Investeringsstrategie voor de informatievoorziening. (Information Economics: Investment Strategy for Information Provision).* Schoonhoven: Academic Service.

Oliver, P., Marwell, G. and Texeira, R. (1985) 'A theory of critical mass I: interdependence, group heterogeneity, and the production of collective action', *American Journal of Sociology,* 91(3): 522–56.

Olson, M. (1965) *The Logic of Collective Action.* Cambridge, MA: Harvard University Press.

Oost, E. van and Van Hoorn, T. (1998) 'De opkomst van de computer' (The emergence of computers), in J. van den Ende (ed.), *Techniek in Nederland in de twintigste eeuw. Deel I, Kantoor en informatietechnologie* (*Technology in the Netherlands in the 20th century. Part 1 Office and Information Technology*). Zutphen: Stichting Historie der Techniek, Walburg Pers. pp. 289–304.

Orlikowski, W. and Hofman, J.D. (1997) 'An improvisational model for change management: the case of groupware technologies', *Sloan Management Review,* (38)2: 11–21.

Orlikowski, W., Yates, J., Okamura, K. and Fujimoto, M. (1999) 'Shaping electronic communication: the meta-structuring of technology in the context of use', in G. DeSanctis, and J. Fulk (eds), *Shaping Organization For: Communication, Connection and Community.* Thousand Oaks, CA: Sage. pp. 135–173.

Orlikowski, W.J. (1992) 'The duality of technology: rethinking the concept of technology in organizations', *Organization Science,* 3(3): 398–427.

Orlikowski, W.J. (2000) 'Using technology and constituting structures: a practice lens for studying technology in organizations', *Organization Science,* 11(4): 404–428.

Paans, J. (1993) *Teleparticipatie, elektronische participatie als vorm van bestuurlijke vernieuwing in de gemeentelijke democratie* (*Tele-Democracy: Electronic Participation as a Model for Administrative Renewal in a Local Democracy*). Leiden: Faculteit Rechtsgeleerdheid Rijksuniversiteit Leiden.

Parker, M. (1996) *Strategic Transformation and Information Technology: Paradigms for Performing while Transforming.* Upper Saddle River, NJ: Prentice Hall.

Parker, M.M., Benson, R.J, and Trainor, H.E. (1988) *Information Strategy and Economics.* Englewood Cliffs, NJ: Prentice Hall.

Peiro, J.M. and Prieto, F. (1994) 'Telematics and organizational structure and process: an overview', in J.H.E. Andriessen and R.A. Roe (eds), *Telematics and Work.* Hove: Lawrence Erlbaum Associates. pp. 175–207.

Petrovic, O. and Kittl, C. (2003) 'Capturing the value proposition of a product or service', position paper for the international workshop on business models, Lausanne, Switzerland, October.

Pettigrew, A. and Whipp, R. (1993) *Managing Change for Competitive Success.* Cambridge, MA: Blackwell.

Picard, R.G. (1989) *Media Economics: Concepts and Issues.* Newbury Park, CA: Sage.

Poole, M. and DeSanctis, G. (1990) 'Understanding the use of group decision support systems: the theory of adaptive structuration', in J. Fulk and C. Steinfield (eds), *Organisations and Communication Technology.* Newbury Park, CA: Sage. pp. 173–193.

Popescu-Zeletin, R., Abranowski, S., Fikouras, I., Gasbaronne, G., Gebler, M., Henning, S., Van Kranenenburg, H., Postschy, H., Postmann, E. and Raatikainen, K. (2003) 'Service architecture for the wireless world', *Computer Communications,* 26(1): 19–25.

Porter, M.E. (1980) *Competitive Strategy: Techniques for Analyzing Industries and Competitors.* New York: Free Press.

Porter, M.E. (1985) *Competitive Advantage: Techniques for Analyzing Industries and Competitors.* New York: Free Press.

Porter, M.E. and Millar, V.E. (1985) 'How information gives you competitive advantage', *Harvard Business Review,* 63(4): 149–160.

Powell, W.W. (1990) 'Neither market nor hierarchy: network forms of organizations', in B. Slaw (ed.), *Research in Organizational Behavior.* Greenwich, CT: JAI Press. pp. 295–336.

Presley, A., Sarkis, J., Barnett, W. and Liles, D. (2001) 'Engineering the virtual enterprise: an architecture-driven modelling approach', *International Journal of Flexible Manufacturing Systems,* 13(2): 145–162.

Quintas, P. (1996) 'Software by design', in R. Mansell and R. Silverstone (eds), *Communication by Design: The Politics of Information and Communication Technologies.* Oxford: Oxford University Press. pp. 74–102.

Qvortrup, L. (1994) 'Telematics and organizational communication: trends in organizational communications', in J.H.E. Andriessen and R.A. Roe (eds), *Telematics and Work*. Hove: Lawrence Erlbaum Associates. pp. 367–390.

Radicati, S. and Khmartseva, M. (2003) 'The IT cost of spam', *The Messaging Technology Report*, 12(8): 2–10.

Raessens, B. (2001) *E-business Your Business. Over de effectiviteit van E-commerce* (*E-business Your Business: On the Effectiveness of E-commerce*). Utrecht: Lemma.

Rappa, M. (2000) *Managing the Digital Enterprise*, http://digitalenterprise.org/index.html.

Rayport, F.J. (1999) 'The truth about business internet business models', *Strategy+Business*, 16 (third quarter): 1–3.

Rayport, F.J. and Jaworski, B.J. (2001) *e-Commerce*. Boston, MA: McGraw-Hill/Irwin.

Reicher, S., Spears, R. and Postmes, T. (1995) 'A social identity model of de-individuation phenomena', in W. Stroebe and M. Hewstonde (eds), *European Review of Social Psychology 6*. Chichester: Wiley. pp. 161–198.

Renkema, T.J.W. (1996) *Investeren in de informatie-infrastructuur – Richtlijnen voor besluitvorming in organisaties* (*Investment in Information Infrastructure Guidelines for Management Decisions in Organizations*). Deventer: Kluwer Bedrijfswetenschappen. retrieved on 6 December 2004 from

Rice, R. (1999) 'Multiple theories, issues, data and methods for understanding the implementation of an information system', *Trends in Communication*, 5: 39–51.

Rice, R.E. (2002) 'Primary issues in Internet use: access, civic and community involvement, and social interaction and expression', in L. Lievrouw and S. Livingstone (eds), *Handbook of New Media*. London: Sage. pp. 105–130.

Rice, R.E. and Rogers, E. (1980) 'Reinvention in the innovation process', *Knowledge*, 1(4): 490–514.

Roach, S.S. (1991) 'Services under siege – the restructuring imperative', *Harvard Business Review*, 69(5): 82–92.

Rogers, E.M. (1983) *Diffusion of Innovations*. New York: Free Press.

Rojo, A. and Ragsdale, R. (1997) 'Participation in electronic forums', *Telematics and Informatics*, 13(1): 83–96.

Sarkar, M.B., Butler, B. and Steinfield, C. (1995) 'Intermediaries and cybermediaries: a continuing role for mediating players in the electronic marketplace', *Journal of Computer-Mediated Communications*, 1(3), http://www.ascusc.org/jcmc/vol1/issue3/sarkar.html.

Sarkar, M.B., Butler, B. and Steinfield, C. (1998) 'Cybermediaries in the electronic marketspace: towards theory building', *Journal of Business Research*, 41(3): 215–221.

Schepers, W. (2002). *Business IT Alignment. Oplossingen voor de productiviteitsparadox* (*Business IT Alignment: Solutions for the Productivity Paradox*). Utrecht: University of Utrecht, Department of Informatics and Information Science.

Schick, A.G., Gordon, L.A. and Haka, S. (1990) 'Information overload: a temporal approach', *Accounting, Organizations and Society*, 15(3): 199–220.

Schmitz, J. and Fulk, J. (1991) 'Organizational colleagues, media richness, and electronic mail: a test of the social influence model of technology use', *Communication Research*, 18(4): 487–523.

Seddon, P. and Lewis, G. (2003) 'Strategy and business models: what is the difference', 7th Pacific-Asia Conference on Information Systems, Adelaide, 10–13 July.

Selz, D. (1999) 'Value webs. Emerging forms of fluid and flexible organisations: thinking, organising, communicating and delivering value on the Internet', dissertation, St. Gallen.

Seybold, P.B. (1998) *Customers.com; How to Create a Profitable Business Strategy for the Internet and Beyond*. New York: Random House.

Shapiro, C. and Varian, H.R. (1999) *Information Rules: A Strategic Guide to the Network Economy*. Boston, MA: Harvard Business School Press.

Shea, R. (1994) *Netiquette*. San Francisco, CA: Albion Book.

Short, J., Williams, E. and Christie, B. (1976) *The Social Psychology of Telecommunications*. London: Wiley.

Simon, H.A. (1957) *Models of Man*. New York: Wiley.

Simons, L. (2001) 'Cisco-case study. Increasing the value of web and call center channels for customer contact', paper presented to 2nd McMaster World Congress on the Management of Electronic Commerce, Hamilton, Canada.

Sitkin, S.B., Sutcliffe, K.M. and Barrios-Choplin, J.R. (1992) 'A dual-capacity model of communication media choice in organizations', *Human Communication Research,* 18(4): 563–598.

Sluis, A. van der (2001) 'Internet communities en communities in een werkomgeving' (Internet community's and community's in the working place), in H. Bouwman (ed.), *Communicatie in de informatiesamenleving* (*Communication in Information Society*). Utrecht: Lemma. pp. 117–138.

Slywotzky, A.J. (1996) *Value Migration: How to Think Several Moves Ahead of the Competition.* Boston, MA: Harvard Business Press.

Snowball, D. (1980) 'Some effects of accounting expertise and information load: an empirical study', *Accounting, Organizations and Society,* 5(3): 323–338.

Spears, R. and Lea, M. (1992) 'Social influence and the influence of the 'social' in computer-mediated communication', in M. Lea (ed.), *Contexts of Computer-Mediated Communication.* Hemel-Hempstead: Harvester-Wheatsheaf. pp. 30–65.

Spears, R. and Lea, M. (1994) 'Panacea or panopticon? The hidden power in computer-mediated communication', *Communication Research,* 21(4): 427–459.

Spears, R., Lea, M. and Postmes, T. (2000) 'Social-psychological theories of computer-mediated communication: social pain or social gain?', in P. Robinson and H. Giles (eds), *The Handbook of Language and Social Psychology.* Chichester: Wiley. pp. 601–623.

Sproull, L. and Kiesler, S. (1986) 'Reducing social context cues: electronic mail in organizaitonal communication', *Management Science,* 32(11): 1492–1512.

Sproull, L. and Kiesler, S. (1991) *Connections; New Ways of Working in the Networked Organization.* Cambridge, MA: MIT Press.

Standish (2000) *Chaos,* http://standishgroup.com/visitor/chaos.htm.

Steinfield, C. (2003) 'Click & brick e-commerce', in B. Preissl, H. Bouwman and C. Steinfield (eds), *E-life after the Dot.com Bust.* Berlin: Physica Verlag. pp. 101–116.

Steinfield, C., Bouwman, H. and Adelaar, T. (2001) 'Combining physical and virtual channels: opportunities, imperatives and challenges', in B. O'Keefe, C. Loebbecke, J. Gricar, A. Pucihar and G. Lenart (eds), *e-Everything: e-Commerce, e-Government, e-Household, e-Democracy.* Proceedings of the 14th Bled Electronic Commerce Conference, University of Maribor, Bled, Slovenia, pp. 783–796.

Steinfield, C., De Wit, D., Adelaar, T., Bruins, A., Fielt, E., Hoefsloot, M., Smit, A. and Bouwman, H. (2001) 'Pillars of virtual enterprises: leveraging physical assets in the new economy', *Info,* 3(3): 203–215.

Stojanovic, Z., Dathanayake, A. and Sol, H. (2001) 'A methodology framework for component-based system development support', in J. Krogstie, K. Siau and T. Halpin (eds), *Proceedings of the 6th Caise/IFIP8.1 International Workshop on Evaluation of Modeling Methods in System Analysis and Design.* Interlaken: EMMSAD'01.

Strassmann, P.A. (1990) *The Business Value of Computers.* New Canaan, CT: Information Economics Press.

Tanis, M. and Postmes, T. (2003) 'Social cues and impression formation in CMC', *Journal of Communication,* 53(4): 676–693.

Tapscott, D. (1996) *The Digital Economy: Promise and Peril in the Age of Networked Intelligence.* New York: McGraw-Hill.

Tapscott, D., Ticoll, D. and Lowy, A. (2000) *Digital Capital: Harnessing the Power of Business Webs.* Boston, MA: Harvard Business School Press.

Tiggelaar, B. (2001) *Internet-strategie 2.0* (*Internet Strategy 2.0*). Amsterdam: Prentice Hall.

Timmers, P. (1998) 'Business models for e-commerce', *Electronic Markets,* 8(2): 3–7, www.electronicmarkets.org.

Timmers, P. (1999) *Electronic Commerce: Strategies and Models for Business-to-Business Trading.* Chichester: Wiley.

Tolido, R. (1996) *IAD - Het evolutionaire ontwikkelen van informatiesystemen (Evolutionary Development of Information Systems).* Schoonhoven: Academic Service.

Trevino, L.K., Daft, R.L. and Lengel, R.H. (1990) 'Understanding managers' media choices: a symbolic interactionist perspective', in J. Fulk and C.W. Steinfield (eds), *Organizations and Communication Technology.* Newbury Park, CA: Sage. pp. 71–94.

Tulder, R. van, and Junne, R. (1988) *European Multinationals in Core Technologies.* Chichester and New York: Wiley.

Turban, E., Lee, J., King, D. and Chung, H.M. (2000) *Electronic Commerce: A Managerial Perspective.* Upper Saddle River, NJ: Prentice Hall.

Tweede Kamer (1990–91) *Beleidsnotitie informatievoorziening openbare sector (BIOS-I). De computer gestuurd (White Paper Information Provision and the Public Sector: The Managed Computer).* TK 1990–1991, 20 644, nrs. 1–2.

Tyre, M.J. and Orlikowski, W.J. (1994) 'Windows of opportunity: temporal patterns of technological adaptation in organizations', *Organization Science,* 5(1): 98–118.

Umble, E., Haft, R. and Umble, M. (2003) 'Enterprise resource planning: implementation procedures and critical success factors', *European Journal of Operation Research,* 146(2): 241–257.

Van den Hooff, B. (2004) 'Electronic coordination and collective action; use and effects of electronic calendaring and scheduling', *Information and Management,* 42(1):103–114.

Van den Hooff, B. (in press) 'A learning process in e-mail use: a longitudinal case study of the interaction between organization and technology', *Behaviour and Information Technology.*

Van den Hooff, B., Elving, W., Meeuwsen, J.M. and Dumoulin, C. (2003) 'Knowledge sharing in knowledge communities', in M. Huysman, E. Wenger and V. Wulf (eds), *Communities and Technologies.* Deventer: Kluwer Academic. pp. 119–142.

Van den Hooff, B.J. (1995) 'For what it's worth: de strategische waarde van communicatie-technologieën voor organisaties' (For what it's worth: strategic value of communication technology for organizations), *Informatie en informatiebeleid,* 13(2): 34–43.

Van den Hooff, B.J. (1997) *Incorporating Electronic Mail: Adoption, Use and Effects of Electronic Mail in Organizations.* Amsterdam: Otto Cramwinckel Uitgever.

Van den Hooff, B.J. (2000) 'Dynamiek in ICT en organisatie: Vier fasen van innovatie' (Dynamics in ICT and organizations: four phases in innovation), *Tijdschrift voor communicatiewetenschap,* 28(4): 318–333.

Van Dijk, J.A.G.M. (1997). *Nieuwe media en politiek, Informatie- en communicatietechnologie voor burgers, politici en ambtenaren. (New Media and politics: Information and Communication Technology for Citizens, Politicians and Civil Servants).* Houten: Bohn Stafleu Van Loghum.

Van Dijk, J.A.G.M. (1999) 'Elektronische Discussies bij Interactieve Beleidsvorming' (Electronic meetings and interactive policy-making), *Bestuurskunde,* 8(5): 1999–2009.

Van Dijk, J.A.G.M. Van (2001a) *De Netwerkmaatschappij, Sociale aspecten van nieuwe media (Network Societ, Social Dimensiosn of New Media).* Houten: Bohn Stafleu van Loghum. (1st edn, 1991.)

Van Dijk, J.A.G.M. (2001b) 'Digitale democratie; illusie en realiteit' (Digital democracy: illusion and reality), in H. Bouwman (ed.), *Communicatie in de informatiesamenleving. (Communication in Information Society).* Utrecht: Lemma. pp 165–190.

Veld, S. van 't (1990) *16 Methoden voor systeemontwikkeling. Een vergelijkend rapport van de NGGO (16 System Development Methods: A Comparative Analysis for NGGO).* Amsterdam: Tutein Nolthenius.

Venkatesh, A. (1999) 'Virtual models of marketing and consumer behavior', paper presented to the ESRC Virtual Society Program Workshop: E-commerce and the restructuring of consumption, London.

Venkatesh, V., Morris, M.G., Davis, F.D. and Davis, G.B. (2003) 'User acceptance of information technology: toward a unified view', *MIS Quarterly*, 27(3): 425–478.

Versteeg, G. and Bouwman, H. (2004) 'Business architecture: a new paradigm to relate business strategy to ICT', paper presented to ECIS 2004, Turku, Finland.

Vinkenburg, H.H.M. (1995) *Stimuleren tot perfectie: kritieke factoren bij het verbeteren van dienstverlening* (*Stimulating to Perfection: Critical Factors for Improving Services*). Groningen: Rijksuniversiteit Groningen.

Viscio, A.J. and Pasternack, B. (1996) *Toward a New Business Model: Strategy and Business*. Booz, Allen and Hamilton, www.strategy-business.cm/research/96201.

Walden, E.A. and Browne, G.J. (2002) 'Information cascades in the adoption of new technology', *Proceedings of the 23rd International Conference on Information Systems*. Barcelona, Spain, pp. 435–443, retrieved from www.aisnet.org, 6 December 2004.

Walther, J.B. (1992) 'Interpersonal effects in computer-mediated interaction: a relational perspective', *Communication Research*, 19(1): 52–90.

Walther, J.B. (1996) 'Computer-mediated communication: impersonal, interpersonal and hyperpersonal interaction', *Communication Research,* 23(1): 3–43.

Walton, R. (1989) *Up and Running, Integration Information Technology and the Organization*. Cambridge, MA: Harvard Business School Press.

Wang, Y. (2002) 'The adoption of electronic tax filling systems: an empirical study', *Government Information Quarterly*, 20(4): 333–352.

Weggeman, M. (1997) *Kennismanagement. Inrichting en sturing van kennisintensieve organisaties* (*Knowledge Management: Design and Management of Knowledge Intensive Organizations*). Schiedam: Scriptum.

Weggeman, M. (2000) *Kennismanagement: de praktijk* (*Knowledge Management: Practices*). Schiedam: Scriptum.

Weick, K.E. (1990) 'Technology as equivoque: sense-making in new technologies', in P.S. Goodman, L.S. Sproull and associates (eds), *Technology and Organizations*. San Francisco, CA: Jossey-Bass. pp. 1–44.

Weill, P. and Vitale, M.R. (2001) *Place to Space: Migrating to E-business Models*. Boston, MA: Harvard Business School Press.

WiFi Alliance (2003) http://www.wi-fi.org/OpenSection/index.asp, retrieved in 2003.

Wigand, R. (2000) 'New business paradigms for the e-economy: evolving electronic commerce models', paper presented to Conference on New Business Paradigms for the e-Economy, Brussels: European Commission, Directorate General Information Society.

Wigand, R., Picot, A. and Reichwald, R. (1997) *Information, Organization and Management: Expanding Markets and Corporate Boundaries*. Chichester: Wiley.

Winston, B. (1998) *Media Technology and Society: A History from the Telegraph to the Internet*. London: Routledge.

Winter, S.J. and Taylor, S.L. (1996) 'The role of IT in the transformation of work: a comparison of post-industrial, industrial and proto-industrial organization', *Information Systems Research,* 7(1): 5–21.

Wit, O. de (1994) 'De beginjaren van het Nederlandse telefoniesysteem' (The early years of Dutch telephony), *Informatie & informatiebeleid* (*Information and Information Policy*), 13(3): 30–42.

Wit, O. de and Ende, J. van den (1998) 'Het kantoor in een stroomversnelling na de tweede wereldoordlog' (The office after World War II), in J. van den Ende (ed.), *Techniek in Nederland in de twintigste eeuw. Deel I, Kantoor en informatietechnologie* (*Technology in the Netherlands in the 20th Century. Part 1 Office and Information Technology*). Zutphen, Stichting Historie der Techniek, Walburg Pers. pp. 271–287.

Wit, O. de and Huiter, H. (1998) 'De opkomst van de moderne administratie' (The emergence of modern administrations), in J. Van der Ende (ed.), *Techniek in Nederland in de twintigste eeuw. Deel I, Kantoor en informatietechnologie* (*Technology in the Netherlands in the 20th Century. Part 1 Office and Information Technology*). Zutphen, Stichting Historie der Techniek, Walburg Pers, pp. 219–235.

Woudstra, E. and Van Gemert, L. (1994) 'Planning van de interne communicatie: Een kader' (Planning of internal communication: a framework), *Handboek interne communicatie (Handbook Internal Communication)*: C5.2.3–C5.2.28.

Yorukoglu, M. (1998) 'The information technology productivity paradox', *Review of Economic Dynamics*, 1(2): 551–592.

Zee, H.T.M. van der (1995) 'De vijf denkparadigma's binnen het opleidings- en ontwikkelingsveld' (Five paradigms in the training and development domain), *Management and Organization*, (2): 107–134.

Zee, H.T.M. van der and Koot, W.J.D. (1989) 'IT-assessment, een kwalitatieve en kwantitatieve evaluatie van de informatieverzorging vanuit een strategisch perspectief' (IT assessment: a qualitative and quantitative evaluation of information management from a strategic perspective), *Informatie (Information)*, 31(11): 805–900.

Zuurmond, A. (1994) *De infocratie, Een theoretische en empirische heroriëntatie op Weber's ideaaltype in het informatietijdperk (Infocracy: A Theoretical and Empirical Reorientation on Weber's Gestalt in the Information Age)*. Den Haag: Phaedrus.

Author Index

Subject Index